Luther Refracted

Additional Praise for *Luther Refracted*

"Martin Luther is a more polyphonic and full-bodied theological figure than ecumenists usually assume. This volume discovers a variety of ways in which the Reformation contributes to the unity of the church. In our multicultural modernity, ecumenism needs the rich powers of theological imagery and imagination present in Luther."

Risto Saarinen
University of Helsinki

"In this important new work, editors Malysz and Nelson daringly hand over the richest treasure in the Lutheran tradition, Martin Luther himself, to a wide range of generous and vigorously engaged ecumenical conversation partners: Catholic, Baptist, Evangelical, and more. They do not, in other words, *tell* their ecumenical partners what their Martin Luther has to say but instead *listen* with patience to a varying series of answers to the question how those partners hear Luther's voice. The result is a Luther ready and able to surprise and to contribute to theology today, a Luther who provokes a constructive pan-Christian conversation that beckons the divided churches beyond mere convergence toward listening and learning together. In short, these essays model a new kind of ecumenical engagement that invites diverse Christian readers to share the task of understanding anew their divided traditions, in the hope that they will be led toward the unity that only Spirit can give. An exciting venture!"

Mickey Mattox
Marquette University

"'Martin Luther is one of those rare Christian theologians who belong to all Christian theology.' With these perceptive words David Tracy concludes his contribution to this remarkable volume on Luther's theology. Malysz and Nelson have assembled contributions of established authors hailing from various denominations who make two points clear: Luther's theology continues to influence and stimulate the whole of Christendom. Though Luther was neither infallible nor a saint, his theological insights provide valuable resources across denominational lines. This book needs to be studied for the benefit of the open-minded reader."

Hans Schwarz
Emeritus, University of Regensburg

"This symposium contributes to the emerging ecumenical consensus that Luther's theology can be a rich resource for all Christian churches and denominations. An aspect of this consensus is that Luther's followers have often diminished his greatness by practicing the art of selective reductionism to prove the superiority of their particular brand of Lutheranism. The pietists reconstructed Luther after their own image and the orthodox did the same. With hindsight we Lutherans must grudgingly admit that Luther was never a good Lutheran, judged by the criteria applied by the various denominations that bear his name."

Carl E. Braaten
Emeritus, Lutheran School of Theology at Chicago

"In this book, world-class theologians move beyond dialogue designed for developing churchly position statements effectuating ecumenical rapprochement. Instead, by means of unguarded and critical engagement with Luther, essayists from a variety of confessional heritages address topics of perennial relevance, such as community, universal priesthood, ministry, faith, divine hiddenness, and the sacraments, and allow a new Luther and a new ecumenism to emerge. From the questions posed to Luther as well as the challenges that Luther poses to us we can foresee a thawing of the current ecumenical winter and the warming of a renewed theological collaboration across confessional lines."

Mark Mattes
Grand View University

"The essays in *Luther Refracted* free Luther from captivity to confessionalist or modernist agendas and engage him in lively contemporary ecumenical-theological conversation. A valuable stimulus for anyone interested in the continuing vitality of Luther's theological legacy."

David S. Yeago
North American Lutheran Seminary and Trinity School for Ministry

Luther Refracted

The Reformer's Ecumenical Legacy

Piotr J. Małysz and Derek R. Nelson, editors

Fortress Press
Minneapolis

LUTHER REFRACTED

The Reformer's Ecumenical Legacy

Cover image: Cranach, Lucas the Younger (1515-1586) Martin Luther. Location: Chiesa Evangelista Luterana, Venice, Italy. Photo Credit: Cameraphoto Arte, Venice / Art Resource, NY

Cover design: Tory Herman

Library of Congress Cataloging-in-Publication Data

Print ISBN: 978-1-4514-9038-1

eBook ISBN: 978-1-5064-0147-8

The paper used in this publication meets the minimum requirements of American National Standard for Information Sciences — Permanence of Paper for Printed Library Materials, ANSI Z329.48-1984.

Manufactured in the U.S.A.

This book was produced using Pressbooks.com, and PDF rendering was done by PrinceXML.

Contents

Abbreviations

BC   *The Book of Concord: The Confessions of the Evangelical Lutheran Church*, ed. Robert Kolb and Timothy J. Wengert (Minneapolis: Fortress Press, 2000).

LW   *Luther's Works*, American Edition, 82 vols. (Philadelphia: Fortress, and St. Louis: Concordia, 1955–).

WA   *D. Martin Luthers Werke*, Kritische Gesamtausgabe, ed. J. F. K. Knaake et al., 57 vols. (Weimar: Böhlau, 1883ff).

Introduction

The fast-approaching 500th anniversary of the Protestant Reformation—to be celebrated, or perhaps lamented, in 2017—has issued in a host of fresh portrayals and retrievals of the man who started it all: Martin Luther. This recent wave of interest in the person and thought of the Wittenberg reformer is, of course, nothing new. The twentieth century saw the emergence of several important schools of Luther interpretation, beginning with the German Luther Renaissance in its early decades. The quincentenary of Luther's birth in 1983 marked the first truly ecumenical celebration of Luther's achievement, following on the heels of post-Vatican II fascination with Luther among Roman Catholic scholars (discussed in the present volume by Jared Wicks) as well as ecumenical dialogue with Eastern Orthodox churches. Those ecumenically minded engagements culminated, in 1999, in the signing of the *Joint Declaration on the Doctrine of Justification* between the Pontifical Council for Promoting Christian Unity and the Lutheran World Federation. Since then, we have seen still newer biographical attempts to understand Luther as, for example, "a rebel in a time of upheaval," cast in relief against the backdrop of the early modern struggle over the role of religion;[1] and we have seen new assessments,

---

1. Heinz Schilling, *Martin Luther: Rebell in Einer Zeit des Umbruchs* (München: C. H. Beck, 2012).

theological and more broadly intellectual, of Luther's thought and the unwitting role he may have played in the emergence of modernity.[2] For some today, "the real Luther" can only be understood when seen as a worthy heir to a formidable theological and exegetical tradition;[3] for others, to grasp Luther means to look forward and to mine the "global" potential of his theology.[4]

Luther's historical significance and the long shadow the Reformation has cast over the shape of modernity go without saying. On this all the contributors to the present volume are agreed. But this book would never have come into existence, if the contributors' conviction did not go significantly beyond merely asserting that Luther's voice is one to be reckoned with. All the essays included here *show* that Luther's remains above all a voice genuinely worth hearing. Five hundred years after the Wittenberg professor called for a public debate on indulgences, Luther still has something to teach us. He still calls today's church to reflection, and does so across denominational boundaries, the presence of which has not infrequently been blamed on him. If only for this reason, Luther's voice remains at the same time in need of being addressed, even from the vantage point of the early 21st century, when the very diverse—and divided—Christian landscape appears to be a simple matter of fact.

What distinguishes the present volume from some earlier ecumenical attempts at rapprochement is that the question of the "real Luther" is decidedly less important. Stripping off centuries' worth

---

2. Hans-Martin Barth, *The Theology of Martin Luther: A Critical Assessment*, trans. L. M. Maloney (Minneapolis: Fortress Press, 2013); and Olli-Pekka Vainio, ed., *Engaging Luther: A (New) Theological Assessment* (Eugene, OR: Cascade, 2010).

3. Franz Posset, *The Real Luther: A Friar at Erfurt & Wittenberg* (St. Louis, MO: Concordia, 2011). For a different account, situating Luther not only in relation to his intellectual antecedents but also in the broader context of the developing Wittenberg theology, see the work of Robert Kolb: *Bound Choice, Election, and Wittenberg Theological Method* (Grand Rapids, MI: Eerdmans, 2005), and *Martin Luther: Confessor of the Faith* (Oxford: Oxford University Press, 2009).

4. Christine Helmer, ed., *The Global Luther: A Theologian for Modern Times* (Minneapolis: Fortress Press, 2009).

xvi

of layers of uncharitable caricature and hagiographic adulation no longer confronts us as a particularly urgent task, as much of it has already been accomplished. This is by no means to suggest that the contributors do not seek, in their own way, to do justice to Luther. They certainly do. But once the caricature, whether positive or negative, falls away, the Luther that emerges, the "real Luther," appears more complex, polyphonic, perhaps even dissonant, more full-bodied than any apologetic or dismissive portrayals might have suggested.

This volume is interested, therefore, in the reception of Luther as a figure that instructs and inspires but also provokes and challenges precisely through the very richness of what he has to offer. To "get Luther right" is to allow *him* to speak, and to hear him in a manner simultaneously critical and constructive. The idea that this can be done in any other way, that one can uncover and recover the true—straightforward and unambiguous—Luther, showed itself to be a fantasy already in the years following Luther's death. As Robert Kolb observes, already in the mid-sixteenth century Luther's authority posed a problem to those who claimed to be his heirs.[5] For one thing, the *corpus* of Luther's writings was too immense for monitoring public teaching in the Church and adjudicating questions of biblical interpretation. More importantly, Luther could be cited against himself. Further, Luther's theology did not develop in a vacuum but was a product of fruitful collaboration with colleagues and intellectually demanding battles with opponents. Consequently, as Paul Hinlicky reminds us in his essay, Lutheranism historically, as a tradition that appeals to Luther and claims his mantle, is at the very least "Luther mediated by Melanchthon."

Even twentieth-century Luther research, undertaken by Lutheran

---

5. Robert Kolb, *Martin Luther as Prophet, Teacher, Hero: Images of the Reformer, 1520-1620* (Grand Rapids, MI: Baker, 1999), 66.

scholars, produced, for all its historical consciousness, diverse portrayals of the reformer, often rather indicative of the scholars' own *Sitz im Leben* and its perceived exigencies. For the Luther Renaissance of the early twentieth century, the framework was largely epistemological and ethical, reflective of the then-dominant Neo-Kantianism. Oswald Bayer has since repeatedly drawn attention to the strongly ontological character of Luther's Christology, rejecting the denuded anti-metaphysical accounts of what the previous generation hailed as Luther's "theology of the cross."[6] For Bayer, the kernel of Luther's thought is found in the realism of the communication of properties between Christ's divinity and humanity and the objective, ecclesially mediated reality of divine promise. The interpretations of the Finnish School, oriented toward *theosis* (deification), constitute another set of ontological claims to what lies at the center of Luther's theological vision.[7]

The contributors to the present volume come from a number of Christian denominations whose reception of the reformer's thought, even as they seek to do justice to it, is even more refracted—and for this reason even more interesting. As the essayists proceed to give Luther a fair hearing, they demonstrate that Luther cannot be heard as a single voice, or addressed from a single perspective. In their at times vigorous engagement, Luther's legacy comes to light not only as variously received but also contradicted, and/or transformed,

---

6. Oswald Bayer, "Das Wort ward Fleisch," Oswald Bayer and Benjamin Gleede, eds., *Creator est Creatura: Luthers Christologie als Lehre von der Idiomenkommunikation* (Berlin: de Gruyter, 2007), 5-34.

7. Inaugurated by Tuomo Mannermaa's *In Ipsa fide Christus adest: Luterilaisen ja Ortodoksisen Kristinuskonkäsityksen leikkauspiste* (Helsinki: Missiologian ja ekumeniikan seuran, 1979). This essay was subsequently translated into German and included in Tuomo Mannermaa, *Der im glauben gegenwärtige Christus. Rechtfertigung und Vergottung. Zum Ökumenischen Dialog* (Hannover: Lutherisches Verlagshaus, 1989). It is available in English as *Christ Present in Faith: Luther's View of Justification*, ed. Kirsi Stjerna (Minneapolis: Fortress Press, 2005). Mannermaa's essay has since been followed by numerous monographs and articles by his own students and now also their students.

only to reemerge as a fruitful leaven that may effect an even further transformation. The putative "real Luther" is thus replaced by Luther the *doctor ecclesiae*, a teacher of the Church.

All the essays were first presented at an Ecumenical Luther conference, convened at Wabash College in the summer of 2014. At the most fundamental level, the goal of the conference was to encourage mutual understanding and appreciation between other Christian traditions and those that claim Luther's legacy. However, the specific focus on the Wittenberg reformer himself, his life and his thought, yielded (as we had indeed hoped) a far richer harvest. It rendered the reciprocity of ecumenical encounters more complex, transcending a mere hammering out of points of convergence and divergence. At the very least, we thought, even if Luther should have nothing surprising to teach all of us, then perhaps he at least still challenges us to constructive engagement with our own Christian identities and the broader Christian tradition. The point turned out to be moot. All the essays presented here are witnesses to the fact that Luther continues to surprise. In this encounter, the Lutherans—represented here by the five Lutheran respondents—come to understand themselves better, and perhaps even more self-critically, through other traditions' engagement with Luther. And in the process they come to appreciate those traditions, not least through the way those traditions lay claim to Luther or respectfully push back. A similarly complex understanding of self and the other is gained by non-Lutherans. To see Luther both as a voice in the church catholic, a voice to be reckoned with, and as a forerunner, for better and for worse, of another tradition that claims his legacy may prove to be a source of deeper insight into one's own identity; more than that, it may offer ways of enriching one's identity and of deploying it more successfully in dialogue with Christian brothers and sisters across denominational lines.

The essays are certainly not intended to call into question official bilateral dialogues between Lutheran Churches and other denominations, or between Christian denominations more generally. Several of the essayists have participated in such official dialogues as delegates of their respective church bodies. Implicit in all the essays is an appreciation for the institutional initiative behind much ecumenical dialogue, and its very specific aim of establishing convergence in matters deemed essential to one's own and one's partner's identity. However, the essays do seek to make a vital contribution to ecumenical dialogue, so understood, by broadening out its scope. This they do, first, in a diachronic fashion by making the implicit argument that one can learn most fruitfully by recovering and engaging the voice of the teachers and by presuming fundamental wisdom on their part. As a *doctor ecclesiae*, Luther remains a teacher not only of the tradition that claims him, whether with considerable admiration or a modicum of unease, but of the *una sancta*, the Christian Church at large. Second, the essays make the implicit argument that true understanding of the other not only zeroes in on the common denominator, while assuming a blessed irrelevance, or even ignorance, of the non-divisive rest. It also consists in the capacity to learn from each other in a more dynamic way: by drawing on each other's heritage, by calling the partner back to the partner's own heritage, and by allowing this heritage to speak to all those concerned in a critical and constructive fashion. Last but not least, insofar as the authors are all scholars and Christians who reflect on beliefs and practices that are very much their own, the essays are an invitation to ecumenical reflection—an invitation extended to all and intentionally informed by one's own and the other's tradition, open to a challenge, and ready for a surprise.[8]

8. The editors note, with gratitude, that the idea for the conference was inspired by the rules with which the late Cardinal Avery Dulles sought to articulate the nature and goals of ecumenical

The first essay offered here is by **Jared Wicks.** Wicks has spent an academic lifetime—indeed, over half a century as a Jesuit theologian—attending to close readings of significant texts in Luther's corpus. His essay in the present volume chronicles shifts in his focus during those decades. Wicks begins with his early fascination with the theology behind Luther's denunciation of indulgence preaching, not just the familiar *Ninety-Five Theses* but the theologically richer *Treatise on Indulgences.* He relates how these early works caused him to realize how deftly, though ever so slightly, the young Luther began to reshape the theology of grace inherited from the late medieval church and give it a new, pastoral twist. What the medieval church called *gratia sanans* (healing grace), Luther now understood firmly, in the context of faith, as a *donum,* a gift that accompanies the fullness of grace. This grace has a re-recreating, re-vivifying effect in the life of the Christian yearning for God's grace, and thus orients all of life's activities.

Far from being separated from the corporate life of the church, however, this life-orientation is nurtured and deepened in participation in the sacraments. Wicks describes and elucidates his discovery of the important notion of *fides sacramenti* (faith in the sacrament) in the early Luther. It is not the sacrament by itself that heals, but also the believer's faith therein, that the sacrament is promised *pro me* (for me). Yet this is not a subjectivizing tendency in Luther; it is, as Wicks shows, due to the objective declaration of promise, such as in the words of institution, that the sacrament elicits faith. Wicks concludes with further reflections on the difficulties (because of Luther's polemics) and resources (because of Luther's

dialogue; in his particular case it was dialogue between Catholics and Evangelicals. Cardinal Dulles' essay, "The Unity for Which We Hope," was originally published in Charles Colson and Richard John Neuhaus, eds., *Evangelicals and Catholics: Toward a Common Mission* (Nashville: Thomas Nelson, 1995), 115-146; its summary can be found in a blog post by Timothy George at http://www.firstthings.com/web-exclusives/2013/07/averys-ten-rules.

catechesis) for Roman Catholic engagement with Luther's understanding of the Church and sanctification in the Holy Spirit.

Brian Brewer, a Baptist theologian and historian, engages an understanding of Luther's famous "priesthood of all believers" doctrine. Noting its origins as an egalitarian, laity-ennobling move, Brewer tracks the evolution of Luther's thought on the common priesthood, especially as the torrents of the 1525 Peasants' War raged. Brewer thinks that Luther never abandoned his key insight—that a priest is made by virtue of baptism and faith, not by ordination or human ordinance—though his emphases and certainly his rhetoric changed over time. However, in order to speak to the Baptist tradition today, Brewer insists that the key feature of the common priesthood for Luther was the way it facilitated mutual accountability and consolation among laypersons. There was no need for an ordained priest to be present for Bible study to happen, nor even confession and absolution of sin among laity. Each, by virtue of his common priesthood, could do that for and with one another.

Such mutuality and shared accountability stand in marked contrast to many recent Baptist understandings of the priesthood of all believers, which have tended to stress individuality and each person's "soul competence," in the words of influential Southern Baptist theologian E. Y. Mullins (1860-1928). Brewer shows that engagement with Luther's understanding of the common priesthood might well safeguard Baptist identity from privatized and subjectivist personal theologies, and help it develop a nascent mutuality in ministry.

Matthew Boulton, a pastor in the Disciples of Christ church, argues that Luther is helpful to other churches primarily in the subtle ways the reformer helps to identify the *enemy* of faith. Very often, Boulton points out, Luther notices how the deepest threat to Christianity comes not from without, but from within, from where the heart of the faith is beating. Because of humankind's penchant for idolatry, the fall from worship to mere observance, from living tradition to dead traditionalism, from righteousness to self-righteousness is an ever-present threat. Boulton thus casts Luther's understanding of sin in a *liturgical* context: distorted, idolatrous human action is an incurvature upon oneself, but genuinely human action, shaped by worship of God, is *excurvatus ad alios*—curved outward in service of others. Luther helps us to see redeemed human nature as a kind of *homo laudans* (praising person) rightly oriented to God in prayer and to one's fellows in humble service.

David Tracy finds in Luther a necessary supplement to Christian theology's insistence that God is fundamentally incomprehensible: God is also hidden, and hidden because God hides Godself. Tracy's essay explores several dimensions of hiddenness. God is revealed as hidden in the crucified Christ, which discloses in a provocative way God's promise of forgiveness. A second dimension is one many Lutherans are quick to elide, but which Tracy affirms: for Luther, theology's God (the *deus theologicus*) also hides beyond this paradoxical revelation. God is also revealed *sub contradictario*, under the form of its contradiction. To speak of this God is to take with utter seriousness the believer's experiences of dread and struggle, or as Luther called them, *Anfechtungen*. Witnesses to a cosmic battle in history between good and evil, the elect and the damned, are sensible to feel uneasy, even terrified of the outcome. God is experienced as hidden in a fearful, not just reason-thwarting, way, as well. Finally there is the dimension of hiddenness closest to the notion of incomprehensibility: his mysterious revelation as Trinity. Drawing on recent scholarship that takes into account the mature Luther's careful disputations on precise meanings of "person" and "relation," Tracy shows that such precision is subjugated to mystery. The second person of the Trinity unifies himself to the believer in faith in a way beyond our comprehension. This union with Christ, which cannot be comprehended, "comprehends" the believer into something like *theosis*.

Matt Jenson, writing in the tradition of American evangelicalism, develops ways in which that tradition can helpfully critique, but more importantly be enriched by engagement with Luther's multifaceted approach to faith. Focusing on Luther's influential Galatians lectures of 1535, Jenson identifies three potential features of Luther's notion of faith that supplement and safeguard American evangelical Christianity from potential languor. "Easy-believism" names the temptation to limit one's faith to a kind of fire-insurance, resting assured that assent to a few Spartan concepts is enough. Another temptation is to turn the gospel into a toilsome, even if therapeutic, law. A third temptation is to focus inwardly on the *pro me* feature of Christ's promise that one forgets it is the objective *Christ* who promises. Engagement with Luther thereby helps Evangelicals to be even more fully who they wish be in the Christian household of faith.

Susan Wood draws on her experiences of ecumenical dialogue to offer an appreciation and critique of Luther on baptism. Noting the Council of Trent's condemnation of certain positions it supposed Luther and his followers had taken, Wood draws on the emerging ecumenical consensus that these anathemas largely missed the mark. On the contrary, receptive Roman Catholics might well appreciate Luther's pastoral theology of baptism that drives one to remember baptism daily, construes baptism as God's promise for new life, and recovers an eschatological orientation of the sacrament. Catholic theology can also clarify Luther's own claims about baptism as it relates to the Word of God, namely, whether grace is a substance or a presence, as well as the continuing claim of God's law on the life of the baptized.

Randall Zachman takes a slightly different approach in his essay from our other contributors. Answering the question, "What did reading Luther do for you (or *to you!*) as a non-Lutheran?", Zachman recounts his coming to grips with Luther's insistence that, while no man is an island, facing death certainly puts him on one. As Luther insisted, each of us must fight our own battle with death by ourselves, alone. This is better than not thinking about death—our own death—at all, for it lends some existential weight to our days, rescuing them from a bland (even if occasionally riotous) flaccidity. And then the force of the Gospel penetrates especially deeply, because a dying person confronted with the need to clear his conscience in the presence of God is so keenly aware of the futility of works and the law at that point.

Further, Zachman's essay seeks to highlight how Luther's views on the conscience and death demand personal responsibility for belief. It is not enough to say, "Well, this is what my church believes." Each of us, then, is asked to stand at Worms and consider what the Christian faith entails to our minds and lives. This places an intense burden on each believer. However, in the paradox of faith the more earnestly we confess our lives and shortcomings to God, the more intensely Christ desires to take them as his own.

Johannes Zachhuber examines Luther's principle of *sola scriptura* and comes to the rather surprising conclusion that an ecumenically acceptable version of it was implicitly affirmed by the Second Vatican Council. Tracing one trajectory of a critique of the "two-source" theory of oral apostolic tradition and written biblical tradition, Zachhuber highlights features of Josef Geiselmann's views on the Council of Trent, and Joseph Ratzinger's appropriation of that sharp criticism. Though the scripture principle is often thought to be the least compelling of the Reformation *solas*, Zachhuber shows that its disparagement is actually a symptom of its success and general acceptance. Despite Karl Barth's protests that, by accepting a historicized continuity between scripture and ecclesial authority, the churches who are inheritors of the Reformation betray the scripture principle, Zachhuber concludes that the Reformation's re-balancing of tradition in a way normatively shaped by scripture actually vindicates the catholic church's long consensus.

Anna Case-Winters discerns many touch-points common to Luther's thought and her own Presbyterian tradition, and finds some of the divergences to be mutually illuminating. There is unfinished business remaining from the Protestant Reformation, and the task, as Case-Winters sees it, is not to celebrate divisive achievements of the sixteenth century, but rather to roll up our sleeves and get to work. On a number of matters, Calvin and Luther are close. Luther thought the Bible pointed to the Gospel; Calvin thought it pointed to the Word. Luther thought the real presence of Christ in Holy Communion was physical; Calvin's real presence was spiritual. What some of Luther's followers have termed the "second use of the Gospel" Calvin's followers term "the third use of the law." Such differences should not be discarded, but neither should they excuse the churches from the patient and methodical work of growth together in unity.

The editors would like to thank all the authors for the seriousness with which they have approached the task of reflecting on the figure and thought of the reformer in the context of their own traditions. Their enthusiastic participation in the Ecumenical Luther conference at Wabash College, from which this volume emerged, made it an intellectually stimulating and personally memorable event. Thanks are also due others at Wabash without whose hard work and dedication the conference would never have taken shape, let alone place. Bev Cunningham was the organizational and logistical brain, while the student interns, Stephen Batchelder and Joe Mount, lent a hand with a host of practical matters. We would also like to extend words of appreciation to Dean Scott Feller at Wabash, and Dean Timothy George and Associate Dean David Hogg at Beeson Divinity School for their abiding support of our research. Thanks go, further, to Libby Manning, David Kubiak, Bronwen Wickkiser, and Michael Wren, as well as Lilly Endowment staff, Chris Coble and Jessicah Krey Duckworth. We can hardly express our immense gratitude to Kelly Nelson for her good cheer and hospitality, as a horde of theologians descended on her home. Finally, warmest thanks are also due to the staff at Fortress Press, especially Will Bergkamp and Lisa Gruenisen, who eagerly embraced this project and affirmed us in our conviction that its fruits deserve to be shared.

We trust that the ecumenical and multi-voice engagement with Martin Luther presented here will enrich the readers' own reflection on their own traditions, just as the contributors have all learned both from and about each other. Such mutual learning, we believe, models Christian witness, not as uniformity at all costs but as reflective, appreciative, critical and constructive dialogue—with those adjectives applying equally to the other and to one's own tradition.

Piotr J. Małysz
Derek R. Nelson

1

———

Catholic Encounters with Martin Luther

Jared Wicks, SJ

Luther's theological insights have been fascinating me for nearly fifty years, with influence on my teaching at the Jesuit School of Theology in Chicago in the 1970s and then at the Gregorian University in Rome. Since I left the Gregorian in 2004, Luther has continued to be a source of theological ideas to communicate to Lutherans and Catholics, and to combine in key ways with my own spiritual formation in the *Spiritual Exercises* of Ignatius Loyola.

This essay does not offer a survey of Catholic Luther scholarship, but is instead a personal memoir, looking back upon my own varied encounters with Luther. I have met him along the way of a life of theological scholarship, teaching, and work on ecumenical commissions. My perceptions of the reformer have led to my published efforts at proper historical reconstruction of Luther's development, at analytical organizing of his teaching, and at framing Luther's theological contributions to sound theology and greater personal depth in Christian believing and acting.

1. Early Encounter with Luther in Münster

My doctoral studies in the mid-1960s were at Münster, where the University had both Catholic and Evangelical theology faculties. It was for me a sustained encounter with Luther's early works and with the Luther scholarship on hand at the time. The work was theological in character, even though I was often surrounded by Reformation historians. For the doctorate in the Catholic faculty, Erwin Iserloh was my mentor, and a demanding one, at a time when he was developing lines of Luther-interpretation going beyond the work of his own mentor, Joseph Lortz.[1]

In my first Münster semester, Iserloh's seminar treated Luther's 1517 intervention on the doctrine and practice of indulgences. My mentor was already famous for contesting, in 1961, the historicity of Luther posting the *Ninety-Five Theses* on the door of Wittenberg's Castle Church on October 31, 1517.[2] The seminar was Iserloh's

---

1. Three substantial contributions by Iserloh to Luther studies are "Sacramentum et exemplum. Ein augustinisches Thema lutherischer Theologie," in *Reformata Reformanda. Festgabe für Hubert Jedin*, 2 vols., ed. Erwin Iserloh und Konrad Repgen (Münster: Aschendorff, 1965), 1:247–64; "Luther und die Mystik," in *Kirche, Mistik, Heiligung und das Natürliche bei Luther*, ed., Ivar Asheim, Vorträge des 3. Internationalen Kongress für Lutherforschung (Göttingen: Vandenhoeck und Ruprecht, 1967), 60–83, in English as "Luther's Christ-Mysticism," in *Catholic Scholars Dialogue with Luther*, ed. Jared Wicks (Chicago: Loyola University Press, 1970), 37–58; and "Gratia und Donum. Rechtfertigung und Heiligung nach Luthers Schrift 'Wider den Löwener Theologen Latomus' (1520)," in *Studien zur Geschichte und Theologie der Reformation. Festschrift Ernst Bizer*, ed. Luise Abramowski and J. F. Gerhard Goeters (Neukirchen: Neukirchener Verlag, 1969), 141–56, and in *Catholica* 24 (1970), 67–83. These and other articles relevant to Luther-Interpretation are in Erwin Iserloh, *Kirche – Ereignis und Institution. Aufsätze und Vorträge* (Münster: Aschendorff, 1985), vol. 2. A full bibliography of Iserloh's publications is now in Uwe Wolff, *Iserloh. Der Thesenanschlag fand nicht statt* (Freiburg, Switzerland: Universitätsverlag, 2013), 247–67.
2. Erwin Iserloh, *Luthers Thesenanschlag. Tatsache oder Legende?* (Wiesbaden: Steiner, 1962), first

workplace for preparing the book whose English version is *The Theses Were Not Posted.*[3]

During that first seminar, I studied a little-known theological treatise by Luther on indulgences and on their rightful (that is, marginal) place in a Christian life of penance. Luther's *Tractatus de indulgentiis* is misplaced in vol. 1 of the Weimar Edition as a sermon of summer 1516, but a Mainz archive preserves it together with Luther's *Ninety-Five Theses* and his letter to the Mainz Archbishop, Albrecht of Brandenburg, sent from Wittenberg on October 31, 1517.[4] I take Luther's short treatise as essential for grasping his theological grounds for drawing up the theses with which Reformation doctrinal controversy began.[5]

Luther's *Tractatus* filled the instructional vacuum left by Tetzel and other preachers on indulgences. Luther highlights a present penitential combat against the residue of sin, while insisting on post-justification penance *and* God's interior healing and renewing

---

given as a lecture in Mainz, November 8, 1961, sponsored by the Institut für Europäische Geschichte.

3. The original German was *Luther zwischen Reform und Reformation. Der Thesenanschlag fand nicht statt* (Münster: Aschendorff, 1966), of which the translation came out from Beacon Press in 1968. Wolff, *Iserloh* (2013), gives Volker Leppin's judgment that Iserloh's amassed Luther texts not mentioning a historical theses-posting clearly outweigh other later texts advanced to prove the historicity of the event (pp. 239–45).

4. Fritz Herrmann, "Luthers Tractatus de indulgentiis," *Zeitschrift für Kirchengeschichte* 28 (1907), 370–73; G. Krüger, "Luthers Tractatus de indulgentiis," *Theologische Studien und Kritiken* 90 (1917), 507–20; Walther Köhler, *Dokumente zum Ablassstreit von 1517* (Tübingen: Mohr-Siebeck,2 1934), 94–99. WA 1 (1883) placed the text among Luther's sermons of summer 1516: WA 1:63–65. Today, the treatise is accessible as part of Luther's correspondence of late October 1517 in *WABr* 12:5–9.

5. My publications on Luther's Treatise began with an introduction, translation, and commentary in "Martin Luther's *Treatise on Indulgences*, 1517," *Theological Studies* 28 (1967): 481–518, which also was part of my dissertation, *Man Yearning for Grace. Luther's Early Spiritual Teaching* (Washington: Corpus, 1968), also published by Veröffentlichungen des Instituts für Europäische Geschichte Mainz, 56 (Wiesbaden: Steiner, 1969), 238–61, with a German translation of the treatise in the Steiner edition on pp. 431–438. I revised and updated my English translation and presentation of the treatise in Jared Wicks, *Luther's Reform. Studies on Conversion and the Church* (Mainz: Ph. Von Zabern, 1992), 87–116.

influence. Luther speaks of a *gratia infusa* that purges concupiscence and unruly affections. Everyone needs this urgently, but indulgences *per se* do not help because, as presented, they remit imposed satisfactory penances—without an interior effect during this life. Regarding the departed souls undergoing purgation, Luther's proposal was that the standard phrase *per modum suffragii*, concerning indulgences applied to the souls by way of petitionary intercession, was an indication of the church's prayer of impetration that God grant these souls the infused grace that will overcome their remaining concupiscent spiritual disorders, turn them to God in pure longing, and so make them ready for seeing God in heavenly beatitude.

Luther's conclusion of his *Tractatus de indulgentiis* became one orientation of my further research on what he had written, taught, and only in part published from 1509 through 1517. This was the era of his early biblical lectures and first anti-scholastic disputations. The last lines of the 1517 treatise on indulgences articulate one recurrent concern of this early work, when it concludes that Christian instruction has to promote a spiritual dedication to penitential purification from the concupiscent affections left after sins are absolved and forgiven. Preaching has to alert people to the danger that indulgences may foster spiritual security, lethargy, and neglect of interior grace. Emphasis has to fall, in ways well known from Augustine's *Confessions* (especially Book X), on reducing sinful drives and replacing them with longing for God, which occurs by the influence of infused, healing grace. The treatise concludes, "Let us incessantly seek his healing grace" (*assidue sanantem gratiam eius quaeramus*). Thus a *gratia sanans* was an important factor in Luther's critical position on indulgences in 1517. This mode of God's influence, with prayer of yearning for this grace, loomed large in my dissertation research as I found it in numerous texts before October

1517. When I handed in my dissertation on Luther's early spiritual teaching, the title included the phrase, *gemitus pro gratia*, in reference to the heaving sigh of desire for God's cleansing, renewing, and orienting influence in the heart of a penitent Christian. In 1967 preparation for publication, the title had the time-conditioned form, *Man Yearning for Grace*,[6] which flattened considerably Luther's Latin phrasing in many accounts of Christian life and penance in his works down to and including the 1517 theses and treatise on indulgences.

I did not realize it during my Münster years, but I was getting more than familiar with an important spiritual trait and dynamic. That earlier study would help me grasp Luther's lifelong thesis that the believer is *simul iustus et peccator*—one of the "hard nuts" we had to crack in preparing and defending the 1999 *Joint Declaration on the Doctrine of Justification*, particularly in Part 4.4, "The Justified as Sinner," which became a model text of "reconciled diversity."[7] The *simul* is not a static condition simply to be endured. For the *iustus simul peccator* struggles over his or her interior disorders, emitting prayerful longing for God's healing influence, later called the *dona* given with God's relational and reconciling *gratia*. The *dona*, earlier called *gratia sanans*, enables a practice of self-denial to counteract life-long sinfulness.[8]

---

6. See the previous note, on this publication.

7. A crucial point is that Catholics do not call remaining concupiscence "sin" in the proper sense, which amounts to a language-rule, about how one predicates "sin," especially in preaching and catechetics. The two sides agree on the ontology of disorder needing to be rectified.

8. Later I presented an account of Luther's *simul* in a seminar at the 1988 congress on Luther-Research at Oslo and amplified this in "Living and Praying as *simul iustus et peccator*. A Chapter in Luther's Spiritual Teaching," *Gregorianum* 70 (1989): 521–546, reprinted in *Luther's Reform*, 59–83. Otto Hermann Pesch then took over parts of this essay in "Simul iustus et peccator. Sinn und Stellenwert einer Formel Martin Luthers," in *Gerecht und Sünder zugleich? Ökumenische Klärungen*, ed. Theodor Schneider and Gunther Wenz (Freiburg: Herder, and Göttingen: Vandenhoeck & Ruprecht, 2001), 146–67. The studies in this work defend the judgment that the *simul* is not a Lutheran-Catholic church-dividing difference, but is open to reconciliation, as the *Joint Declaration* states.

Luther on Christian Living: Research of 1964–1966

My study in Münster of Luther's early works repeatedly yielded impressive theological and spiritual explanations on Christian living, praying, and struggling with interior disorders of the person. At the time, Luther-research did not have the term *Frömmigkeitstheologie* ("theology for piety"), later introduced by Bernd Hamm, but this is an accurate category for characterizing what Luther regularly presented in his early works.[9]

Luther's lectures on the Psalter (1513–15) and Romans (1515–16) show that the 1517 conclusion of the *Treatise on Indulgences*, on the urgency of seeking God's healing grace, arose from themes of Luther's early biblical work. Christian instruction should include personal concern about one's endemic sinfulness, leading to prayerful longing for God's therapeutic influence to free one's heart from the drive of concupiscence and instill righteous movements of willing.

Along with the *Treatise on Indulgences*, another concise expression of Luther's early theology came in theses of 1517, prepared for a September 4 "Disputation against Scholastic Theology."[10] These too rest on God's infused and operative grace and on the spirituality of "incessantly seeking God's healing grace." But the target here is not, as was the case with indulgences, preaching that disorients. Targeted instead are the views of certain Scholastics, especially Gabriel Biel, on

9. Bernd Hamm, *Frömmigkeitstheologie am Anfang des 16. Jahrhuderts. Studien zu Johannes von Paltz und seinem Umkreis* (Tübingen: Mohr-Siebeck, 1984), which I reviewed in *Gregorianum* 65 (1984), 200–204. In 1984 I made connections linking Hamm's study of Paltz and Staupitz with Luther's development, in "Fides sacramenti – Fides specialis: Luther's Development in 1518," *Gregorianum* 65 (1984), 53–87, at 58–59; reprinted with small modifications in *Luther's Reform*, 117–147, at 121-22.

10. *WA* 1:224–228, giving ninety-seven theses. But Helmar Junghans divides the text into one hundred theses in Martin Luther, *Studienausgabe*, ed. H.-U. Delius et al. (Berlin: Evangelische Verlagsanstalt, 1979), 1:165–172, in which the notes lead to the relevant texts in the scholastic authors against whom Luther directed his theses. However, a different enumeration does not lead to different contents. I follow the text and enumeration of the theses in *WA* 1 because of their wider accessibility.

a capability of fallen human beings to make moral efforts good, and so "by one's natural powers alone" (*ex puris naturalibus*) to become well-disposed to receive justifying grace.[11] Against this Luther posits that the fallen human person is a bad tree that can only will and do evil (Thesis 4). The Scholastics have imported Aristotelian ideas into theology, forgetting that human beings stand in need of redemption (Th. 40-44, 50-53).

Luther's theses of September 1517 contain eleven counter-pointed assertions which ascribe to God's grace—not to moral effort—a re-creative, revivifying effect in the human spirit. This is the positive, constructive element underlying in Luther's anti-scholastic polemic.[12] The theses of early September 1517 tell of the work of infused or healing grace, which was a key notion as well in Luther's treatise on indulgences.[13]

To the present day, Luther's penitential conception of Christian

11. In the margins, "Contra Gabrielem" identifies the adversary of eleven theses. Luther's marginal notes to Gabriel Biel's *Collectorium*, on *Sentences*, Bk. III, dist. 27, treat the human ability to love God. *WA* 59:40, 27–47, 40. The nub of the problem is Biel's erroneous assumption that the human will is healthy and needs no healing: "insulse arguit, sanam voluntatem praesupponens" (45, 40).

12. I was critical of Leif Grane's monograph on this disputation, *Contra Gabrielem* (Copenhagen: Gyldendal, 1962), for its neglect of the renewing efficacy Luther ascribed to grace, for example, on grace making righteousness abound, because it instills good-pleasure toward observing the law: "Gratia autem dei facit abundare iustitiam per Ihesum Christum, quia facit placere legem" (Thesis 75, *WA* 1:227, 33–34).

13. In the September theses, prevenient divine grace, not the fallen human nature and will, is the source of authentic love of God, termed "the love of friendship" (Th. 20), in which the person is converted to God (Th. 27). Grace must coexist with human actions for the latter to have value as meritorious (Th. 54). The reason for these and the following conclusions about grace is that it is never a static or idle presence, but is active as "a living, moving, and operative spirit" (*vivus, mobilis et operosus spiritus*) (Th. 55a). To be sure, such grace does not fully suppress the anger and lust of fallen humans (Th. 65b), but it works at such suppression (Th. 67). In fact, by such grace, righteousness abounds through Jesus Christ (Rom 5:15), because it instills good pleasure in observing the law (Th. 75). Therefore, "blessed are all those who carry out the works of God's grace" (Th. 80). Because the imperatives of the law grate on fallen human nature, grace must enter as a *mediatrix* to reconcile the will to the law (Th. 89). Such grace guides and directs the will, lest it make erroneous choices in loving God (Th. 90). Thesis 91 specifies that grace not only facilitates a life of love of God but is in fact the essential and irreplaceable cause of any elicited act of love of God (Th. 92). Breaking out of the Scholastic vocabulary of *amicitia, voluntas*, and *gratia*, Luther's Thesis 84 specifies in a Pauline way how the law becomes a good

living, enabled by God's sanative interior influence, is a valued part of my own life. It enters my preaching during Lent and my guiding of persons through the Ignatian *Exercises*. I hope it will become more widely known as people approach the commemorations coming in 2017, because it represents the doctrinal and spiritual basis of Luther's 1517 criticism of preaching on indulgences.

2. Discovery of Luther's *fides sacramenti*: 1969 and After

I was able in 1969 to undertake extensive study of Luther's works beyond 1517, during six months at the Institut für Europäische Geschichte in Mainz, then directed by Joseph Lortz. Reading Luther in Mainz, I concentrated on the reformer's sacramental theology in 1518–1519, attending especially on how the sacraments make their impacts on Christian living.

Luther's main innovation of 1518–1519 was his insistence that the believer is to take hold, in personal faith, of central words of sacramental conferral, especially absolution spoken to the person upon confessing his or her sins. Absolution is God's means of conferring his grace, that is, of accosting the repentant sinner with an open and unambiguous word of forgiveness, consolation, and assurance—it is "gospel" in dense concentration. God reveals himself openly and calls for faith in what he conveys—which becomes valid *pro me* in receptive faith. A dialectic of hiddenness *sub contrario* is marginal here, since here God is *not* justifying under the outward form of judgment, as in several of Luther's earlier comments on the Psalter and Romans.[14] A visit to Tübingen during my Mainz fellowship led to an evening with Oswald Bayer, who soon published

---

way of life in love, for "the love of God is poured into our hearts by the Holy Spirit" (Rom. 5:5).

14. I presented Luther's early theology of the sacramental word and faith amply and appreciatively in "*Fides sacramenti – fides specialis*: Luther's Development in 1518," (n. 9, above), which began as a seminar paper during the 1983 Luther Research Congress in Erfurt. This involved several

his *Promissio* on Luther's reformation *Wende*. He and I agreed on Luther's turn to the objective, forgiving word and on the dependent *pro me* of faith.[15]

Luther defended his insight into "faith in the sacrament" (*fides sacramenti*), with its insistent personalizing of the *pro me*, in texts of 1518 that climax in his *Acta Augustana*, countering a critique by Cardinal Cajetan, the Papal Legate to the German Imperial Diet in Augsburg. To ground his thesis, Luther cited numerous biblical texts on faith in a present effect, as when Jesus healed those in need. Luther also claimed he was not innovating, but was in fact applying a well-known, probative axiom, "*Non sacramentum, sed fides sacramenti iustificat*" (It is not the sacrament, but faith in the sacrament that justifies). On a visit to Heidelberg during my Mainz fellowship, I met Kurt-Victor Selge, who showed me evidence that at Augsburg in 1518 Cardinal Cajetan, after insisting that Luther must retract his innovation on *fides sacramenti*, in fact withdrew this demand, because Luther's position could be interpreted in an orthodox way.[16]

Most importantly, Luther's 1519 works moved toward integrating this new aspect of faith into the spirituality he had developed in works I had studied earlier. My Mainz study yielded a positive evaluation of

revisions of critical judgments I had made earlier on Luther's notion of *fides*, when I was influenced to an extent by the Münster professor Paul Hacker.

15. See Oswald Bayer, "Die reformatorische Wende in Luthers Theologie," *Zeitschrift für Theologie und Kirche*, 66 (1969): 115–150, and *Promissio. Geschichte der reformatorischen Wende in Luthers Theologie* (Göttingen: Vandenhoeck & Ruprecht, 1971). Knowing Bayer's Luther-interpretation confirmed for me that an innovation occurred in Luther's theology in 1518. Bayer and I agreed extensively on the contours of the teaching that preceded this, which I set forth in *Man Yearning for Grace*, and I came to hold a positive view of Luther's new departure in and after 1518.

16. K.-V. Selge reviewed Gerhard Hennig, *Cajetan und Luther. Ein historischer Beitrag zur Thomismus und Reformation* (Stuttgart: Calver, 1966), in *Archiv für Reformationsgeschichte*, 60 (1969): 217–274. Selge told on p. 273 about Cajetan's change, related in a letter from Augsburg of Georg Spalatin, published in the Wittenberg edition of Luther's German works, Part 9 (1560), p. 36a. Selge gave a fuller citation of Spalatin's information in "La chiesa in Lutero," in *Martin Lutero*, ed. Massimo Marcocchi (Milan: Vita e pensiero, 1983), 31–32, note 30.

this *fides sacramenti* during Luther's transitional years of 1518–1519, which I featured in the 1970s and 1980s in several broader accounts of Luther on justification.[17]

This Luther-theme also correlates with Ignatian spirituality. For in the *Spiritual Exercises* the Nativity meditation—a model for contemplating Gospel scenes—leads one to consider our Lord's whole life and suffering unto death on the cross, "and all this *for me.*"[18]

Advocacy for Luther, 1969–1979

Upon my return to America after the 1969 fellowship in Mainz, my book-reviewing on Luther studies began in earnest. In several reviews, I became an advocate for Luther's emphatic objectivity concerning the word of God in the encounter of justifying faith, especially in absolution and the Lord's Supper. Against a claimed "subjectivism" in Luther (the old shibboleth of Lortz), I urged attention to his sacramental theology, which is "centered in an objective and utterly reliable word of forgiveness."[19] The English translation in 1970 of Gerhard Ebeling's short introduction to Luther gave me the opportunity to call attention to Luther's notion of *fides sacramenti*, which is all but absent from Ebeling's account, but which Luther took as central in justification. God's word comes to the believer most concretely in the assuring communication, "Your sins are forgiven." I claimed that the reader who goes from Ebeling's introduction to reading Luther's major works may well be astounded

17. I inserted the 1518 works on *fides sacramenti* into the entry, "Luther," *Dictionnaire de Spiritualité*, 9 (1976), 1206–1243; into "Justification and Faith in Luther's Theology," *Theological Studies* 44 (1983): 3–29 and *Luther's Reform* (n. 5, above), 15–42; and into *Luther and His Spiritual Legacy* (Wilmington, Del.: Michael Glazier, 1983), 130–37.

18. Ignatius of Loyola, *Spiritual Exercises*, no. 116. But under Ignatius's instruction the sacraments play no great role, while Luther is emphatic on the Gospel being expressed personally to one being baptized or absolved and receiving Holy Communion.

19. *Catholic Historical Review* 57 (1971–72): 637, in a review of Riccardo Garcia Villoslada, *Raices históricas del luteranismo* (Madrid: Biblioteca de Autores Cristianos, 1969).

by Luther's serious and extensive attention to the sacraments and to their role in the believer's life of faith.[20]

My account of Luther in *Dictionnaire de Spiritualité* stressed how Luther's personalizing of Christ's saving work applied *pro me* can be rightly understood only when one connects it with "the objective, mediating instruments through which one grasps the message of salvation. The certitude and confidence of Lutheran faith rests on the word and sacraments. . . . The heart of Lutheran spiritual experience is hearing quite specific words in faith."[21]

Most recently, I spoke a word of advocacy for Luther, based on his conception of *fides sacramenti* in June 2008, at the theological symposium preceding the Eucharistic Congress at Quebec in Canada. In presenting ecumenical exchanges on the Eucharist, I featured Luther's account of the Lord's Supper, with his emphasis on the Gospel expressed in Christ's words over the bread and cup. An earlier intervention by the Lutheran theologian Albrecht Peters was critical of the Lutheran-Catholic ecumenical dialogue on the Lord's Supper for its neglect of the words of institution, which are for believing listeners "Christ's word of effective promise which elicits faith."[22] Also, study of responses by Lutheran churches to the

---

20. *Journal of the American Academy of Religion*, 39 (1971): 366, and *Journal of Ecumenical Studies* 8 (1971): 421–422, in reviews of Gerhard Ebeling, *Luther: An Introduction to His Thought* (Philadelphia: Fortress Press, 1970).

21. "Luther," *Dictionnaire de Spiritualité*, 9 (1976), col. 1234, as I stated in the original English text, which I incorporated into *Luther and His Spiritual Legacy* (1983, as in n. 17), 132, in a section on "The Mediated Promise." Juan Alfaro, esteemed Gregorian University professor, showed that what Trent ruled out as "certitude of grace" differed notably from what Luther proposed in 1518 and after. See J. Alfaro, "Certitude de l'espérance et 'certitude de la grâce," *Nouvelle Revue théologique* 104 (1972): 3–42. Another positive Catholic reading of Luther on *fides sacramenti* was in Wolfgang Schwab's Munich dissertation, *Entwicklung und Gestalt der Sakramententheologie bei Martin Luther* (Frankfurt/M.: Peter Lang, 1977), 365–89, especially 383–89.

22. Jared Wicks, "The Eucharist in Ecumenical Dialogues: Advances and New Tensions," in *L'Eucharistie, don de Dieu pour la vie du monde* (Ottawa: Canadian Conference of Catholic Bishops, 2009), 306–35, on 323, drawing on Albrecht Peters, "Einheit im Herrenmahl?" *Theologische Revue* 75 (1979): 183–90, which was critical of the Lutheran-Catholic dialogue document, *Das Herrenmahl* (Paderborn: Bonifatius & Frankfurt: Lembeck, 1979), published in

Eucharist section of the Faith and Order Commission's *Baptism, Eucharist, Ministry* (1982) led me to sympathize with Lutheran objections that *BEM* does not know Christ's "role as Lord of the Supper, who stands before the church to face it and give forgiveness and assurance in virtue of his once-for-all saving self-sacrifice." At the central moment, believers receive in faith "Christ's saving word and gift of himself."[23] I proposed at Quebec that Catholics should receive instruction from Luther's profound insight into the soteriology of the sacrament through the grace-bearing institution narrative and the reception of Holy Communion.[24]

3. Insights from Luther on the Church's Life and the Creed, 1979 and After

For the 450th anniversary of the *Augsburg Confession* in 1980, I studied the Confession's "abuse" articles (nos. 22–28), mainly because everybody else was studying the doctrinal articles (nos. 1–21).[25] Another factor in approaching the 1530 clash over "abuses" and their practical reform was a perception resulting from my reading, during the 1970s, on the sixteenth-century Protestant reforms and the eventual Catholic reforming initiatives as both being accelerators of social change and adaptations of Western Christianity amid the broader evolution of early modern European social structures and life.[26] This led me to consider the history-of-impact

English in Harding Meyer and Lukas Vischer, eds., *Growth in Agreement* (New York: Paulist & Geneva: World Council of Churches, 1984), 190–214.

23. "The Eucharist in Ecumenical Dialogues," 329. The Lutheran responses to *BEM* are spread through Max Thurian ed., *Churches Respond to BEM*, 6 vols. (Geneva: WCC Publications, 1986–1988). Martin Seils studied them in *Lutheran Convergence?* (Geneva: Lutheran World Federation, 1988).

24. Wicks, "The Eucharist in Ecumenical Dialogues," 332–33.

25. Jared Wicks, "Abuses under Indictment at the Diet of Augsburg 1530," *Theological Studies*, 41 (1980): 253–302, and in *Luther's Reform* (n. 5, above), 223–77.

26. For example, Keith Thomas, *Religion and the Decline of Magic* (New York: Scribner, 1971); Jean Delemeau, *Catholicism between Luther and Voltaire* (London: Burns & Oates, 1977; original

(*Wirkungsgeschichte*) of Luther's work, that is, how his instructions came to be implemented in church life in the Protestant territories and free cities. This is part of the total phenomenon of Martin Luther. An ecumenical recognition of the values of Luther's reform has to attend to churches and groups of churches, which worked out in the sixteenth century a reconfigured form of life and worship and created a social ethos passed on and still living in the present. This ecumenical motivation made it important to begin with the churches that presented the *Augsburg Confession* in 1530 and to see these in their historical context. Thereby one could understand how Luther's message and teaching became social "flesh" in corporate bodies that were realizing many of the widespread aspirations for reform of that day.[27]

In 1986 I joined the world-level dialogue set up by the Lutheran World Federation and the Vatican Secretariat for Promoting Christian Unity. This motivated another effort of research on the Augsburg Diet of 1530, which led to a detailed narrative of the colloquy in quest of unity between Lutheran and Catholic representatives, from August 16 to 30, 1530. This first Lutheran-Catholic dialogue was more than a doctrinal face-off between defenders of the Lutheran Confession and of the Emperor's *Confutation*, since the dialogue came to treat the concrete shape that church life was taking in the reformed territories and cities.[28] In

French, 1971); and Peter Burke, *Popular Culture in Early Modern Europe* (New York: New York University Press, 1978). Charles Taylor treats a broad ranging "drive to reform," beginning in the late medieval period and cresting in Calvinistic efforts to re-order whole societies. See Charles Taylor, *A Secular Age* (Cambridge, Mass.: Belknap-Harvard University Press, 2007), 61–89 and 142–45. The *Augsburg Confession*, following hard on the first parish visitations in Electoral Saxony, exemplifies the reforming drive in the Confession's articles 22–28.

27. The main outcome of this phase of my work is "Abuses under Indictment at the Diet of Augsburg 1530."

28. My study came out as "The Lutheran *forma ecclesiae* in the Colloquy at Augsburg, August 1530," in *Christian Authority. Essays in Honor of Henry Chadwick*, ed. Gillian R. Evans (Oxford: Clarendon Press, 1988), 160–203; reprinted in *Luther's Reform*, 279–316.

their colloquy, Melanchthon and Eck reached doctrinal agreements during the first two days regarding justification, church-membership of baptized sinners, the mediation of forgiveness by word and sacrament, good works by the justified, and heavenly intercession by the saints (but not on prayers invoking them).[29] But on "abuses" and their reform, treated in Articles 22-28 of the Confession and *Confutation*, sharp differences emerged over offering the chalice in Holy Communion, holding only community masses, celebrating according to the traditional canon of the mass, and then fasting, holy days, confession, and especially the jurisdiction of bishops. The two sides discussed compromises, which aimed to preserve peace and a degree of mutual toleration until a General Council brought definitive clarifications, but these were not satisfactory to the leaders who had commissioned the dialogue-members.[30]

Later Study of Luther's Pastoral and Creedal Instructions

After accepting a call to teach at the Gregorian, I began living and working in Rome in 1979. In the 1980s Martin Luther became present to Italian readers in a new way, through an Italian translation by Stefano Cavallotto of nine works in which the reformer provided instruction on everyday religious living.[31] This became an occasion for me to speak and write appreciatively of Luther in a way opposed the widespread Italian image him as a proto-liberal apostle of freedom

---

29. Wicks, "The Lutheran *forma ecclesiae*," *Luther's Reform*, 289–94.

30. Ibid., 294–311. When the colloquy changed on August 23 from involving fourteen members (seven Lutherans and seven Catholics), to just six (three from each side), progress was impeded by the Catholics' having no new proposals and by Lutheran opposition, especially from Prince Philip of Hesse and the city of Nürnberg, to making concessions on the *obligation* of receiving Communion from the cup and on admitting even a limited restoration of episcopal jurisdiction.

31. Martin Luther, *Scritti pastorali minori*, ed. & trans. Stefano Cavallotto (Naples: Ed. Dehoniane, 1987). I spoke at the book's "launch" in Naples in late 1987 and published my text as "Lutero e la religiosità vissuta," *Gregorianum* 70 (1989): 120–26, published in English in 1992 as "Luther and Lived Religiosity," *Luther's Reform*, 189–96, and in condensed form in *Luther Digest* 3 (1995): 104–5.

and anti-hierarchical proponent of priesthood of each individual. In his polemics, Luther was clearing the ground for living the faith. In the reformed communities, pastors took guidance from his short pastoral works, of which Cavallotto offered a selection in Italian, on baptism, catechesis and professing the faith, confession, marriage, daily prayer, enduring temptation and discouragement, and finally preparing well for death.[32] This was one more step in my own concentration on the church life of Lutherans to which Luther gave focus and depth by his genial accounts of the basic elements of Christian faith and practice.

In the late 1980s, while I was taking part in the official world-level Lutheran-Catholic dialogue on the church and justification, I turned to Luther's instructions on the Church in the Creed's third article for a lecture in Münster in 1990 on the occasion of Erwin Iserloh's seventy-fifth birthday.[33]

Taking up a position advanced often by Iserloh, I noted a contrast between some well- known works by Luther in the "breakout" years 1520–1525 and his later works in the years before and after the *Augsburg Confession* of 1530. To this day, the earlier tracts pose problems for our Catholic rapprochement because of their polemics, especially on the church and ministry, in which, for example, Luther can even speak of the "invisible church" which only faith can perceive.[34] But a self-correcting process set in after 1525, leading

---

32. Continuing along this line, I turned to Luther's deathbed instructions in a seminar paper on his work, as compared with 15th century texts on the *ars moriendi*, at the 1997 Heidelberg Congress on Luther Research, published as "Applied Theology at the Deathbed," *Gregorianum* 79 (1998): 345–68.

33. Jared Wicks, "Heiliger Geist—Kirche—Heiligung: Einsichten aus Luthers Glaubensunterricht," *Catholica* 45 (1991): 79–100, published in English as "Holy Spirit—Church—Sanctification: Insights from Luther's Instructions on the Faith," *Pro ecclesia* 2 (1993): 150–72; condensed in *Luther Digest* 1 (1993): 138–40, and reprinted in full in *Luther's Reform* (n, 5, above), 197–220.

34. *WA* 7:710, 2. K. Hammann noted the potential for misunderstanding in Luther's polemics at this time, in *Ecclesia spiritualis. Luthers Kirchenverständnis in den Kontroversen mit Augustin von Alveldt und Ambrosius Catharinus* (Göttingen: Vandenooeck & Ruprecht, 1989), 85, 108,

to Luther's repeated affirmation of the common doctrinal heritage. From these later works, especially Luther's catechetical works, the ecclesiology of both Catholics and Lutherans can be positively promoted.

Luther began publishing catechetical sermon-series as early as 1520, with the church regularly explained within the third article of the Creed.[35] Here the church results from the missions of Christ and the Holy Spirit, as a holy community on earth, which the Spirit assembles, preserves and rules, increasing it daily by the sacraments and word of God. The community is a vital network of mutual help and bearing of burdens, marked especially by the forgiveness of sins through the keys.[36] Luther's later accounts of the Creed, before, in, and after his catechisms of 1529, offered engaging accounts of the church within the earthly economy of the Holy Spirit.[37] The overall unifying concept is that of the Spirit's work of sanctification carried out in the assembly that the same Spirit gathers. For sanctifying, the Spirit has equipped the assembly with effective "gifts and endowments," such as baptism, the gospel-centered sermon, the altar-sacrament, absolution in virtue of the keys, and ministries of mutual consolation and encouragement.[38]

Luther even ascribed to the church an instrumental service as

122–123, and 235. Erwin Iserloh presented Luther's early polemical ecclesiology in "Martin Luther und die römische Kirche," in *Luther und die politische Welt*, ed. Erwin Iserloh and Gerhard Müller (Stuttgart: Steiner, 1984), 173–86.

35. *Eine kurtze Form . . . des Glaubens*, Das dritte Teil; *WA* 7:218, 20–220, 5.

36. Jared Wicks, "Holy Spirit—Church—Sanctification," *Luther's Reform*, 200–202.

37. In the main section of my text, I drew on Luther's 1523 and 1528 sermons on the creed (*WA* 11:48–54; *WA* 301:2–94), his Confession of faith in 1528 (*WA* 26:499–509), his two catechisms of 1529 (*WA* 301:182–89 and 292–99), and his Pentecost sermons of 1529, 1531, and 1538 (*WA* 29:359–376; *WA* 341:458–468; *WA* 46:360–372).

38. What Luther calls "gifts and endowments," Vatican II calls "elements of sanctification and truth," in *Lumen Gentium* 8, affirming that several ecclesial realities are present and operative beyond the limits of the Catholic Church. *LG* 15 goes more into detail on these "elements" which are salvific in the communities not in full communion with the Catholic Church. The study-document of the world-level dialogue, *The Apostolicity of the Church* (Minneapolis: Lutheran University Press, 2006), noted this identity of Luther's "gifts or endowments" with

believers' nurturing mother, who of course is subordinated to the Spirit in administering Christ's gifts. "The Holy Spirit is the one who outwardly and visibly baptizes, making use of the word and applying the keys. These are his tongues of fire."[39] In the larger economy, the Holy Spirit is the executor who completes the redemptive work of Christ on earth, with the Spirit working unceasingly until the last day through the community's preachers and sacraments.[40] After drawing out the ecclesiology of his catechetical works, I expanded on Luther's teaching on sanctification, in order to further clarify issues in our dialogue on justification around 1990.[41]

I concluded "Holy Spirit – Church – Sanctification" with an insistence that Luther's ecclesiology rested on comprehensive principles of mediation, which the Holy Spirit poured out at Pentecost and keeps bringing into operation. The church's task involves announcing forgiveness of sins, helping personalize faith's relation to God, and promoting sanctification as penitential observance of the commandments, along with expecting the eschatological fullness of salvation. These insights can "notably enhance for all Christians both their theology of the church and their lives as people assembled in the church."[42]

Concluding Reflection: How Can This Be?

One might ask just how a Jesuit theologian who for a quarter-century taught Catholic Fundamental Theology at the Gregorian University in Rome could coherently develop a source-based

---

Vatican II's "elements" on pp. 69–70. Since these are apostolic in origin, they make the ecclesial body administering them *apostolic*.

39. Pentecost Sermon (1538); *WA* 46:425, 3–5.

40. Sermon on the Creed (1528); *WA* 301:93, 11-14.

41. Wicks, "Holy Spirit – Church – Sanctification," *Luther's Reform*, 202–211 (the constructive ecclesiology) and 211–218 (the Spirit's work in hearts, even to overcoming endemic sin and living by the Decalogue, although in ways falling short of perfection).

42. Wicks, "Holy Spirit – Church – Sanctification," *Luther's Reform*, 220.

interpretation of Luther's thought and regularly present it to a variety of Catholic and Lutheran publics.

One key to my half-lifetime with Luther is the formative impact made upon me by the Second Vatican Council's Constitution of Divine Revelation, *Dei Verbum*, promulgated November 18, 1965, near the mid-point of my Luther research for the doctorate in Münster. In fact, in regularly offered courses at the Gregorian and in my research and writing on the Council, I have probed genetically and systematically that high-level Catholic teaching document. I take *Dei Verbum* as a fundamental part of Vatican II's legacy for the ongoing work of Catholic theology and, because of this, my encounters with Luther have been greatly facilitated. Three *Dei Verbum* teachings enter this relationship in major ways.

First, Chapter 1 of the Constitution, on God's self-revelation and the response of faith, treats the word of God to humankind as personal, historical, and centered in Christ. In no. 4, the defining content of all God's revelation comes from the Christ-event. Most importantly, this content is unmistakably soteriological in impact, in Vatican II's momentous account of *what* revelation conveys, namely, "that God is with us to free us from sin and death and raise us to eternal life." The cognitive and authoritarian emphases of Vatican I's account of revelation have given way to accentuating God-with-us and God-for-us in Christ. A positive correlation with Luther's central account of the Gospel is obvious and not difficult to elaborate.

Second, Chapter 2 of *Dei Verbum* affirms the Gospel as the one source of all saving truth and guidance for humane and holy living. Then the document reconceptualizes tradition in a decided move away from highlighting "unwritten apostolic traditions" (as at the Council of Trent) to focus on the Christian community's self-perpetuation through the generations of believers by its teaching, life, and worship. The contribution of this tradition, according to no. 9 of the Constitution, is not to reveal contents supplementary to Scripture, but instead to provide certainty in holding to revelation as transmitted. Here, avenues are open to meeting Luther and his own legacy as it is moving through history.

Third, Chapter 6 of *Dei Verbum*, which gives pastoral conclusions on the role Scripture should have in the Church's life, affirms that all preaching ought to be nourished and ruled by Scripture, because it brings God lovingly near to faith-communities as their support, strength, and spiritual sustenance. In no. 25 the Constitution urges, emphatically (*vehementer*), the practice of assiduous, meditative, and prayerful reading of Scripture by all the faithful. The chapter even ends with a Reformation slogan about the Word of God, "which abides forever" (*quod manet in aeternum*). Again, Vatican II offers a doctrinal and pastoral instruction that makes easy a positive correlation with Luther as one part of my theological work to enrich the thinking and discourse Catholics and all other Christian theologians.[43]

This essay has sketched a Catholic, Jesuit theologian's "affair" with Martin Luther, lasting over half a lifetime, but still not completed. I hope this presentation will contribute constructively, for Lutherans, Catholics, and many others, in their commemoration in 2017 of the 5th centenary of Luther's protest to the Archbishop of Mainz about indulgence preaching. The protest came in the dual form of both Luther's *Ninety-Five Theses* and—*nota bene!*—his theological gem of a treatise on indulgences in penitential living.

---

43. For my 2009 "primer" on theological sources and method, called *Doing Theology* (Paulist Press), I had head-shot pictures placed on the cover of Athanasius, Thomas Aquinas, Luther, Newman and Yves Congar. The opening chapter surveys basic types of theological work, among which Luther exemplifies theology concentrated on a single truth applicable across a wide range of theological topics (pp. 13–14).

2

Spirituality, Ontology, and the Church: A Response to Jared Wicks

Piotr J. Małysz

I. Spirituality: From 'healing grace' to 'faith alone'

Jared Wicks's rich and multilayered presentation is a particularly fitting piece to serve as the opening chapter of the present volume. It neither offers a mere diachronic overview of the central themes of Luther's theology, nor does it present a dispassionate account of convergences and divergences between Luther's reforming program and the theology of the Church of Rome, whether then or now. What it does offer is something far more exciting. The essay conveys a palpable sense of adventure Luther's theology offers. And it depicts a scholarly journey as one that takes place not only in the company of books but also among conversation partners: with some one may travel only for a season and yet be left with cherished memories and lasting insights. In Wicks's case, this adventurous journey (it surely must have felt like that for a young Jesuit!) has lasted for almost half a century. This alone should give us Lutherans pause. For we often presume familiarity (and presumption is not infrequently only how far things go); but just as often we seem to have lost our sense of wonder. If today a Lutheran university, in search of an enticing and marketable self-image, can reduce Luther's theology to a bare emphasis on freedom, then something is certainly amiss! That aside, what Wicks has given us, above all, is a glimpse into a scholar's journey, with all its excitement and diversions, that is not merely an intellectual affair but, if I may say so, a transformative and spiritual pilgrimage. A theologian may already have arrived at the end of all things and, in the words of Paul, have already "fathomed all mysteries and all knowledge" (1 Cor 13:2), but still, the theologian dare not forget that he or she, too, is only a *homo viator* in this life.

The spiritual dimension of Wicks's engagement with Luther, indicative of its very depth, is something I wish to highlight. This is not to suggest, of course, uncritical reception, or the absence of differences and uneasiness. I am highlighting spirituality because, on the one hand, it signals both a superficial continuance, and a profound transformation, of the Roman-Catholic preoccupation with the subjective elements of Luther's thought. The roots of this preoccupation lie in sixteenth-century *ad hominem* repudiations of Luther as a depraved and resentful monk. Attempts to find in Luther's personality the key to his protest continued well into the twentieth century. Behind this interpretive paradigm—and gradually less so, the tone—stood the truculent Johannes Cochlaeus (1479-1552), author of *De actis and scriptis Martini Lutheri* (1549). Initially, the change came when denunciations of malice were replaced by a pity-evoking concoction of psychological problems: pathological fear, a father complex, and megalomania.[1] Luther's portrayal began to change in earnest with Franz Xaver Kiefl (1869-1928), who still saw the immediate roots of the Reformation in Luther's psyche but came to view his protest as theologically motivated, rather than as a symptom of moral perversity or a pathological disorder. "Musing about Luther's personality," which Daphne Hampson holds to be "largely a Catholic preoccupation,"[2] thus finally gave way to an interest in Luther's piety and spiritual sensibilities.

Retrieval of Luther's "theology for piety," however, posed challenges of its own. There was much, as Wicks notes, that was commendable in the *young* Luther up to the time of and just after the indulgence controversy, such as his strong emphasis on a posture of humility and the healing effect of grace on the self. But this spirituality seemed rapidly, around 1518, to have yielded to what Paul Hacker denounced as a reflexive, anthropocentric faith—a faith that seemed to make everything fine just as long as one knew it was there. Wicks conveys his initial disappointment with this change: "I regretted the 'turn' that Luther took in 1518, in which I saw a loss for Christian spirituality."[3] Indeed, it must have seemed like a radical break! Instead of "a *metanoia* of self-estimate," healing grace (*gratia sanans*), the cultivation of the church's prayer life to accompany indulgences, Luther now staked the entirety of the Christian life on faith—which appeared only to reinforce anthropocentrism, individualism, self-absorption, and self-congratulation.

---

1. In the works of Heinrich Denifle (1844-1905) and Hartmann Grisar (1845-1932). For a broader overview, see Theo M. M. A. C. Bell, "Roman Catholic Luther Research in the Twentieth Century: From Rejection to Rehabilitation," in *The Oxford Handbook of Martin Luther's Theology* ed. Robert Kolb et al. (Oxford: Oxford University Press, 2014), 584-97.
2. Daphne Hampson, *Christian Contradictions: The Structures of Lutheran and Catholic Thought* (Cambridge: Cambridge University Press, 2001), 104.
3. The quotation comes from an earlier and longer version of Fr. Wicks's essay: "Half a Lifetime with Luther in Theology and Living," *Pro Ecclesia* 22, no. 3 (Summer 2013): 307-36, 319.

Well-entrenched post-Kantian strands of Lutheran theology and Luther interpretation could only strengthen further the impression that preoccupation with one's self was what Luther had intended with his concept of faith. In his study of the believing self in Luther's theology, for example, Paul Hacker goes on to criticize Gerhard Ebeling for making "faith … reflexive to the point of being man-centered."[4] Whether Hacker does justice to the nuance of Ebeling's thought is beside the point. Suffice it to say that, for Ebeling, the event of the Word about the cross, as this Word is heard and received in the conscience, is what awakens faith and confronts one with a decision about "the whole of reality—the decision between assurance and despair, between freedom and servitude, between life and death."[5] In the theater of the conscience, where this confrontation takes place, faith's knowledge of itself is essential. What concerns us, however, is where Hacker lays the blame. "It is ultimately the impact of Luther's doctrine of reflection that has in modern usage narrowed the meaning of the word 'existential' to denote what decisively concerns the existence of a *human* individual in a crucial *individual* situation."[6] The blame specifically falls on Luther's antithetical juxtaposition of sin and grace, law and gospel, despair and assurance, etc., elevated by Ebeling (according to Hacker) to the status of an interpretive principle for the reformer's thought.

Admittedly, in this light, Luther's "turn" to faith must seem, on the one hand, to place an impossible burden on the individual. This is captured even more pointedly in Rudolf Bultmann's demand that each and every one of us, as "those who have the modern world view live as though [we] had none," that each should "believe …

---

4. Paul Hacker, *The Ego in Faith: Martin Luther and the Origin of Anthropocentric Religion* (Chicago: Franciscan Herald, 1970), 134.
5. Gerhard Ebeling, "Faith and Unbelief in Conflict about Reality," *Word and Faith*, trans. J. W. Leitch (Philadelphia: Fortress Press, 1963), 384.
6. Hacker, *The Ego in Faith*, 134.

in spite of experience," and go through life with the interminable and unmitigated burden of "a new understanding of [one's] personal existence."[7] Alternatively, it could just as easily seem that Luther was blithely unconcerned about good works and had no place for them. This latter accusation goes back to Luther's earliest opponents, who interpreted his notion of faith within the schema of infused grace. That is, they thought what Luther had in mind was a theological virtue, a habit located in the soul of the believer. To say that one was saved by faith *alone* would then have meant, incomprehensibly, that the disposition remained inoperative and without a healing effect, and even more contradictorily, that one could actually remain blissfully unconcerned about the concrete shape of one's Christian life. Bonhoeffer's worry about "cheap grace" may have stemmed from the fact that also some Lutherans had come to see faith as their inalienable and all-too-sufficient property and right.[8]

All this is to acknowledge that Luther's turn to faith *may* seem like a fatal move. But whether faith is seen as a tall order, or an all-too-easy way into heaven, we also need to observe that it will seem so only when the notion is articulated without any ontological underpinnings, in epistemological but not also in metaphysical terms. In this context, I highlight the spiritual aspect of Wicks's engagement with Luther in order to draw attention, first, to how the long-standing Catholic concern with Luther's personality has been transformed into appreciation of Luther's spiritual motivation and then into an even broader, edifying retrieval of the reformer's spirituality. However, I highlight this also in order to put in perspective Wicks's own eventual pushback against metaphysically

---

7. *Jesus Christ and Mythology* (New York: Charles Scribner's Sons, 1958), 85, 84, 73.

8. Dietrich Bonhoeffer, *Discipleship*, Chapter One. For the critical edition, see *Dietrich Bonhoeffer Works*, vol. 4, ed. Martin Kuske et al. (Minneapolis: Fotress Press, 2001), 43-57. It is not insignificant, in light of the argument I am advancing here, that for Bonhoeffer cheap grace is less a threat to the individual Christian than it is the enemy of the church!

denuded, and thus spiritually dubious, accounts of Luther's view of faith and the Christian life. What brought about this change of perspective was Wicks's new appreciation for Luther's *fides sacramenti*. Surely, Luther had not blithely surrendered spiritual concerns for the sake of a painstakingly reflexive or carelessly permissive notion of faith alone, as both Catholic and Lutheran theology seemed to convey in the mid-twentieth century. In the course of his research, Wicks has come to reject as false Ebeling's portrayal of "Luther as promoting an interiorization that overcame Catholic sacramental reality."[9] For, once Luther's appreciation for the objective reality and validity of the sacraments and the word of absolution, as concrete forms of the gospel, was brought into the picture, things changed quite drastically. The fruit of this nuanced charting of Luther's own spiritual journey, leading to yet further engagement with Luther's pneumatology and ecclesiology, was Wicks's 1983 volume, *Luther and His Spiritual Legacy*, especially its appreciative discussion of Luther's mature spirituality.[10]

For Luther, the sacraments are *public* acts that proclaim God's goodness and, in doing so, elicit trust in God's promise; more than that, they are locales of *God's own ongoing action* through which God not only attests to his own grace but also himself dispenses spiritual gifts. As Luther says against those who would turn Baptism into a testimony to their own faith, and thus their own work, Christ himself "is present at baptism and in baptism, in fact is himself the baptizer."[11] In this light, what initially seemed to be a disappointing turn to mere faith gives way to a view of Baptism, the Lord's Supper, and absolution as the objective means through which God himself

---

9. Jared Wicks, SJ, "Recent Theological Works on Luther," *Pro Ecclesia* 21, no. 4 (Fall 2012): 448–56, 452.

10. Jared Wicks, SJ, *Luther and His Spiritual Legacy* (Wilmington, DE: Michael Glazier, 1983).

11. Martin Luther, *Concerning Rebaptism* (1528); *LW* 40:242; *WA* 26:156.

publicly reiterates the gospel of his Son and the faithful grasp it by faith. The *fides sacramenti* is "faith which grasps personally the powerful work of salvation Christ is carrying out on our behalf."[12] For their deeply personal aspect, the sacraments and absolution thus point to the church, not the treacherous recesses of an individual heart, as the primary locale of the Holy Spirit's work. They also point to the community: the church is the place where faith is neither a feat nor an excuse, but where faith lays hold of Christ and is conformed to him. As Wicks suggests, the absolution and the sacraments thus displace and crucially reorient access to God through speculative knowledge and explication of God's demands, together with their subjective counterparts, the cultivation of a mystical ascent and an ethical posture.[13] This indispensable connection of the church's public acts to the clear proclamation of Christ, who gives himself to us even now, is something, Wicks notes, Catholics can learn from: "What Luther discovered about absolution and Eucharistic institution can help Catholics clarify an essential element in faith," that is, the words of institution as a particularly pointed expression of the gospel of Christ.[14] The Lutherans also have much, if not more, to learn here.[15]

II. Irreconcilable Ontologies?

God's justification of the sinner, for Luther, has its proper locus in an ecclesial context, as faith grasps God's ongoing public work on the sinner's behalf. But Luther's notion of faith is grounded on more than ecclesial foundations. It must be appreciated in tandem with the reformer's insistence on the *communicatio idiomatum* between Christ's divine and human natures.[16] The communication forms the

---

12. Wicks, *Luther and His Spiritual Legacy*, 126.
13. Ibid., 121-5, 135.
14. Wicks, "Recent Theological Works on Luther," 453.
15. Jared Wicks, SJ, "Holy Spirit – Church – Sanctification," *Pro Ecclesia* 2, no. 2 (Spring 1993): 150-72, esp. 171.

ontological basis for understanding the person of faith. Just as Christ's humanity shares in his divinity, while God can now be said to have died,[17] so also faith takes possession of Christ's righteousness, life, and salvation, indeed Christ's whole person,[18] while Christ takes upon himself the sinner's own person in what for the believer is a happy exchange (*feliciter commutans*).[19] Christ in truth becomes "the greatest thief, murderer, adulterer, robber, desecrator, blasphemer, etc., there has ever been anywhere in the world."[20] Further, the specific character of this exchange must be clarified through the lens of the Finnish emphasis on union with Christ as ontologically defining the believer. Being united to Christ through "the wedding ring of faith"[21] means that the person's self is now significantly enlarged; it gives rise not only to what Daphne Hampson calls "a double *sense* of self" but to a truly *new* self.[22] In trusting, as a sinner, in God's gracious favor, one now grasps one's self both in its Christ-formed newness and in its old, but always real, possibility of

16. Oswald Bayer has done much to retrieve this aspect of Luther's theology over against the epistemologically weighted Luther Revival of the early 20th century; see Oswald Bayer and Benjamin Gleede, eds., *Creator est Creatura: Luthers Christologie als Lehre von der Idiomenkommunikation* (Berlin: Walter de Gruyter, 2007).

17. *On the Councils and the Church* (1539); *LW* 41:103-4; *WA* 50:590.

18. "He took upon Himself our sinful person and granted us His innocent and victorious Person" (*Lectures on Galatians* [1531]; *LW* 26:284; *WA* 40I:443). "The chief article and foundation of the gospel is that ... you accept and recognize [Christ] as a gift, as a present that God has given you and that is your own. This means that when you see or hear of Christ doing or suffering something, you do not doubt that Christ himself, with his deeds and suffering, belongs to you. On this you may depend as surely as if you had done it yourself; indeed as if you were Christ himself" (*A Brief Instruction on What to Look for and Expect in the Gospels* [1521]; *LW* 35:119; *WA* 10I/1:11). "[Christ] gave to all who believe, as their possession, everything that he had. This included: his life, in which he swallowed up death; his righteousness, by which he blotted out sin; and his salvation, with which he overcame everlasting damnation." (*Preface to the New Testament* [1522], *LW* 35:359; *WA DB* 6:4).

19. *LW* 26:284; *WA* 40I:443b.

20. *LW* 26:277; *WA* 40I:433b.

21. *The Freedom of a Christian* (1520); *LW* 31:352; *WA* 7:55; Cf. "Faith takes hold of Christ and has Him present, enclosing him as the ring encloses the gem" (*LW* 26:132; *WA* 40I:233b).

22. Hampson, *Christian Contradictions*, 99. Since Hampson largely disregards the ecclesial dimension of Luther's notion of the self (which the present paper seeks to retrieve), this leads her to construe the self in terms that are excessively noetic and futurist.

unfaithfulness, of being a self over against God. Precisely in this sense the Christian is *simul iustus et peccator* (at once a saint and a sinner)[23]—in the concreteness of his or her extrinsic self.

Union with Christ, understood as a dynamic exchange sustained in an ecclesial context, forms the essential backbone of Luther's understanding of faith alone. If we accept that the believer thus undergoes a fundamental ontological transformation, then we cannot avoid querying the relatively more recent paradigm for construing Lutheran and Catholic thought. The paradigm juxtaposes, on the one hand, Lutheran theology as more *existential* in its thought structure (no narrow existentialism is implied here but rather vibrant lived piety) and, on the other hand, Catholic theology, which is said to be *sapiential* (oriented to dispassionate metaphysical precision). This ingenious distinction between existential Lutheranism and sapiential Catholicism allowed Otto Hermann Pesch to accept as orthodox the Lutheran understanding of the believer as *simul iustus et peccator*.[24] For can a Christian approach God in prayer as anything but a sinner?[25] But is this lens still heuristically valid, now that it can hardly be denied that ontology forms an intrinsic part of Luther's theological

---

23. *LW* 26:232, 234; *WA* 40I:368b, 370b.

24. Pesch characterizes existential theology as "a theology given to psychologizing our relations to God, and thereby opposed to the more objective sapiential theology." He insists that "The distinction between existential and sapiential theology must be an essential hermeneutical element in the systematic comparison of the theologies of martin Luther and Thomas Aquinas." See Otto Hermann Pesch, "Existential and Sapiential Theology – the Theological Confrontation between Luther and Thomas Aquinas," in *Catholic Scholars Dialogue with Luther*, ed. Jared Wicks (Chicago: Loyola University Press, 1970), 78, 80. The chapter by Pesch represents the concluding section (pp. 935-48) of his dissertation, *Theologie der Rechtfertigung bei Martin Luther und Thomas von Aquin. Versuch eines systematisch-theologischen Dialogs* (Mainz: Matthias Grünewald Verlag, 1967).

25. This remains the essence of Pesch's appropriation of Luther's dictum; see his *Hinführung zu Luther*, 3rd ed. (Mainz: Matthias-Grünewald, 2004), Chapter 11. Pesch's conclusion is largely repeated in a recent Polish monograph-length treatment of Luther's formula: Tomasz Jaklewicz, *Święty grzesznik: Formuła Marcina Lutra „simul iustus et peccator" w kontekście ekumenicznym* [Holy Sinner: Luther's Formula in an Ecumenical Context] (Lublin: KUL, 2006). Jaklewicz, however, also suggests that "being in Christ" may be an equivalent periphrastic formula acceptable to both the confessions.

vision, while Pesch himself admits that "Thomas' sapiential theology is itself another form of existential theology ... it is 'existential' in being the expression and incarnation of a heartfelt commitment to God"?[26] Lutheranism may, in fact, represent a genuine "paradigm change" from the Augustinian view of the self as a substance endowed with an intellect. In the Augustinian schema, this substance, through an initial bestowal of grace (*gratia infusa*) and through its exercise as an intrinsic property, is able by works of love to give concreteness to its belief in God. Can this view of the self *in via* be reconciled with Luther's extrinsic, justified self, for which sin is not, at its root, a failure of love and internal disorder but rather inability to trust in the goodness of God for me and to take possession of it? Or do we have here a case of contradictory paradigms, as both Stephan Pfürtner[27] and Daphne Hampson have argued? According to Hampson, "It becomes fundamentally impossible, for philosophical reasons, for Catholicism to acknowledge the truth that Lutheranism proclaims," namely, that the believer is at once totally a saint and totally a sinner.[28] I doubt Wicks would wish to draw such a radical conclusion, and neither for that matter do I. Yet there is in Wicks's discussion of Luther's mature spirituality an implicit recognition that a different ontological paradigm may, in fact, be at issue. Wicks acknowledges, albeit from a more action-oriented perspective, that in Luther "the ultimate ground of the new life of faith [is] a ground outside of oneself in Christ and in God's promise"; and he goes on to affirm: "Justification by faith is a relation, not a substantial amalgamation."[29]

---

26. Pesch, "Existential and Sapiential Theology," 81.
27. Stephan Pfürtner, "The Paradigms of Thomas Aquinas and Martin Luther: Did Luther's Message of Justification Mean a Paradigm Change?" in *Paradigm Change in Theology*, ed. Hans Küng and David Tracy, trans. Margaret Köhl (New York: Crossroad, 1989), 130–60.
28. Hampson, *Christian Contradictions*, 91. She adds that "the attempt to understand the Lutheran/Catholic distinction as one of an ontology versus speaking existentially may well act as a diversion from considering the difference in structure of Lutheran and Catholic faith" (120).

Where do we go from here? I do not think we need to be defeatist, even if Pesch's idea for a rapprochement is no longer quite viable. In the rest of this paper, I would like to suggest an ecclesiological path along which a mutual understanding and genuine agreement can be pursued. Hampson's insistence, however insightful, on "a double sense of self"—a self both living out of the future and confronting the present—is both too epistemological in orientation and too individualistic. Her understanding of faith in Lutheran theology is too beholden to Bultmann for her to be able constructively to take into account the ecclesially inflected ontology at work in Luther's notion of faith. In other words, Lutheran and Catholic theology may very well exhibit two divergent thought structures and two conceptions of the self. But what seems divergent when the believer is considered in isolation may actually reverse its orientation toward a rapprochement, when the ontological implications are worked out in their proper, ecclesial context.

III. The Church: Where Nature and Grace Converge

Louis Dupré suggests a promising way forward. "Luther," he writes, "was among the first fully to perceive the magnitude of the problem created by the split between nature and grace. His entire theology addresses it." If Dupré is right, then we can regard both Catholic and Lutheran theology not simply as irremediably divergent but, more appreciatively, as engaged in the same project. Now, Dupré is skeptical that Luther actually succeeded in closing the breach because of the dialectical nature of the reformer's solution: "the dialectical opposition between a totally corrupt nature and a divine justification" only converted the religious tension between nature and grace "into

29. Wicks, *Luther and His Spiritual Legacy*, 136, 139.

the very essence of a new Christian piety."[30] But perhaps Dupré, too, overplays the dialectical character of Luther's thought.

When Luther describes the believer as *simul iustus et peccator*, it is not to assert that divine justification is a mere forensic verdict that leaves the nature untouched. Neither does Luther imply that faith is an infused virtue which becomes one's property, quality, and disposition—in the words of Trent, a "vain confidence" (*inanis fiducia*) if left to itself.[31] Rather, Luther views the believer as *simul* to insist on a genuinely *Christ-formed self* in face of the very real possibility that one can be a *self over against God*, or even without God. In other words, what the formula expresses is not a contradiction or paradox or a prayerful posture, but the asymmetrical reality of union with Christ and, more broadly, *essential*, though *extrinsic*, rest in divine self-donation. This union is always threatened, on our part as historical beings, with dissolution into an ontology of self-contained essences. Added to this persistent threat is the fact that, in the context of early modernity, humans actually can aspire, both conceptually and existentially, to be "pure natures" over against or without God. Luther seriously reckons with this possibility. It is important to note here that, like Thomas Aquinas, Luther does admit a purely philosophical concept of nature; but he is equally insistent that, were it to be realized as such, it would produce an ambiguous, deeply inhuman, and ultimately unbearable reality. For Luther, the concept of a mere nature cannot but subvert itself, for it requires that one be simultaneously creator and creature.[32] Before we turn to Luther's

---

30. Louis Dupré, *Passage to Modernity: An Essay in the Hermeneutics of Nature and Culture* (New Haven: Yale University Press, 1993), 208-9.

31. *The Canons and Decrees of the Council of Trent*, trans. H. J. Schroeder (Charlotte, NC: TAN Books, 2011), 35 [Sixth Session: Decree Concerning Justification, Chapter IX].

32. For all the relative security one might enjoy, human life without Christ is, according to Luther, an existence exclusively under sin, the curse, death and the devil (*LW* 26:281ff; *WA* 40I:440ff). At their mercy, one is doomed to a life of self-creation and self-justification through one's own works (a self-contradictory idea in which one attempts to be simultaneously the material

articulation of the Christ-formed self and its inalienably ecclesial context, let us consider his thought in light of this very concern about nature's self-subverting emancipation.

We begin by noting that Dupré's charge of a new, dialectical piety applies far more accurately to Luther's successors and other Protestant followers. It was they who again conceptualized the human as a substance in a fashion at once Aristotelian and early modern. But this came at a cost, and the cost was precisely a dichotomy of nature and grace characterized on both ends by severe theological overcompensation. To preserve the completeness of justification the Protestants now had to restrict the imputation of Christ's righteousness to a merely *forensic verdict*; otherwise, righteousness would become a quality of the self-standing nature and thus only partial righteousness. At the same time, they could no longer argue that sin was fundamentally unbelief, that is, inability and unwillingness to find one's self extrinsically in God's goodness; that sin, in other words, was self-justification and self-creation at the root of one's being. Within the substance framework, they could only argue for the reign of sin in in a rather demoralizing way by insisting that *total depravity* flowed necessarily from occasional, or even habitual law breaking. At bottom, to thrust Luther's *simul* into a substance-based framework either leaves the believer to his or her own devices, demanding that he or she perform the existential feat of living from pure grace in face of what is dismissed as a depraved and recalcitrant nature; or it makes the believer complacent, for all the believer's works, despite appearances and the believer's own self-perception, are dismissed as falling short of the divine law. It is

and the worker) (*LW* 26:259; *WA* 401:407b). Thus one is constantly under the law, delivered, first of all, up to oneself, to one's being less than one seeks. As such, it is, in the end, a life of standing unremittingly accused by God's very law (cf. Luther's *Fifth Set of Theses against the Antinomians* [1538], where Luther denies that an existence outside the law is humanly possible: *WA* 391:354-7).

hard to understand why, within this kind of personal ontology, one would not rather embrace the more compellingly realist Augustinian, i.e., transformational, view that the believer is partially a saint and partially a sinner, a *viator* doing his or her best to put to work the grace received and awaiting in hopeful expectation God's justifying verdict.[33]

The Augustinian-Aristotelian paradigm is certainly tempting! But perhaps Luther's extrinsic view of the self as united to Christ and completely justified, while in itself remaining a sinner, is not totally without merit (the pun being very much intended). It is possible to view Luther's critique as seeking to overcome Augustinianism's own propensity to consider the human in a self-contained and isolated fashion. To view the human as a microcosm within which the drama of personal salvation essentially plays itself out may unwittingly reinforce the deceptive self-sufficiency of the self. This holds true for theologies *indebted* to both the young Augustine's ideal of an internally ordered self[34] and the mature Augustine's notion of a self in face of a selectively and individually predestining God.[35] Both, it

---

33. Gerald Strauss, *Luther's House of Learning: Indoctrination of the Young in the German Reformation* (Baltimore: Johns Hopkins, 1978), details the theological and practical difficulties (bordering on incoherence and certainly eliciting incomprehension) that the propagators of the Reformation faced in trying to express its message within the framework of the old, Augustinian conception of the self, without awareness of Luther's ecclesial-ontological notion of the person. "Preachers and catechists seemed to be telling their ... auditors that even though God demanded nothing of them but love, trust, and faith, they would be well advised to support their claim to a place in heaven with a lifelong record of laudable deeds" (Strauss, 220).

34. Emblematically, *De doctrina Christiana* (A.D. 396): The body's "concupiscence, which is its evil habit, should be completely conquered so that it is rendered subject to the spirit as the natural order demands. ...Thus the spirit acts in dominating the flesh that it may destroy the evils of habit as if they constituted a perverse covenant, and it crates the pace of good custom" (Augustine, *On Christian Doctrine*, trans. D. W. Robertson, Jr. [Upper Saddle River, NJ: Prentice Hall, 1997], 21 [I.xxiv.25]).

35. Again, emblematically, *Grace and Free Choice* (A.D. 426): "God works in the hearts of human beings to incline their will to whatever he wills, whether to good actions in accord with his mercy or to evil ones in accord with their merits" (in *Answer to the Pelagians IV*, trans. R. J. Teske [Hyde Park, NY: New City Press, 1999], 102 [§43]; on God's gratuitous choice of some from the "mass of perdition," see *Rebuke and Grace* in the same volume).

seems, culminate in the need for the self's self-execution. In regard to the former type, a recent monograph on "creation, freedom, and grace in Western theology" draws attention to Luther's christological actualism as a critique of infused grace (which as a divinely created habit comes to replace Augustine's notion of God's direct presence in the soul). "Luther recognized," Joshua Davis comments,

> that, if it is the case that the creature must produce its own act of charity, then charity could never be an actuality for the soul. If the infusion of the *habitus* of charity was merely an accidental rather than substantial transformation of the natural drive to self-preservation, charity would remain only an abstract ideal for human activity, an infinite and unrealized demand. ... Luther saw that the scholastic conception of *habitus* actually implied the opposite of what it was taken to mean.[36]

It is in this light that we must interpret Luther's insistence that *work does not make a person but rather the person, first made through faith, does works.*[37]

The self is faced with a similar predicament when grace is construed as the mysterious impact of God's predestining choice on an individual's will. Augustine's fateful move, as Robert Jenson observes, was to give the will a hypostatic character.[38] The will is a reality sheerly as such: we *have* it and it is *in* us. Whether serving evil

---

36. Joshua B. Davis, *Waiting and Being: Creation, Freedom, and Grace in Western Theology* (Minneapolis: Fortress, 2013), 110. Cf. Luther: "however much of this love I may have, it is never enough" (*LW* 26:144; *WA* 40I:251b). Davis's intuition about Luther's christological actualism is certainly right, but in his articulation, unfortunately, it remains an abstract postulate. Davis is, in the end, unable to give a concrete account of Luther's Christ-formed conception of the self because he leaves out of his account Luther's emphasis on the sacraments and the church.

37. *LW* 26:255; *WA* 40I:402b; cf. "*Fides facit personam ... opus non facit personam, sed persona facit opus*" (*Zirkulardisputation de veste nuptiali* [1537]; *WA* 39I:283). See also Philip Melanchthon's and Luther's critique of Augustine's understanding of faith as internal renovation in *WA BR* 6:98–101.

38. This paragraph is based on Robert W. Jenson, "Thinking Freedom," *On Thinking the Human: Resolutions of Difficult Notions* (Grand Rapids: Eerdmans, 2003), 38–39. Jenson's own discussion draws on Augustine's *Grace and Free Choice* and *The Predestination of the Saints*.

or good, the will remains "continuous through the transformation from the adjectivally bad will to the adjectivally good will." This "hyper-neutral will" then, as a personal reality, in itself "must surely be a will that does not will." Even so, "it never appears in a character of its own but only as one or the other of two actual willings." Where actual willing is concerned, Augustine affirms that divine willing and human wiling in the state of grace do not compete but rather, operating on a different plane of being, "God freely chooses that we shall freely choose and what he chooses us to choose." But so formulated, Jenson argues, Augustine's notion of a *divinely assisted* will, though not wrong, is "frustratingly empty." It asserts only what is the case when one's will as such is free. That this encourages introspection is one thing. More problematic is what is presupposed: the impact of grace cannot be sought conclusively in actual, polyvalent willing but in the inaccessible depths of the will itself, for it is there that God's will opposes the human will and irresistibly *makes* it free.[39] But to see grace as transforming a will that is abstracted from willing (and as such remains a rather mysterious entity) is to make the work of grace incomprehensible and reflexively unavailable. Small wonder, Jenson notes further, that one then easily falls into classical Calvinism's attempt to reason back from one's works to one's graced status. Here, too, the imperative one confronts is to deploy one's self in order to grasp the self's actuality: in a circular fashion, one must secure that which was to ground the self in advance.[40]

---

39. "He works ... without us so that we will, but when we will and will so that we do the action, he works along with us; nonetheless, without his either working so that we will or his working along with us when we will, we can do nothing in terms of works of piety" (*Grace and Free Choice*, 94 [§33]; compare this with the quotation in note 35).

40. In practice Augustine does emphasize the importance of Baptism, over against speculation, though as such Baptism is not decisive: (1) it brings the forgiveness of sin but not complete renewal (*The Punishment and Forgiveness of Sins and the Baptism of Little Ones* [A.D. 412], II.44), and (2) its grace may, in the end, prove ineffective (*Grace and Free Choice*, §45). Still, one is to

Jenson believes the hypostatization of the will distracts Augustine from seeing freedom in more positive terms as "the glorious freedom of the children of God" to which God's grace liberates us (cf. Rom. 8:21). "To say that we are free," Jenson asks, "must we say we 'have' freedom or free will, or that there is free will 'in' us?" He argues that it is only on the assumption that *we* are the foundationally free ones that a need emerges to posit in ourselves an entity called the free will. But what we rather have is a "dispositional property for being apt for willing action." Importantly, that our willing is free rather than unfree, good rather than evil, can only be enabled by a community to which we belong. Alluding to Luther's *De servo abitrio*, Jenson insists freedom is "not an individual possession at all; it is something that happens to us by the provocation of another; it is a phenomenon of community."

In light of all this, Luther's insistence on the *simul*—his actualist view of the self in essential, yet extrinsic, union with Christ—may be viewed as a critique of the scholastic tendency to construe the individual under grace in isolation, a tendency exacerbated further by broader philosophical developments. Its upshot is not only the emancipation of the individual but also the individual's elevation, as a doer, to a status over against God. Latent in both the Augustinian types is the possibility of an isolated self, and it is precisely this that Luther seeks to overcome as ultimately incoherent. This is not to suggest that, for Luther, the human cannot also be regarded in his or her particularity. Yet, especially where the self's relation to grace is at issue, the threat is that grace will become abstract and the self will thus be delivered up to itself. Regardless of whether one views grace as infused or mysteriously granted, on the former view grace becomes all too easily assimilated to nature, whereas on the latter

put the best construction and to consider others "chosen when they believe, are baptized, and live godly lives" (*Rebuke and Grace*, §16).

view one flees from the unreliability of nature to the mystery of grace—only to have to fall back on nature. In both, the need for self-actualization emerges in a viciously circular way. This threat of making grace into an abstraction and thus delivering the self up to itself is, in early modernity, exacerbated further by the sweeping metaphysical replacement of the participatory notion of form with that of substance.[41] As Eberhard Jüngel puts it, "the basic theological aporia of the modern age" is that "in our experience ... man can be human without God."[42] Luther thus reckons with the possibility of human being without or over against God—only to dismiss it as a deficient ontology, possible solely through obscuring the question of humanity's efficient and final cause.[43] An isolated and self-contained nature is less than a nature for it is always the result of a subtraction.[44]

When we consider the negative aspect of Luther's *simul* and view it as critical of scholastic anthropologies, the impression that two paradigms are at stake is unavoidable. However, of even greater importance is the positive side of Luther's critique. It is a strong plea to understand graced and free existence as communally and ecclesially constituted. Luther's insistence that the self, created through union with Christ, is a fully formed and actualized self can only be understood in the context of the church. On this score, Lutherans need to take seriously the Roman-Catholic critique of faith alone, which, in fact, recalls them to their own rich ecclesiology.

---

41. Louis Dupré, *Religion and the Rise of Modern Culture* (Notre Dame, IN: Notre Dame University Press, 2008), 6-14. This is not to say that somehow participation in the form could already be considered grace.

42. Eberhard Jüngel, *God as the Mystery of the World: On the Foundation of the Theology of the Crucified One in the Dispute between Theism and Atheism*, trans. D. L. Guder (Grand Rapids: Eerdmans, 1983), 16.

43. See Thesis 13 in Luther's *Disputation Concerning Man* (1536); *LW* 34:138, 140; *WA* 391:175, 177.

44. To residual ambiguities in Luther's own theology and that of his successors which ultimately led to the minimization of the impact of both sin and grace, elevating mere nature to an independent standing and endowing it with residual righteousness, see Piotr J. Małysz, "Sin, between Law and Gospel," *Lutheran Quarterly* 28:2 (Summer 2014): 149-78.

They must also think constructively with Luther. The point is not to reject faith alone but, first, to comprehend the ease with which faith alone—in the modern context of seemingly self-sufficient natures—devolves into an existential dialectic. When it does, then grace stands only for the self's reflexive feat of not succumbing to resignation in face of an ungodly and recalcitrant reality, or the sinner is simply declared "irrevocably affirmed and authorized to affirm himself" without (the need for) further implications.[45] Either nature or grace becomes, in the end, irrelevant.

But for Luther faith alone does not mean the believer alone. For it is in the assembly at worship that freedom from the old self takes place as a communal identity, and faith conforms to Christ in a way that also "extends" his deed.[46] Here grace and nature converge. What constitutes the assembly is the proclamation of the Word, in its character of absolution, and the celebration of the sacraments, especially the Lord's Supper. It is to these external and public realities that Luther directs those who are desperate to discern within themselves the workings of divine grace.[47] Through the Word God himself reiterates his promise: his forgiveness and his faithfulness. The

---

45. The phrase is Eberhard Jüngel's. But, as Jüngel makes clear, justification, understood as God's unconditional recognition of one as a person, by no means implies freedom to abandon all restraint or complacently to maintain the *status quo*. Rather, through divine recognition one is distinguished from God for one's own sake – which gives rise to an entire life structured by and flowing from worship. See "Hoffen, Handeln – und Leiden," *Beziehungsreich* (Stuttgart: Radius, 2002), 23; and *Justification: The Heart of the Christian Faith*, trans. J. F. Cayzer (Edinburgh: T&T Clark, 2001), 266-77.

46. Christians not only "understand the deed of Christ ... receive and preserve it, use it to [their] advantage" but *also* "impart it to others, increase and extend it" (*Confession Concerning Christ's Supper* [1528]; *LW* 37:366; *WA* 26:506).

47. "For God did not come down from heaven to make you uncertain about predestination, to teach you to despise the sacraments, absolution and the rest of the divine ordinances. Indeed, He instituted them to make you completely certain and to remove the disease of doubt from you heart, in order that you might not only believe with the heart but also see with your physical eyes and touch with your hands. ... If you have [Jesus], then you also have the hidden God together with Him who has been revealed. And that is the only way, the truth, and the life. Apart from it you will find nothing but destruction and death" (*Lectures on Genesis* [1535-45], *LW* 5:45; *WA* 43:459; cf. "Preface to Romans" [1522], *LW* 35:378; *WA DB* 7:22-4).

sacraments are God's own acts of self-attestation to his favor and goodness; they are means of grace. In contrast to the preached Word, the sacraments have an intensely public dimension: the recipients are drawn out of themselves to grasp God in the act of distributing his gifts, and only in this way are the sacraments then also intensely personal.[48] To put it in a biblical idiom, the sacraments belong to God's single action which had its beginning in the rising of Jesus from the dead as the first fruits and whose culmination will be the universal resurrection.[49] Importantly, the New Testament thematizes this divine action, stretching from the resurrection of the One to the universal rising of all, as the new creation. For the New Testament, the resurrection is underway, for it is *already in the present* that we truly are buried into Christ's death and raised with him to newness of life (Rom 6).[50] And it is already in the present that grain and grapes yield not only bread and wine, but a heavenly feast, as Irenaeus states so eloquently![51] God at work in the here and now is what, for Luther, constitutes the gospel, the good news of the new creation already being called into being: "for God Himself together with Christ, His dear Son, and the Holy Spirit are in Baptism."[52]

---

48. In Wicks's apt summary: "The sacraments express the same Gospel message preached before the community as a whole; their eminence rests on the way they personally apply the benefits of Christ to individuals" (Wicks, *Luther and His Spiritual Legacy*, 132). Wicks substantiates this conclusion with a citation (extended here) from Luther's *The Sacrament of the Body and Blood of Christ – Against the Fanatics* (1526): "When I preach his death, it is in a public sermon in the congregation, in which I am addressing myself to no one individually; whoever grasps it, grasps it. But when I distribute the sacrament, I designate it for the individual who is receiving it; I give him Christ's body and blood that he may have forgiveness of sins, obtained through his death and preached in the congregation. This is something more than the congregational sermon; for although the same thing is present in the sermon as in the sacrament, here there is the advantage that it is directed at definite individuals" (*LW* 36:348; *WA* 19:504-5).

49. Luther emphasizes the unity of Christ's action, embracing his as well as humanity's resurrection, in his *Commentary on 1 Corinthians 15* (1534), vv. 20-21, *LW* 28:107-114; *WA* 36:542b-53b.

50. "when by faith [I] consciously take hold of Christ Himself . . . I have risen again" (*LW* 26:157-8; *WA* 40I:270b).

51. Irenaeus, *Against Heresies*; *ANF* 1:527-8 [Bk. V, Ch. 2].

52. *LW* 28:78; *WA* 36:501b.

Importantly, through and around this Gospel, humans are being gathered as a people made by God unto himself. God's unceasing work of exchange on behalf of his creation transforms us from our former nothingness, rescues us from our empty ways, and renews us in our minds. It is our new birth in Christ, *extra nos*. Luther's language is strikingly realist:

> This attachment to [Christ] causes me to be . . . pulled out of my skin, and transferred into Christ and into His kingdom. . . . Because He lives in me, whatever grace, righteousness, life, peace, and salvation there is in me is all Christ's; nevertheless, it is mine as well, by the cementing and attachment that are through faith, by which we become as one body in the Spirit.[53]

And even if death may still be our lot, it is now no different from sleep. "Now that Christ reigns, there is in fact no more sin, death, or the curse – this we confess every day in the Apostles' Creed when we say [note the ecclesiological emphasis]: 'I believe in the holy Church.'"[54] What is already underway, indeed "more than half finished,"[55] will find its completion in no less than bodily incorruption.

What must be noted is that the new creation itself, to which the ecclesial mediation of grace gives rise, is likewise a social reality. Those justified by God, who lay hold of their selves in Christ, now depart from the altar to share righteousness with the neighbor.[56] To possess Christ by faith is, even in the flesh, to live "the life of Christ, the Son of God."[57] In this, Christians re-present a creative economy

---

53. *LW* 26:167-8; *WA* 40I:283. The ecclesiological dimension of Luther's statements is, admittedly, often only implicit, and his descriptions of the afflictions of sin are not infrequently focused on the individual's predicament. The latter aspect comes across quite strongly in Wicks's account of the daily expulsion of sin in Luther's theology: Wicks, *Luther and His Spiritual Legacy*, 144-8.

54. *LW* 26:285; *WA* 40I:444b.

55. *LW* 28:110; *WA* 36:547b.

56. "Das groest [werck der liebe] ist das, wenn ich mein gerechtigkeit hyn gib und dienen lassz des nechsten sünde" (*Predigt am 3. Sonntag nach Trinitatis* [1522]; *WA* 10III:217).

of grace that transcends mere legal and contractual structures. For this reason, Luther finds it inconceivable that Christians—as those who have been freed from the need to justify themselves because they share in an excess of alien righteousness—would not perform spiritual service in public vocations, especially in the household and the state, and transform them from the inside out, give them depth and analogical correspondence to God's own creative work.[58] Joshua Davis gives an apt summary: "In creating, God assumes the good of the existence of the other as God's own, but by grace the creature assumes that same good as its own."[59]

Last but not least, by living from God and mediating God's justice to those in need—by sharing in God's grace and participating in God's new creation—Christians also justify God. In their new being, in their communal nature, they display not only God's redemption but God's very act of new creation. They thus do justice to God as true Redeemer and Creator, indeed, and with their being they proclaim him as the giver of all good gifts. It is in this sense that Luther can say that faith "consummates the Deity."[60] It is God's creation-transforming presence through the faithful as the body of Christ. In the church, as a community oriented to the world, grace and nature are united.[61]

---

57. *LW* 26:172; *WA* 40I:290b.

58. *Temporal Authority: To What Extent It Should Be Obeyed* (1523), *LW* 45:94-95; *WA* 11:253-4.

59. Davis, *Being and Waiting*, 129. For all its insightfulness, Davis's discussion exhibits what, from the perspective the argument advanced here, are three flaws. He falls short of constructively articulating the sacramental and ecclesiological location of the union of grace with nature. This is, in part, a consequence of his neglect of the sacramental thrust of Luther's christology. Neither does Davis appreciate that the creature's affirmation of God's work, as the creature's own goal, has the integrative structure of *exitus* and non-identical *reditus*.

60. "[Faith] is the Creator of the Deity, not in the substance of God but in us. For without faith God loses His glory, wisdom, righteousness, truthfulness, mercy, etc., in us; in short; God has none of His majesty or divinity where faith is absent," for he either is regarded as an idol, or his mercy and goodness go unacknowledged (*LW* 26:227; *WA* 40I:360b).

61. For an exploration of human partnership with God, articulated in the context of Luther's eucharistic theology and Milbank's theology of gift as delayed and non-identical repetition of a prior unilateral gift, see Piotr J. Małysz, "Exchange and Ecstasy: Luther's Eucharistic Theology

When one comes to appreciate Luther's insistence on the *fides sacramenti*—faith *alone* in its proper sacramental and ecclesial context—it will hardly seem an impoverishment to piety. Here I could not agree more with Wicks's view, though I have also sought more explicitly to ground it in Luther's ontological concerns. Luther's *simul* emphasizes the eschatological reality of the self in essential communion with the God who is making all things new in a world that is now conclusively old. Luther concretizes this new structure of selfhood through a rich sacramental piety utterly inseparable from a vocational ethos woven into its fabric. Faith lays hold of Christ, and in the conclusiveness of this self-enlarging gesture, the self is at the same time actively conformed to Christ. To say that Christ is the form of faith, that faith alone justifies, is to assert this unity of grace and nature actively radiating into all creation.

IV. Conclusion

By way of conclusion, let me ask again: Are the ontologies underwriting Luther's and Roman-Catholic spirituality irreconcilable? Should we simply accept that we have here two different ways of structuring Christian thought, two different ways of understanding the self? Essentially this is true. But even as we admit this, we must, first and foremost, acknowledge the theologies' fundamentally shared purpose to give a coherent account of the unity of nature and grace. And we must be attentive to the various ways in which they resonate with each other, for in this resonance they call each other to be better at what they already do and remind each other of their mutual blind spots. The encounter is certainly not one

in Light of Radical Orthodoxy's Critique of Gift and Sacrifice," *Scottish Journal of Theology* 60:3 (August 2007): 294-308.

of incomprehension, but, as Jared Wicks's lifelong engagement with Luther has shown, it can be an altogether fruitful and joyful affair.

3

"The" vs. "All": Baptist Appropriations and Distortions of Martin Luther's Universal Priesthood

Brian C. Brewer

The Baptist tradition has no single founder. While other Christian traditions may debate the interpretations of their foreparent's intentions and the degree to which the denomination must follow in his or her footsteps, Baptists have no one name to honor as their heritage's theological fount, to turn to for clarity of purpose and identity in the midst of strife, to follow slavishly without critical reflection, to rebuff rebelliously in favor of "progress," to insidiously distance itself from out of neglect, or even continuously to hold, if not embrace, as a competent dance partner even as the world plays new rhythms. When forced to admit it, Baptists are both jealous of and relieved when it comes to having one such winsome founder.

However, the consequence of having no single forefather makes not only Baptist theology but even Baptist history and identity enigmatic. There is no original set works to turn to for understanding the movement's cause and purpose for being. Baptists even debate amongst themselves their origin. Do they come from some tributary of the Anabaptist stream? Balthasar Hubmaier seems a likely theological precursor. But after his martyrdom in 1528 in Austria, Hubmaier's congregation in Moravia soon dissipated. Do the Baptists then find their origins from John Smyth (Baptists even debate the pronunciation of his last name!) who, when persecuted by James I for non-conformity, led a group of English Separatists to Holland in 1607? Or do they find their origin in Thomas Helwys, the English layman in Smyth's flock who returned from Holland to England only a few years later, in 1609, with a remnant of this same congregation after Smyth and the majority decided to join the Waterlander Mennonites in Amsterdam? Or did the real Baptists begin a generation later under the auspices of a group of Puritan Calvinists who were apparently the first in England to insist on credobaptism by immersion—a rite that is now a touchstone of the Baptist tradition? How one answers this question of provenience depends upon how the respondent perceives the basic makeup of Baptist identity. The Baptist heritage, then, is inscrutable, controversial and messy.

If truth be told, the majority of the doctrines that comprise Baptist theology is not original to the tradition. Like a hungry deacon at a church potluck dinner, Baptists have assembled a full plate from the ecumenical smorgasbord of Anabaptist, Lutheran, Separatist and Calvinist dishes, later seasoned by American Frontier revivalist spices.[1] The Baptists have mixed these distinctive doctrinal entrees

1. James Leo Garrett astutely observed that Baptists "seem to have been indebted to various

into a strange mélange and proudly declared the concoction their own,

> mostly forgetting the respective kitchens in which each was baked. One notable Baptist leader even quipped: "There's no single doctrine that is unique to Baptists, but their collective beliefs are distinctive. No other denomination holds this specific 'recipe' of convictions."[2]

Even though one might trace the origins of what now comprises Baptist thought to disparate sources, there is arguably no one person whose thought would ultimately influence Baptist theology more than the "father of Protestantism," Martin Luther. So influential are Luther's ideas to most Baptists that the latter have come to believe such core doctrines as *sola fide*, *sola gratia*, and *sola scriptura* to be their very own.[3] In other words, most Baptists unquestionably perceive their devotion to the authority of scripture alone and to the doctrine of justification by grace through faith alone to be uniquely Baptist, and they are strikingly oblivious to their progenitor.

The adoption of much of Luther's theology is undoubtedly now unobserved in many Protestant traditions, naturally because Luther created a foundation upon which subsequent reformers built distinctive structures of Protestant traditions by sometimes rejecting, sometimes accepting, and sometimes nuancing or reworking Luther's initial designs. Baptists are no exception. While perhaps

magisterial Reformers: Luther for the supremacy of the Scriptures over tradition, for justification by grace through faith, and the priesthood of all Christians; Zwingli for a memorialist understanding of the Lord's Supper; Bucer for church discipline as essential to the true church, and Calvin for predestination as a major doctrine. Continental Anabaptist influence can most clearly be seen in believer's baptism as constitutive of a truly ordered church, church discipline as necessary, the New Testament as superior to the Old Testament, and religious freedom for all humans." See Garrett, *Baptist Theology: A Four-Century Study* (Macon: Mercer University Press, 2009), 22.

2. Russell H. Dilday, *The Baylor Line* (December 2007), 6.

3. Baptist historian Bill Leonard observes that Luther's "concern for the primary authority of Scripture, the priesthood of all believers, and the evangelical dimension of faith had profound impact on the Baptist understanding of the nature of Christian belief." See Leonard, *Baptist Ways: A History* (Valley Forge: Judson Press, 2003), 18.

accentuating and developing its doctrines differently, the Baptist tradition has historically held fast not only to Luther's positions on justification and the supreme role of Scripture vis-à-vis tradition, but it also has assumed Luther's ideas of *simul iustus et peccator*, the theology of the cross, the importance of faith preceding the sacraments (which Baptists typically called "ordinances"), the recovery of immersion as the best symbol for baptism,[4] the importance of preaching the Word in gathered worship, the Christian vocation of all God's people, Christian ethics as sanctification, and much of Luther's distinction between Law and Gospel. This list could undoubtedly be lengthened several times over. However, perhaps other than the traditional "solas,"[5] Baptists have most tenaciously adopted, maintained and, regretfully, distorted Luther's momentous doctrine of the priesthood of all believers.

The Development of Luther's Universal Priesthood

Among his most important reforms, Luther precipitated a massive theological and ecclesiological shift from a dominating church

4. For instance, in his *Babylonian Captivity of the Church* (1520) Luther recommends: "It is therefore indeed correct to say that baptism is a washing away of sins, but the expression is too mild and weak to bring out the full significance of baptism, which is rather a symbol of death and resurrection. For this reason I would have those who are to be baptized completely immersed in the water, as the word says and as the mystery indicates. Not because I deem this necessary, but because it would be well to give to a thing so perfect and complete a sign that is also complete and perfect. And this is doubtless the way in which it was instituted by Christ" (*LW* 36:68; *WA* 6:534, 18-24).

5. One could argue that the priesthood of all believers is actually not only a doctrine Baptists have held in addition to the "solas" but, more rightly understood, *in relationship with* or *because of* them. Mark Rogers observes that Luther's doctrine of the universal priesthood is grounded in Christ's priesthood and pertains to our union with Christ, that it was community-centered, as each individual works to "priest" the others in the congregation in order to "maintain justifying faith throughout life," and that the doctrine is Word-centered, the Word becoming the empowering message of each Christian's priesthood. "Therefore," Rogers argues, "we see that three main points of Evangelical theology come together in one area of Luther's doctrine: biblical authority, salvation by faith in Christ alone, and the priesthood of all believers." See Rogers, "A Dangerous Idea? Martin Luther, E. Y. Mullins, and the Priesthood of All Believers," *Westminster Journal of Theology* 72 (2010): 123.

hierarchy to an ordered but egalitarian priesthood of all. Utilizing 1 Peter 2:9 ("You are a chosen race, a royal priesthood, and a priestly royalty"), in 1520 Luther famously concluded: "Therefore we are all priests, as many of us as are Christians."[6] For Luther, the entire church, clergy and laity, are "priests," ordained by virtue of their baptisms into this order. Said Luther in 1523:

> For a priest, especially in the New Testament, was not made but was born. He was created, not ordained. He was born not indeed of flesh, but through birth of the Spirit, by water and Spirit in the washing of regeneration [John 3:6f; Titus 3:5f.]. Indeed, all Christians are priests, and all priests are Christians.[7]

While laity and clergy often play different roles in their daily lives because of each person's unique vocation, there is no fundamental distinction between the two in terms of status.[8]

Luther's understanding of the universal priesthood was predicated on his theology of freedom granted through the divine gift of grace through faith. Justified by Christ's alien righteousness which frees each believer from the bondage to sin and the law, as Mark Kolden observes, "faith spontaneously springs [the Christian] into acts of love, according to Luther. It does not let us remain 'in heaven' but returns us to earth. This is another way of saying that the gospel frees us from the law for the law. The gospel returns us to the law; it frees us to the [l]aw for the good of our neighbor."[9]

It is worth noting that Martin Luther never used the actual phrase, "priesthood of all believers." Additionally, his initial development of

---

6. *The Babylonian Captivity of the Church*; LW 36:113; WA 6:564, 11.
7. *Concerning the Ministry*; LW 40:19; WA 12:178, 26-29.
8. Alister McGrath, *Christianity's Dangerous Idea: The Protestant Revolution – A History from the Sixteenth Century to the Twenty-First* (New York: Harper One, 2007), 52-53.
9. Marc Kolden, "Luther on Vocation," *Word and World* 3 (1983), 385. Gustaf Wingren concurs: "Freedom in externals is freedom to the law, to the full hands of the work of one's vocation, unto bondage before one's neighbor" in *Luther on Vocation* (Philadelphia: Muhlenberg, 1957), 94.

the idea came in his 1520 treatise "To the Christian Nobility of the German Nation Concerning the Reform of the Christian Estate," wherein Luther dismissed the spiritual state as belonging exclusively to the "pope, bishop, priests and monks" to pry open its sacred doors widely enough to include "princes, lords, artisans and farmers," indeed ultimately claiming "all Christians are truly of the spiritual estate."[10] While Luther's arguments might well be construed at this juncture as politically motivated in order to empower the leaders of the temporal estate to act independently of Rome, the reformer had already begun to consider aspects of the universal work of the ministry for all Christians as early as his Romans lectures of 1515-16, before the political turmoil between Saxony and the Papal See had ensued. He there hinted at the idea of a shared ministry in such phrases as: "Every word which proceeds from the mouth of a leader of the church *or from the mouth of a good and holy man* is the Word of Christ, for He has said, 'He who hears you hears Me.'"[11]

As he enlarged the notion of the universal priesthood, Luther was careful to describe this designation as carrying both high privilege and critical responsibility for each believer. The Christian, he stated paradoxically, is both "the most free lord of all, and subject to none," while also "the most dutiful servant of all, and subject to every one."[12] Believers are "worthy to appear before God, to pray for others, and to teach one another"[13] the substance of the faith. This revolutionary shift in ecclesial power became what Alister McGrath would later call "Christianity's Dangerous Idea,"[14] an idea that liberated laity to participate in the functions of ministry, to pray for and forgive one another, to read and interpret Scripture without clerical

10. *To the Christian Nobility*; LW 44:127; WA 6:407, 10-12, 13-15.
11. LW 25:238; WA 56:251, 25-26 (emphasis added).
12. *Freedom of a Christian* (1520); LW 31:344; WA 7:49, 22-25.
13. LW 31: 355; WA 7:57, 25-26.
14. McGrath, title and throughout, but esp. 50-56.

hegemony—an idea which democratized the church in early modern Saxony. Additionally, the layperson is seen to have equal access to God as any clergyman and may freely come before God's presence.

Luther saw this as an important status shared by all, but one that was not intended to disqualify or make redundant the role of the clergy. Instead, as historian Robert G. Torbet remarked, it served less to "defrock the clergy as it ordained the laity."[15] The laity were elevated to become clergy's equal. Even while clergy served the functions of preaching and dispensing the sacraments, they did so because of their particular gifting observed by, and performed on behalf of, the rest of the "priests" in the wider congregation. For the purpose of good order, only the properly ordained priest was, under normal circumstances, to minister the Word in public worship.[16] However, the layperson was always to minister the Word in private, in his or her daily life, vocation, family and activities.[17] Nevertheless, Luther was protective of the work of the clergy as a particularly public role and one that should be kept from charlatans and from those who misinterpreted the "priesthood of all" as conveying a kind of universal theological authority. Scolding any who might attempt to shape or reprove the direction of the pastor's homilies, for instance, Luther wrote: "You fool, you simpleton, look to your own vocation;

---

15. Robert G. Torbet, *The Baptist Ministry: Then and Now* (Philadelphia: Judson Press, 1953), 9. Likewise, Karlfried Froehlich wrote: "Luther did not eliminate priests or do away with the priesthood. Instead he eliminated the laity!" See Froehlich, "Luther on Vocation," in *Harvesting Luther's Reflections on Theology, Ethics, and the Church,* ed. Timothy J. Wengert (Grand Rapids: Eerdmans, 2004), 127.

16. Luther would maintain in his treatise *Concerning the Ministry,* "The community rights demand that one, or as many as the community chooses, shall be chosen or approved who, in the name of all with these rights, shall perform these functions publicly. . . . Publicly one many not exercise a right without consent of the whole body or of the church" (*LW* 40:34; *WA* 12:189, 21-27).

17. Luther argued, for instance, "If you are a manual laborer, you find that the Bible has been put into your workshop, into your hand, into your heart. It teaches and preaches how you should treat your neighbor. . . . Indeed, there is no shortage of preaching. You have as many preachers as you have transactions, goods, tools, and other equipment in your house and home" (*The Sermon on the Mount, LW* 21:237; *WA* 32:495, 19-21, 36-38).

don't you take to preaching, but let your pastor do that."[18] While in emergencies any Christian should preach and baptize, the selected minister(s) are particularly chosen by each congregation to teach what the church needs to hear. These individuals are selected to be "ministers, deacons, stewards, [or] presbyters," but they are not "priests," for all Christians are priests.[19] Therefore, no one individual can arise within the congregation by his own authority and assume alone what belongs to the entire church. Yet in one's own vocation and family relations, each "preaches" and ministers to the other.

When rightly understood, however, this elevation of the laity was not to be seen as mere privilege. Luther importantly underscored this designation as empowerment to act, to minister, to serve. Although the individual Christian need not seek out her ordained pastor to confess her sins, she should still seek out a fellow Christian to do so. And the fellow Christian, in turn, should bring words of absolution in response to such heartfelt repentance. "I have no doubt," Luther would write, "but that every one is absolved from his secret sins when he has made confession, privately before any brother."[20] Christians should pray for one another, help one another, and, when need be, even baptize one another. This new (or renewed) designation was not merely Christian honor but also Christian work, not merely elevated spiritual status but also heightened spiritual responsibility.

Important to note is that Luther's doctrine of the universal priesthood is not developed in a vacuum but rather is connected to Luther's Christology and the Christian's union with Christ. As Paul Althaus has noted: "The church is founded on Christ's priesthood. Its inner structure is the priesthood of Christians for each other. The priesthood of Christians flows from the priesthood of Christ."[21]

---

18. *Exposition of John 1 and 2*; *WA* 46:735; cited in Wingren, *Luther on Vocation*, 114.
19. *LW* 40:36; *WA* 12:190, 14-23.
20. *LW* 36:88; *WA* 6:547, 17-19.
21. See Paul Althaus, *The Theology of Martin Luther* (Philadelphia: Fortress Press, 1966), 313-14.

Yet, in a relatively underappreciated move, Luther also argued that Christians have a similar share in Christ's royal rule: "Wherefore we are priests, as he is Priest, sons as he is Son, kings as he is King. For he makes us to sit with him in heavenly places, as companions and co-heirs with him, in whom and with whom all things are given us."[22] Christians have the promise of having all things in common with Christ, expressed powerfully in the "one loaf, one cup, one body, members of his body, [and] one flesh, bone of his bone."[23] Consequently, as fellow priests, we all share in the priestly functions of teaching and preaching the Word; baptism; the administration of the Supper; the binding and loosing of sin; the common presentation of our bodies, too, as sacrifices in and as the Church; the ministry of intercessory prayer; and, finally, the charge to "judge and pass on doctrines" and spirits.[24]

Because the church shares this responsibility of spiritual discernment, it follows that Luther's early ecclesiological development allowed each community of faith to select and approve its own clergy to carry out these tasks publicly on behalf of the gathered congregation. But because the congregation would choose its leaders, it would follow through their judgment of teaching and preaching, that, as Luther wrote, "a minister may be deposed if he proves unfaithful. On the other hand he is to be permitted in the ministry as long as he is competent and has the favor of the church as a whole. . . ."[25] This function of authority and discernment is always a corporate act. "Publicly one may not exercise a right without consent of the whole body or of the church," yet, theologically and privately, "all Christians are priests in equal degree."[26]

22. *LW* 40:20; *WA* 12:179, 19–21.
23. *LW* 40:20; *WA* 12:179, 22–24.
24. *LW* 40:21–32; *WA* 12:180–88.
25. *LW* 40:35; *WA* 12:190, 25–30.
26. *LW* 40:34 and 21; *WA* 12:189, 25–27 and 179, 39.

Luther was forced to clarify, nuance and perhaps reinterpret this doctrine as Saxony experienced political turmoil at the advent of the German Peasants' War in 1525. Consistently against violence, Luther had heretofore maintained that religious sects and nonconformity were outgrowths of a free society. But following the peasants' rebellion, where many commoners had been stirred up by the preaching of Thomas Müntzer and the Zwickau prophets and where perhaps 100,000 people were ultimately killed, Luther lost faith in the common person's gift of discernment, and his ecclesiology was reshaped further. Such a reaction may be understandable, as Luther perceived that the masses had misconstrued his theological terminology of "freedom" and his sentiment towards greater egalitarianism regarding the work of the church as then applying also to the political realm.[27] For his part, the reformer pressed for an orderly society. Luther was always irascible but following the revolt became qualmish; he would occasionally refer to German commoners as "stupid folk" and "uncouth, undisciplined, shameless people"[28] who were incapable of interpreting the Word on their own without the presence of sound theological guidance of the properly ordained and appointed clergy. Distrustful of the layperson's abilities without such teaching, the later Luther seemed to gravitate away from his earlier proto-congregationalism where churches might raise their own clergy, while underscoring what he perceived as the

27. As Diarmaid MacCulloch wrote, "Luther, the champion of the ordinary Christian, had been transformed into an apologist for official savagery . . . [because of] his uneasy and unspoken knowledge that without his Reformation the events of 1524 and 1525 would never have happened. His own ideas had fueled the fire." See MacCulloch, *The Reformation: A History* (New York: Viking, 2003), 156. Hans-Martin Barth critiques Luther just on this point, saying: "Of course Luther, in his programmatic writing on 'the freedom of a Christian,' which stirs us still today, was not concerned with social or political problems. Nevertheless we have to ask how it was that he took so little notice of concrete situations of unfreedom among his fellow human beings who were not members of his class." See Barth, *The Theology of Martin Luther: A Critical Assessment* (Minneapolis: Fortress Press, 2013), 50.

28. *Infiltrating and Clandestine Preachers* (1532); *LW* 40:392; *WA* 30III:526, 35-36 and 527, 4-5; here cited after Rogers, "A Dangerous Idea?" 126.

temporary necessity of an orderly state-church hierarchy to ascertain and certify clerical callings. Although he never abandoned his earlier notion that all Christians should be accountable to one another, minister to and pray for each other, such liberties, Luther ultimately believed through his experience, must be exercised only under the guidance of an orthodox and attentive clergy and those more mature in their faith. Consequently, as Hans-Martin Barth observes, "Luther's interest in the universal priesthood declined remarkably in his later years, probably because of his experience in the Peasants' War."[29] Interpreters of Luther, then, often make the mistake of reading only Luther's early works regarding the ministry of the laity. As Mark Rogers has rightly observed:

> Many later Protestants, focusing exclusively on the pre-1525 writing of Luther, have presented an inaccurate description of Luther, which emphasizes the right of private interpretation, congregationalism, and the ability of common Christians to discern right teaching on their own. . . . Luther's mature doctrine of the priesthood of all believers still held to the priesthood of every Christian, but his hierarchical ecclesiology and distrust of the common Christian's ability was far from [what McGrath had called] a "democratizing agenda."[30]

Individuals, who can so easily be led astray, cannot and should not develop their own personal interpretations and theologies, he believed. They need the collective church, especially of those more mature and properly competent. In summary, then, when viewing all of his life's work, the Wittenberg reformer often highlighted both the privilege for the individual in his or her priesthood but also the importance of one's submission to one another in an orderly polity as comprising the substance of the universal priesthood. Luther was

---

29. Barth, *The Theology of Martin Luther*, 55–56.
30. Rogers, "A Dangerous Idea?" 126–27.

scrupulous to maintain a careful balance of privilege and obligation in his understanding of the priesthood of all Christians.

Early Baptist Appropriations of Luther's Doctrine

There is ample historical evidence that the Baptist movement, though differing from Luther in many respects, adopted aspects of his principles on the priesthood of all believers in their nascent theology in the seventeenth century. Baptists derived most directly out of English Separatism, a movement which repudiated the notion of a state church and a hierarchical government for what they viewed as biblical authority, a redeemed church membership, and a church polity which included the participation of all its members. With these tenets as central to Baptist beginnings, it is interesting but not surprising that Luther's idea of a joint-kingship with Christ was the most developed portion of this doctrine for the earliest Baptists. John Smyth, the leader of an English Separatist congregation in Dutch exile, would write in 1608 that "the visible Church by the Apostle is called a Kingly preisthood [sic]. I pet. 2.9. and the Saynts are Kings & Preists vnto God Revel. 1.6. The Saynts as Kings rule the visible Church. 1. Cor. 5.12 psal. 149.9 Mat. 18. 15-17. 1. Cor. 6.1-9." Rejecting John Calvin's threefold office of elders (pastors, teachers and rulers) as "none of Gods ordinance but mans devise," Smyth held that the proper polity would allow for only one type of clergy, that plainly of "elder," adding that those who would claim "that all Elders of the Church are Pastors: & that lay[people are simply] Elders (so called) are Antichristian."[31] But even here, the man often credited with founding the first Baptist congregation in the world held that no clergyman stood as a mediator between any Christian and God,

---

31. John Smyth, "Differences of the Churches of Separation" (1608), as cited in *A Sourcebook for Baptist Heritage*, ed. H. Leon McBeth (Nashville: Broadman Press, 1990), 15.

and he stipulated that the elders are subordinate to the "kings of the church," the gathered congregation.[32] Notes David Bebbington:

> This principle, the kingship of all believers, is perhaps Smyth's most enduring legacy. He accepted the general Reformation conviction of the priesthood of all believers, the status that gives access to the Father, but he added an entirely different point. Christians, he held, share in the kingly role of Christ as much as in his priestly role. Together they possess the authority of their ascended Lord to rule each local congregation. That, for Smyth, was the true foundation of church government.[33]

While Bebbington is correct in his assessment that Smyth underscored an unusual doctrine, as we have already seen, the mutual kingship of the gathered church was not foreign to but actually present in Luther's early writings. Because Christ is the High Priest, his flock is the royal priesthood, and because Christ is King, so the church exercises Christ's royal authority as a gathered community. Important to note is that, like Luther, this authority is always interpreted by Smyth to be communal, not individual. Only as the gathered "Saynts" may the body of Christ exercise Christ's kingly work in and as their church polity. All church members would play a role in governing the churches of the General Baptist tradition ("general" meaning they adhered to a general atonement)—the tradition which traced its origins back to Smyth. Importantly, their polity was then not original but based on their reception of the Reformation doctrine of the priesthood of all believers.

However, even before Smyth was the central actor in his proto-Baptist scene on the world stage, other English Separatists had made their way to Amsterdam as early as the end of the sixteenth century

---

32. See Smyth, *The Works of John Smyth: Fellow of Christ's College, 1594-8*, vol. 1, ed. W. T. Whitley (Cambridge: Cambridge University Press, 1915), 315.
33. David W. Bebbington, *Baptists Through the Centuries: A History of a Global People* (Waco: Baylor University Press, 2010), 33.

to avoid persecution from the English government. Upon arriving in Amsterdam without their pastor, because England allowed for emigration of these congregations only if without their pastor, one congregation chose from amongst its ranks Henry Ainsworth to become its new leader. In order to clarify the church's theology and ecclesiology, Ainsworth penned a new creed entitled *A True Confession* on behalf of his exiled church. Marked by a Calvinism typical of its Puritan origins, the confession demonstrated many doctrinal convictions developed from the previous decades of the Reformation. The Church's union with Christ, whose offices were Prophet, Priest and King, was highlighted. As the Priest, Jesus was the "acceptable sacrifice" who had "brokē dovvn the partition vvall, & thervvith finished & [has now] removued al those legal rites, shadovves, & ceremonies," in order to "bee reconciled to his elect. . . ." While Christ now makes intercession for the Church before the Throne of God, Ainsworth notes, he also "maketh his people a spirituall hovvse, an holy Priesthood, to offer up spirituall sacrifices, acceptable to God through him, . . . communicating and applying the benefits, virtue and frutes of his prophecy and Priesthood vnto his elect. . . ."[34]

Like the General Baptists before them, the Particular Baptist tradition[35] developed an even stronger link between baptism, the priesthood and kingship of all believers, and church polity. Borrowing heavily from Ainsworth's *True Confession*, in 1644, the seven Particular Baptist churches in London collectively agreed upon a statement of faith, now called *The London Confession*, which acknowledged not only Christ's own offices of Prophet, Priest and King, but also "that all beleevers are a holy and sanctified people, and

---

34. See Ainsworth, *A True Confession*, nos. 10, 14, 15, and 17; in *Baptist Confessions of Faith*, ed. William L. Lumpkin (Philadelphia: Judson Press, 1959), 84–86.
35. The name derives from their shared Calvinist conviction on particular atonement for the elect.

that sanctification is a spiritual grace of the new Covenant"[36] granted by their High Priest. By virtue of their participation in his covenant work, "every Church has the power given them from Christ for their better well-being" both to choose their ministers and as "his whole Church to receive in and cast out, by way of Excommunication, any member; and this power is given to every particular Congregation, and not one particular person, either member or Officer, but the whole."[37] While admittedly focusing the privilege of the shared priesthood on the right to congregational polity and church discipline and not on one's own access to prayer and collective ministry to one another, the point should not be lost that the confession demonstrated how early Baptists saw the power given in this doctrine of priesthood (and kingship) of all believers as one to be exercised only as a community.[38] This doctrine, originating in Luther's great Reformation works, apparently links English Particular Baptists to their Protestant foreparents in English Puritanism and Separatism.[39]

Another notable Baptist theologian, Thomas Collier, a paradoxically Arminian Particular Baptist,[40] wrote in 1646 that "all the body ought to watch over each other, thus the Elder is to watch

---

36. *London Confession* (1644) XXIX; in Lumpkin, *Baptist Confessions*, 164.
37. *London Confession*, XXXVI and XLII; in Lumpkin, *Baptist Confessions*, 166, 168.
38. It is important to note again that *The London Confession* was unquestionably based upon the 1596 Separatist confession, *A True Confession.* Ainsworth wrote in the latter that the design of the church was such that "the Ministers and people thus remayne together in this holy order and christian communion, ech one endeavoring to do the will of God in their calling, & thus to vvalke in the obedience of faith. . . .", Ainsworth, *A True Confession*, 27; in Lumpkin, *Baptist Confessions*, 90.
39. See Garrett, *Baptist Theology*, 19, and Ainsworth, in Lumpkin, *Baptist Confessions*, 88-93. Though Ainsworth's confession shows some similarities to the Anabaptist *Waterlander Confession* (1580), likely because of geographic proximity, and like the latter refers to Christ's offices of prophet, priest and king, the Anabaptist document makes no mention of the priesthood of all believers. This indicates that the doctrine of universal priesthood derived from English Separatism via Puritanism from the continental Reformation, and its source was ultimately Martin Luther.
40. See Garrett, *Baptist Theology*, 80-83.

over the body . . . and thus may, nay, and ought, the whole Church to watch over (and if occasion be) reprove, admonish &c. the Elder. Thus is the Kingly office of Christ, carried along sweetly in the church of Christ."[41] Differing greatly from one another in polity, soteriology, and even, initially, mode of baptism, both the early General and Particular Baptists were nevertheless in strong agreement on the notion of a shared priesthood of the congregation as a royal authority given by Christ.[42] Although the early Luther would have particularly highlighted the individual's privileged access to God as a priest along with the collective role in the function of ministry all Christians share, the early seventeenth-century Baptists interpreted the common ministry in terms of authority, polity and church discipline. Thus, all confessing members of a congregation play a role in attending to the concerns of the church as well as the matters of mutual admonition and correction of each individual. As we have seen, such an idea had already been developed by Luther. For him, the congregation is to discern God's truth and also to exercise the power of the keys, binding and loosing, together. "For what," says Luther, "is to loose, if not to announce the forgiveness of sins before God? What is to bind, except to withdraw the gospel and to declare the retention of sins?"[43] For early Baptists, this mutual admonition was the exercise of the "kingship of all believers" in union with Christ, the King.

Contemporary Baptist historians have sometimes been led astray from observing this corporate understanding amongst early Baptists because of the latter's arguments for the freedom of conscience. For instance, in insisting upon the freedom of religious expression

---

41. Thomas Collier, *The Exaltation of Christ in the Dayes of the Gospel* (London: Giles Calvert, 1646), 234; cited both in Barrington R. White, "Thomas Collier and Gangraena Edwards," *Baptist Quarterly* 24 (1971), 106, and in Bebbington, *Baptists Through the Centuries*, 62.

42. Bebbington, *Baptists Through the Centuries*, 62.

43. *LW* 40:28; *WA* 12:184, 33-35.

in England, Thomas Helwys intrepidly addressed his 1612 treatise *The Mystery of Iniquity* to the king, stating, "if the Kings people be obedient and true subjects, obeying all humane lawes made by the King, our Lord the King can require no more: for men's religion to God is betwixt God and themselves; the King shall not answer for it, neither may the King be judge between God and man."[44] However, such a statement is an argument for the freedom of conscience, not the singular priesthood of the believer. It was incumbent upon all neophytes to the Baptist tradition that they enter into the community freely and submit themselves with no reservations to the baptism of believers, which represented the mutual discipline, theology, and practice of the corporate church. Each person must do so voluntarily, not by compulsion of the state or any other power.

Although it is unknown if they were aware of its theological derivation, seventeenth century Baptists also rehearsed Luther's idea of baptism theologically serving as one's ordination to the universal priesthood. This was particularly meaningful in that early Baptists consistently initiated only confessing adults who had demonstrated a readiness voluntarily to submit themselves to the mutual discipline and ministry of the church. To demonstrate this theology in their liturgical practice, some early Baptist congregations in the first few decades of the seventeenth century would follow each baptismal service with a rite of the laying on of hands, emphasizing a new convert's calling now to minister to the others[45] and to give "expression that all believers are called to witness in a general sense."[46] Understanding this ritual broadly, both General and Particular

---

44. Thomas Helwys, *A Short Declaration of the Mystery of Iniquity* (1612), ed. Richard Groves (Macon: Mercer University Press, 1998), 53.
45. See Leonard, *Baptist Ways: A History*, 7.
46. Historian Robert G. Torbet articulated this reasoning in "The Beginnings of Baptist Churches," in *What Is the Church? A Symposium of Baptist Thought*, ed. Duke K. McCall (Nashville: Broadman Press, 1958), 130; cited in William L. Pitts, Jr., "The Priesthood of All Christians in the Baptist Heritage," *Southwestern Journal of Theology* 30:2 (Spring 1988): 36.

Baptists perceived a kind of ordination for all initiated Christians to serve and keep one another accountable in the faith, echoing Luther's own statement, "all of us that have been baptized are equally priests."[47]

To a great extent, the necessity of the collective kingship and priesthood remained intact in Baptist thought, confessions and catechisms for the subsequent centuries. Occasionally, warnings were sounded against distorting the freedom of the individual at the loss of community. Thomas Grantham (1634-92), one of the greatest General Baptist theologians, emphasized the "form of godliness" through the corporate liturgical actions of baptism, communion, and the laying on of hands represents the necessity of the entire church for sustaining each Christian's faith. Without these practices of corporate worship and with only an individual determining his or her beliefs and practice, he wrote,

> religion will in a little time either vanish, or become an unknown conceit, every man being at liberty to follow what he supposes to be the motions of the Spirit of God, in which there is so great a probability of being mistaken, as in nothing more; for man's ignorance being very great, and Satan very subtle, and the way of the Lord neglected, men lie open to every fancy which pleaseth best.[48]

Without the priesthood of all, there could be no priesthood of the individual. As one Baptist historian has noted, "the idea of the priesthood of all Christians is so pervasive in Baptist thought that it works as an assumption or presupposition";[49] the term has come to be assumed but not always specifically mentioned in Baptist confessions. For instance, in the *Philadelphia Confession of Faith*, ratified in 1742, members of the oldest Baptist association in America never utilized

---

47. *LW* 36:112; *WA* 6:564, 6-7.
48. Thomas Grantham, *Christianismus Primitivus: or The Ancient Christian Religion* 1678 [II/I/1]; in *Baptist Roots: A Reader in the Theology of a Christian People*, ed. Curtis W. Freeman et al. (Valley Forge: Judson, 1999), 89.
49. Pitts, Jr., "The Priesthood of All Christians in the Baptist Heritage," 34.

the term "priesthood" or even "kingship" of all believers but would still note that the church is made up to those who "willingly consent to walk together according to the appointment of Christ, giving up themselves to the Lord and one to another, by the will of God, in professed subjection . . . to the ordinances of the gospel."[50] The confession stipulates that the work of preaching is assigned both to the ordained bishops and pastors as well as to "others also, gifted and fitted by the Holy Spirit."[51] Additionally, it notes, "as all believers are bound to join themselves to particular churches, . . . so all that are admitted unto the privileges of a church, are also under the censures and government thereof, according to the rule of Christ."[52] In 1813 the Philadelphia Association adopted the *Philadelphia Catechism*, based generally on the confession, which asked: "Are the saints of God commanded to live together in close harmony? and answered: "Yes, they are bound to maintain a holy fellowship and communion in the worship of God, as well as serving their fellow saints."[53]

One historian described the Baptist movement in America during the eighteenth century this way: "Egalitarian, anti-institutional, and anti-clerical, it shared the belief in the priesthood of all believers, in lay ordination, and in lay participation through the exercise or improvement of spiritual gifts in preaching and prayer."[54] Isaac Backus (1724-1806), a significant Baptist pastor and preacher during the American Revolution, argued strenuously for the priesthood of all believers, decried all attempts which placed the minister in any respect over any other church member and stipulated that the pastor

---

50. *Philadelphia Confession of Faith*, Chapter XXVI, no. 6; in *The Philadelphia Confession of Faith with Catechism* (Grand Rapids: Associated Publishers and Authors, Inc., n.d.), 49.
51. *Philadelphia Confession of Faith*, Chapter XXVI, no. 11.
52. *Philadelphia Confession of Faith*, Chapter XXVI, no. 12.
53. "The Philadelphia Baptist Catechism," Chapter XXVII; in *The Philadelphia Confession of Faith with Catechism*, 116.
54. William G. McLoughlin, *Isaac Backus and the American Pietistic Tradition* (Boston: Little, Brown and Co., 1967), 93.

"hath no more power to Decide any case or controversy in the church than any private brother." Every Christian in the community might also be gifted to pray and to preach in public gatherings (something Luther would undoubtedly have frowned upon!) and "every saint is commanded to be faithfull to improve all the gifts & graces that are bestowed on them in their proper place & to their right end."[55] Thus, while each member must recognize his or her individual role, Baptists maintained a sense of communal responsibility, each to the others, essentially until the advent of the twentieth century.

Contemporary Alterations to the Baptist Understanding of the Universal Priesthood

Numerous theories might explain why the Baptist understanding of the universal priesthood was changed from the priesthood of all believers to that of the singular believer. Undoubtedly Baptists, like many other Christians, were influenced by the growing spirit of individualism, especially as Baptists in democratic America played a hegemonic role in shaping their tradition's identity world-wide during the twentieth century. At the advent of the industrialization of American society, the U.S. became increasingly urban and mobile, affecting the stability of the family, the church, and the rural community. And during the early twentieth century no one theologian was more influential among Southern Baptists, the largest Protestant tradition in the US, than E. Y. Mullins.[56] Numerous

---

55. All citations of Backus here taken from McLoughlin, *Isaac Backus and the American Pietistic Tradition*, 43.

56. Mullins would serve as a pastor to three churches and then as president of Southern Baptist Theological Seminary from 1899 to 1928. He additionally served as president of the Southern Baptist Convention denomination (1921 to 1924) and as president of the world-wide entity, the Baptist World Alliance (1923-1928). He founded the journal, *Review and Expositor,* and he chaired the committee that wrote the Baptist Faith and Message in 1925. Though edited twice since then, this latter document still serves as the primary doctrinal statement used by Southern Baptists today.

Baptist observers have noted Mullin's sway over the entire denominational tradition, topped by Harold Bloom's hyperbolic claim that Mullins was "the most neglected of major American theologians . . . the Calvin or Luther or Wesley of the Southern Baptists."[57] Despite such embellishments, Mullins's work was instrumental in shaping modern Baptist theology.

In his most influential theological work, *The Axioms of Religion*, Mullins demonstrated his awareness of Luther's contribution to Protestant thought. Mullins praised Luther not simply for his disputations with perceived Catholic abuses but for his "revolt against spiritual tyranny" to reassert "the fundamental truth of our religious axiom that all souls have an equal right to direct access to God." Mullins recapitulated Philip Schaff's observation that Luther underscored three fundamental Protestant principles: "the supremacy of the Scriptures over tradition, the supremacy of faith over works, and the supremacy of the Christian people over an exclusive priesthood,"[58] the latter of which, Mullins explained, "means of course that there can be no priestly class in the church of God. All are priests alike. . . . Romanism stood for indirect and the Reformation for direct access to God on the part of man."[59]

The *Axioms*, notably subtitled: *A New Interpretation of the Baptist Faith*, placed long-held Baptist doctrines in a new light, or—perhaps more accurately—subjugated traditional doctrines under certain "axioms" or overarching principles, the most important of which was

---

57. Harold Bloom, *The American Religion: The Emergence of the Post-Christian Nation* (New York: Simon and Schuster, 1992), 199; cited in Rogers, "A Dangerous Idea?" 127. Indeed, Rogers also cites Al Mohler as stating, "More than any other individual, E.Y. Mullins shaped the Southern Baptist mind during the first half of the twentieth century," and Rogers himself concedes that "through his denominational leadership and his influential theologian writings, Mullins impacted the course of Southern Baptist life and thought for the rest of the twentieth century," 127. See also R. Albert Mohler's introduction in E. Y. Mullins, *The Axioms of Religion*, ed. Timothy and Denise George (Nashville: Broadman & Holman, 1997), 20.

58. See Schaff, *History of the Christian Church*, 6:16, as cited in Mullins, *Axioms*, 106.

59. Mullins, *Axioms*, 106-7.

what Mullins labeled "soul competency."[60] In the previous centuries, Baptists had developed a belief in soul competency as centered in the doctrine of judgment. That is, Baptists perceived each person as answerable for his or her own faith, and each individual would be judged according to his or her own actions.[61] One could not depend upon the covenant or proxy faith of her parents for salvation and forgiveness. Instead, each human was answerable to God for her own beliefs.[62] But at the turn of the twentieth century, Mullins reshaped this doctrine from essentially spiritual admonition to one of spiritual privilege. For Mullins, competency meant that each person is fit to believe, read Scripture, interpret the Bible, pray to God, and live the Christian faith himself. And soul competency became the axiom under which church polity (properly understood as democracy), church-and-state relations (properly understood as the separation between the two), private judgment, freedom of conscience, and the priesthood of all believers all fell. In turn, soul competency also tended to reject creedal enforcement (though not creeds themselves), a church hierarchy of authority, government power, and any form of compelled religion. Noted Mullins: "Democracy and the priesthood of all believers, again, have been urged as the fundamental Baptist

60. Mullins would argue that "the candid reader will recognize without difficulty that [soul competency] is a distinguishing mark of the Baptists" (*Axioms*, 59).

61. For example, the nineteenth-century Baptist theologian, preacher, and president of Brown University, Francis Wayland, wrote regarding what was then known as "private judgment" that each Christian has a responsibility to read the Bible himself so "he has, therefore no excuse for disobedience. He can not plead before God that he could not know his will. He can not excuse himself before his Judge on the ground that his ministers deceived him. The revelation was made to the man himself, and the means were provided for his understanding of it. 'Every one of us must give account for *himself* unto God.' Such are the views which we [Baptists] have always entertained." Wayland, *Notes on the Principles and Practices of Baptist Churches* (1857; New York: Arno Press, 1980), 133.

62. While there are numerous seventeenth century examples, *The Standard Confession of 1660* depicted the Last Judgment as appearing before Christ "at which time judgment which is unalterable, and irrevocable, every man shall receive according to the things done in body (2 Cor. 5:10)," originally cited in Lumpkin, *Baptist Confessions*, 231; here cited in C. Douglas Weaver, "Early English Baptists: Individual Conscience and Eschatological Ecclesiology," *Perspectives in Religious Studies* 38:2 (Summer 2011): 151.

view. Unquestionably they are of vital importance and grow directly out of our fundamental position. But they are corollaries to a prior truth" of soul competency.[63]

To be fair, while obviously radicalizing much of Luther's intentions for the universal priesthood, the Wittenberg reformer himself still described something of the privilege of individuality that Mullins echoed. For instance, in discussing the need to "beware of false prophets" [Matt. 7:15], Luther himself sounds to be arguing a kind of soul competency:

> What else does [Jesus] mean than that each of us shall have regard for his own salvation and be sure of Him in whom he believes and whom he follows? Each is a most free judge of all who teach him, if he himself is inwardly taught of God. . . . For you will not be damned or saved by the teaching of another, be it true or false, but by your faith alone. Anyone may teach as he pleases, but what you believe is your responsibility whether it result in your peril or your benefit.[64]

Thus, Luther also demonstrated the necessity of private judgment in certain contexts, as Randall Zachman's essay in the present volume explores. Yet, Luther's interpretation of "priesthood" seemed to favor the duties of Christians *for one another*. "The priesthood," he said, "is nothing but a ministry. . . . [W]hoever does not preach the Word ... is no priest at all."[65] The priesthood was thus, for Luther, not something possessed but something done: "to teach, to preach and proclaim the Word of God, to baptize, to consecrate or administer the Eucharist, to bind and loose sins, to pray for others, to sacrifice, and to judge all doctrines and spirits."[66]

Regardless, Mullins changed the course of Baptist understanding

---

63. E. Y. Mullins, *The Axioms of Religion: A New Interpretation of the Baptist Faith* (Philadelphia: American Baptist Publication Society, 1908), 53.
64. *LW* 40:32; *WA* 12:188, 13-19.
65. *LW* 36:113; *WA* 6:564, 13.
66. *LW* 40:21; *WA* 12:180, 2-4.

of priesthood, shifting the focus of the doctrine from the collective, communal responsibility of ministry and pastoral care to one of access to God unfettered by priest, tradition, sacrament, or creed.[67] Such a sentiment was not unheard of either in Luther (especially in his pre-1525 works, as we have seen) or in earlier Baptist tradition. It simply was secondary to the corporate work of the congregation. The church, Mullins even states, is "a group of individuals," which organizes for a shared mission.[68] Yet, the priesthood is no longer a collective notion of "kings" in Christ, who discern God's truth and Christian ethic collectively. The priesthood of the singular believer implies, says Mullins, "Man's capacity for self-government in religion," and he reduces religion to "a personal matter between the soul and God."[69]

The effects of Mullins' project on Baptist ecclesiology, in terms of both pastoral and congregational authority, have been profound. Mullins was quick to note that the church must still select pastors "to perform certain specified duties for the sake of convenience or expediency in the church,"[70] but he developed no place for distinctive pastoral insights in Scripture or for the pastor's role in leadership for the church. All decisions, all discernment, was what he called the "consensus of the competent."[71] So, as one scholar astutely observed, while Mullins undoubtedly viewed the pastoral office as important, "it seems he struggled . . . to articulate a strong view of the pastorate in light of his radically democratized ecclesiology."[72] The exclusively democratic ecclesiology Mullins espoused undoubtedly reflected more of Luther's more youthful Protestant passion than his mature,

---

67. Mullins, *Axioms,* 54.
68. Ibid., 55.
69. Ibid., 55 and 54, respectively.
70. Ibid., 93.
71. Ibid., 56.
72. Rogers, "A Dangerous Idea?" 130.

more nuanced ideas of the collective priesthood under the guidance of good pastors, a nuance which was forged under the crucible of the violent uprising of the Peasants' War. Fisher Humphreys rightly critiqued Mullins as "intoxicated by personal freedom, even by personal rights—a category which owes more to the Enlightenment than to the New Testament—even to the loss of the indispensability of society and relationships for personal life."[73] And Winthrop S. Hudson wryly noted that "the practical effect of the stress upon 'soul competency' as the cardinal doctrine of Baptists was to make every man's hat his own church."[74]

Baptists of various theological persuasions, post-Mullins, have been largely shaped by his work, emphasizing the priesthood of *the* believer instead of the collective priesthood of *all* Christians in the community. For instance, the contemporary conservative leader Paul Pressler argues that

> No individual could believe more strongly in the priesthood of the believers than do those in the conservative [Baptist] movement. . . . [The] believer . . . has the right to go to the Word of God and let the Holy Spirit, who wrote it, interpret it to that person. The priesthood of the believer means that a believer can have direct contact with God and does not need to go through any priest, pope, ecclesiastical organization, or anything or anyone else.[75]

So strongly have modern Baptists associated soul competency with the priesthood of all believers, that they often use the words contiguously and even synonymously. For instance, one moderate Baptist theologian explains, "The idea of soul competency or

---

73. Humphreys, "E.Y. Mullins," in *Baptist Theologians*, ed. Timothy George and David S. Dockery (Nashville: Broadman and Holman, 1990), 346.

74. Winthrop S. Hudson, ed., *Baptist Concepts of the Church* (Chicago: Judson Press, 1959), 216.

75. Paul Pressler, *A Hill on which to Die* (Nashville: Broadman & Holman, 1999) 155; cited in Elizabeth Newman, "The Priesthood of All Believers and the Necessity of the Church," in *Recycling the Past or Researching History?: Studies in Baptist Historiography and Myths*, ed. Philip E. Thompson and Anthony R. Cross (Milton Keynes: Paternoster, 2005), 50.

priesthood of the believers is that you are accountable to God for the interpretation you make and how you live it out and how you understand the Bible. It is a liberty issue. It's about freedom from a religious tyrant or people imposing their beliefs and practices on us."[76] Absent here is not only Luther's emphasis on the shared ministry of one priest to another but also Smyth's, Ainsworth's and Collier's belief in mutual admonition and the necessity of church discipline as apportionments of the church's kingly role.

Elizabeth Newman correctly observes, "The fact that soul competency has been identified so overwhelmingly with 'private interpretation' of Scripture and 'direct access' to God reveals the deep influence of modernity's understanding of religion."[77] And the outcome of Mullins' work has undoubtedly contributed both to ecclesiastical confusion and to the willing privatization of faith in the postmodern era. It has also led to the unfortunate sentiment of viewing the priesthood of the believer as a right to which every person is entitled, leading many a Baptist to the colloquialism: "Ain't nobody but Jesus going to tell me what to believe!" But Luther's intention behind the priesthood of all believers was to appreciate the doctrine, not as a right, but as a gift possessed only as we have an unmerited share in Christ's own roles of High Priest and divine King.

Signs of Hope

Hyper-individualism in the Baptist tradition abides. Nonetheless, some desire for theological course correction has appeared. In 1988 the Southern Baptist Convention began to voice concerns over the post-Mullins interpretations of the doctrine as stressing singularity.

---

76. Fisher Humphreys, former professor at Beeson Divinity School, here cited in John Armistead, "HED: Soul Competency: Historic Baptist Concept Premeates [sic] Debates," in *The Daily Journal / Northeast Mississippi News* (July 29, 2000).

77. Newman, "The Priesthood of All Believers," 58.

At their annual convention meeting in San Antonio, Texas, the SBC adopted a statement which condemned modern interpretations of the priesthood of the singular believer as "a recent historical development" which contradicts a proper understanding, as they viewed it, of the authority of the pastor in any congregation.[78] While this denominational statement did little to advance Luther's emphasis of shared responsibility (as opposed to individual privilege on the one hand or pastoral authority on the other), a subsequent 1994 Presidential Study Report of the SBC clarified:

> Every Christian has direct access to God through Jesus Christ, our great High Priest, the sole mediator between God and human beings. However, the priesthood of all believers is exercised within a committed community of fellow believers – priests who share a like precious faith. The priesthood of all believers should not be reduced to modern individualism, not used as a cover for theological relativism. It is a spiritual standing which leads to ministry, service, and a coherent witness in the world for which Christ died.[79]

Such an emphasis on shared ministry and responsibility, instead of a focus on mere individual privilege or pastoral authority, seems promising for correcting contemporary Baptist distortions of the Protestant doctrine.

Likewise, in 1997 a group of Baptist theologians in the American South issued a statement entitled "Re-envisioning Baptist Identity: A Manifesto for Baptist Communities in North America," which also repudiated the hyper-individualistic tendencies of contemporary Baptist theology and practice and issued a call to recover both Baptist confessionalism and corporate responsibility of one Christian to

---

78. http://www.sbc.net/resolutions/872.
79. *Report of the Presidential Theological Study Committee*, adopted by the Southern Baptist Convention (Meeting in Session, June 1994), 6, at http://www.baptistcenter.net/confessions/Report_of_the_Presidential_Theological_Study_Committee_1994.pdf.

another. Among their affirmations, the authors of the Manifesto asserted:

> 1) We affirm Bible Study in reading communities rather than relying on private interpretations or supposed 'scientific' objectivity 2) We affirm following Jesus as a call to shared discipleship rather than invoking a theory of soul competency 3) We affirm a free common life in Christ in gathering, reforming communities rather than a withdrawn, self-chosen, or authoritarian ones.[80]

These two late twentieth century statements, urging the Baptist tradition to reconsider its modern assumptions regarding the place and responsibility of the individual in the context of a community of clergy and laity, are signs of hope for recovering a more historically Protestant and collective priesthood of mutual understanding and accountability as Luther and other reformers had outlined. Unfortunately, these drafted statements calling for reform of the notion of serving as a priest to one's self are exceptions which prove the rule, reflecting a tradition that was and to a great degree is still ensconced in hyper-individualistic understandings of epistemology and identity. While recent Catholic critics[81] have argued that privatization and relativism of the faith are inevitable, though unintended, consequences of the Protestant project, such claims do not necessarily follow and are, in fact, contradictory to Luther's ecclesiological and vocational emphases.

A Need for Recovery of Luther's Doctrine Amongst Baptists

Baptists and other Christians who have fallen victim to modern forms of hyper-individualism may find recourse and correction in returning

---

80. These affirmations are cited in Steven R. Harmon, *Towards Baptist Catholicity: Essays on Tradition and the Baptist Vision* (Milton Keynes: Paternoster, 2006), 12.

81. See in particular Brad S. Gregory, *The Unintended Reformation: How a Religious Revolution Secularized Society* (Cambridge, MA: Belknap/Harvard University Press, 2012), esp. 74–128.

to the fount of the Protestant doctrine of universal priesthood by reviewing the works of the early reformers, especially those of Luther himself. Paul Althaus summarizes Luther's notion:

> The priesthood means: We stand before God, pray for others, intercede with and sacrifice ourselves to God and proclaim the word to one another. Luther never understands the priesthood of all believers merely in the 'Protestant' sense of the Christian's freedom to stand in a direct relationship to God without a human mediator. Rather he constantly emphasizes the Christian's evangelical authority to come before God on behalf of the brethren and also the world. The universal priesthood expresses not religious individualism but its exact opposite, the reality of the congregation as a community.[82]

Luther would have undoubtedly rejected Mullins', subsequent Baptist, as well as relativistic understandings of the privatization of the faith.[83] For instance, when he expostulated his position in favor of "secret confession" to replace obligatory confession to a priest, Luther outlined that in this act "we have laid bare our conscience to our brother and privately made known to him the evil that lurked within" and, in so doing, "we receive from our brother's lips the word of comfort spoken by God himself."[84] Thus, even "private" confession and absolution require community. Christians then intercede for one another because Christ intercedes for humanity at the right hand of God, and believers enjoy a share in Christ's holy priesthood and

---

82. Althaus, *The Theology of Martin Luther*, 314.

83. Nancy Ammerman states: "While Martin Luther and the other reformers did, indeed, intend to impress on us that each of us can and must go directly to God, I doubt that any of them would have expected the kind of defiant individualism of the twentieth century—'nobody can tell me what to believe; me and Jesus, that's all I need.' The sixteenth and seventeenth century reformers never envisioned solo believers standing figuratively alone before God in prayer and Bible reading. They talked about the priesthood of *all* believers, emphasizing the equality, not the aloneness." See Ammerman's sermon, "Priests and Prophets," in *Proclaiming the Baptist Vision: The Priesthood of All Believers*, ed. Walter B. Shurden (Macon: Smyth & Helwys, 1993), 56 (italics hers).

84. *LW* 36:86; *WA* 6:546, 14-16.

kingship: "We are priests as he is Priest, sons as he is Son, kings as he is King."[85]

Seventeenth-century Baptists especially appreciated Luther's injunction to the community to carry out church discipline, to bind and to loose sins, "to proclaim and to apply the gospel" to one another, and to hold each church member accountable for her actions.[86] Such ideas need not mitigate the axiom of the individual conscience, which appears to be Mullin's primary concern, but actually should support such a principle. If no religion is to be compelled, then the individual may freely acquiesce to the mutual discipline, correction, interpretation, and reproof in the community of his own choosing. In baptism, one is truly professing his own belief in Christ before voluntarily submitting himself symbolically to die to his own self-centeredness and to arise in the newness of life in both his Savior and Christ's Church. In this rite, he is also ordained and charged to minister to the others in his congregation.

The work of recovering Luther's egalitarian community would not be a departure from the Baptist tradition but a recovery. Again, John Smyth, the Baptists' first leader, emphasized that it was "the visible Church" that was to be "called a Kingly preisthood [sic],"[87] and *The Philadelphia Confession of Faith* called upon Baptist congregations to "consent to walk together according to the appointment of Christ, giving up themselves to the Lord and one to another . . . in professed subjection . . . to the ordinances of the gospel."[88] Instead, modern notions of soul competency have mingled with contemporary hyper-individualism and relativism to beget the contemporary Baptist idea of priests as spiritual lone rangers. After Baptists have appropriated

85. *LW* 40:20; *WA* 12:179, 19.
86. *LW* 40:27-28; *WA* 12:184, 31-36.
87. Smyth, "Differences of the Churches of Separation" in McBeth, *A Sourcebook for Baptist Heritage*, 15.
88. *The Philadelphia Confession of Faith*, Chapter XXVI, no. 6.

Calvin's "once saved always saved" doctrine along with the modern reinterpretation of soul competency for individual worship and spiritual life, it is surprising not only that Baptists are the largest Protestant tradition in America but even that Baptist churches exist. For modern Baptist theology has given little reason to its adherents for maintaining active church participation following their conversions of faith. Baptists have sacrificed their notion of community and ecclesiology, church discipline, and mutual priesthood at the altar of self-identification, self-determination, and individual spirituality. Without Luther's corporate corrective, the Baptist identity will only apply to the individual, and any collective understanding of the faith would be rendered meaningless because of the wide diversity of application of faith-keeping by each individual amongst the Baptist people. As Elizabeth Newman articulately noted:

> As long as the church is secondary to Baptist self-understanding, then the priesthood of the believer will remain a description primarily of the *individual*, and worship will be understood primarily as that which takes places between an individual and God. With the Reformers, however, we must emphasize not unmediated access to God, but rather the sole priesthood of Christ, in which the church as a royal priesthood corporately participates.[89]

While Luther does not deny the privilege of the individual priesthood of each Christian, one may only possess such divine access through the priesthood of Christ and the joint-priesthood of his gathered Church. The priesthood of the individual is then always in unity with Christ's office primarily and is a derivative of the priesthood of all Christians secondarily, a priority Baptists would be wise to reclaim.

---

89. Newman, "The Priesthood of All Believers," 64 (italics hers).

4

———

Angels of Light: Luther's Liturgical Attack on Christendom

Matthew Myer Boulton

In Martin Luther's work, particularly in his later years but not only there, the figures of "the Turk" on the one hand and "the Jew" on the other are vivid, hateful specters. Indeed, these two ghosts haunt the whole of the reformer's legacy and serve as emblems for the troubling ways he could conceive Christianity's enemies to be located outside the Christian camp. As such, these two caricatures are among the most intolerable and irretrievable aspects of Luther's thought, particularly from the point of view of constructive theological development in the twenty-first century. Here, we might say, we find Martin Luther at his worst, and the shadows of these two ghastly figures fall across not only his own body of work but also the wider history of the sixteenth-century European reformations. As we approach the 2017 quincentennial and its various remembrances, we will do well to reckon with these shadows candidly, and with repentance.

And yet, at the very heart of Luther's theology, particularly although not exclusively in his early years, there is a theme that runs in what we might call the opposite direction. That theme is Luther's adamant and repeated emphasis on the ways in which Christianity's principal enemies characteristically—and even preeminently—arise *within* the Christian camp, in and through patently Christian ideas and activities. At times, this component of Luther's thought takes the form of vitriol directed at his Christian opponents, effectively putting "the Papist," for example, alongside "the Turk" and "the Jew" in his pantheon of abominations. But at other times, and indeed quite frequently, Luther applies the theme not to any subset of Christianity, but to Christian life in general and as such. Here, I contend, we can find Luther at his best, as well as fertile soil for constructive theological development in the twenty-first century. To anticipate, for Luther, the devil comes, but he comes most typically, insidiously, and effectively as an angel of light (2 Cor. 11:14). Accordingly, with respect to sin and evil, for Luther the most treacherous territory is supposedly "sacred" territory, Christian territory, holy ground at the very center of the sanctuary, at the core of the church, in and through our prayers and songs and celebrated ceremonies. Precisely there, in the midst of our most exalted religious activity—and indeed not only in the *midst* of it but also in the *form* of that activity—we should expect to find and confront the reality of sin and death.

At the same time, of course, according to Luther we should also expect to find there the even greater reality of grace and life in Jesus Christ. But wherever God builds a church, Luther once quipped, the devil builds a chapel.[1] As Luther understood it, the most sinister and characteristic forms of sin are spiritual forms, religious forms, *Christian* forms. This basic idea is not strictly original to Luther, of course, but he developed and expanded it to a remarkable, provocative extent—and further elaboration of the idea today in constructive theology is both promising and compelling. So ambitious, in fact, was Luther's thinking in this regard that we find in his work the outlines of an attack not simply on the Roman church or on more radical reformers but on Christendom itself—an attack, we might say, on the catholic church with a small "c," that is, the visible church universal. And further, Luther's is a *liturgical* attack on Christendom, since for him the most decisive, signature spiritual battleground is marked out and epitomized by those prestigious liturgical actions in God's churches and the devil's chapels. In this respect as well—that is, Luther's liturgical way of thinking through these major themes of sin and grace, perdition and salvation—his work is ripe for constructive theological retrieval and development.

Briefly, then, my argument is this: part of what is most useful and promising in Luther's work is that in it we find resources for a thoroughgoing theological critique or attack on Christendom, and that this attack is fundamentally cast in liturgical terms. Indeed, for Luther, the attack's liturgical character is not incidental, instrumental, or secondary, but rather is primary, substantive, and constitutive to the attack itself and the ways Luther understood it to play out in Christian lives. In this chapter I want to flesh out these ideas, as well as reflect on why I consider them to be so potentially useful for theological work today.

The paper will proceed in three parts: first, some brief background and contributing context; second, a sketch of Luther's account of sin as consummately Christian; and third, notes on how Luther works

---

1. *Commentary on Psalm 101* (1534); *LW* 13:159; *WA* 51:211.

out these ideas via liturgical terms and gestures, even to the point of suggesting an account of the human subject as what we might call a liturgical subject, a doxological subject with a particular stance and bearing.

Part I: Some Background and Contributing Context

Part of what drove Luther to think in terms of a liturgical attack on Christendom was his experience as a friar who found the monastery to be less a sanctuary of freedom, piety, and righteousness, and more a kind of cave along the river Jabbok, a site of wrestling, anxiety, temptation, and struggle. Famously, for Luther the matrix of these difficulties was comprised not of supposedly impious actions but rather of supposedly pious ones, even hyper-pious ones. In other words, Luther's own personal experience was that some of the greatest and most threatening forms of impiety manifest in and through acts of alleged piety, and this particular background no doubt made him especially alert to what he would come to consider the profound and indelible ambiguities of Christian life. For Luther, God's church and the Devil's chapel often were not two separate buildings side-by-side, but rather one and the same house of prayer. For example, toward the end of *The Freedom of a Christian* (1520), we find this striking little sentence: "a man must live . . . in the midst of ceremonies, that is, in the midst of dangers."[2] Luther goes on to affirm the propriety and necessity of ceremonies in Christian life, of course, but at the same time underlines their continually perilous character—and so we find in Luther this stark sense of deep and abiding ambiguity.

A second dynamic that drove Luther's thinking as he developed it was the fact that many of his most formative theological disputes

2. *LW* 31:375; *WA* 7:72.

were fought directly and indirectly over vexed questions of ecclesial action and authority, and those debates created occasions for him (even, we might say, created lures for him) to craft increasingly broad critiques of the ways in which the outward forms of Christian life can be distorted and disoriented: clerical and monastic hierarchies, for example, or councils, or the Mass, or allegedly good works. In these disputations, the more his opponents emphasized the merit of works and the key role played by that merit in human salvation, the more Luther emphasized the contrary, declaring, for example, that human beings bring nothing but "sins, death, and damnation" to the "joyous exchange" with Jesus Christ that constitutes human salvation.[3] Or again, the more his opponents emphasized the ecclesial hierarchy's authoritative role in interpreting Scripture or adjudicating doctrinal disagreements, the more Luther emphasized the fallibility, and indeed the ongoing sinfulness, of the church, even and especially in its most exalted visible forms: hierarchies, councils, and of course the Mass. Reading Luther and tracking his development over time, one gets the impression that in certain respects, at least, these theological disputes could have a kind of catalyzing, intensifying effect on his rhetoric and on the substance of his thinking—and this dynamic, combined with Luther's taste for a contrastive dialectical style (not to mention his sharp tongue, vulgar wit, and penchant for hyperbole), led him to explore and develop his ideas in bold, ambitious ways.

The point is not that Luther's ongoing debates somehow coerced him into making sweeping claims, but rather that these debates formed a kind of frame around which the canvas of his theological imagination could be wrapped and stretched, and then upon which he could paint with the bold, broad strokes he found consistent with the Gospel. On that canvas he painted, for example, in his own

---

3. *LW* 31:351-2; *WA* 7:54-5.

particular dialectical style, his theology of the cross explicitly defined over against any and all "theologies of glory"—a move that itself may be understood as laying thematic foundations for an attack on a kind of "Christendom" (that is, an attack on any "Christianity of Glory"). Or again, on that canvas he painted his signature account of both the individual Christian and the church collectively as simultaneously fully justified and nevertheless fully sinful, *simul iustus et peccator*. The *simul* doctrine puts the whole of Christian life—without remainder—in a kind of double light, on one hand justified (though please note, this is *justificatio impii*, justification of the *impious*), and on the other hand squarely under divine judgment and therefore subject to theological critique. And finally, on that same canvas Luther painted his portrait of sin as characteristically manifesting in and through religious forms, spiritual forms, Christian forms, practical forms—and in that sense liturgical forms, provided "liturgy" is properly understood not as a special province of activity cordoned off from everyday life, but rather one in which the basic gestures and dispositions of everyday life are distilled and epitomized for the sake of reflection and formative training.

We turn now to these latter two points in more detail, one at a time: first, Luther's portrait of sin as characteristically manifesting in and through Christian forms; and second, the ways in which he casts this phenomenon in liturgical terms.

Part II: Sin as Consummately Christian

Borrowing from Augustine, Luther often describes sin and its effects this way: the sinner is *incurvatus in se*, "deeply curved in upon oneself," such that he or she coopts and consumes and uses all things strictly "for [his or her] own purposes."[4] *All things*. And so it follows,

---

4. *Commentary on Romans* (1515-16); *LW* 25:291, 345; *WA* 56:304, 356.

as Luther understands it, that the consummate form of sin would be to take the highest things—even and especially the holy things of Christianity—and turn them toward our own ends, our own advantages, our own narrow self-interest. Not in any crude or conspicuous way, of course, since that would hardly advance our self-serving purposes. No, the method must be covert, the camouflage impeccable. The attempt to acquire must take the outward form of generosity. Self-serving pride must take the form of selfless humility. Blasphemy must take the form of orthodoxy. And so on. Accordingly, for Luther, the extremity of human sin is by no means an escape from Christianity, but rather an escape into it. Here is how he puts the point in his *Lectures on Romans*:

> [O]ur nature has been so deeply curved in upon itself because of the viciousness of original sin that it not only turns the finest gifts of God in upon itself and enjoys them ... indeed, it even uses God Himself to achieve these aims, but it also seems to be ignorant of this very fact, that in acting so iniquitously, so perversely, and in such a depraved way, it is even seeking God for its own sake.[5]

In the background here are those famous passages in Augustine's *De doctrina christiana*, in which Augustine frames what has gone wrong in human life in terms of disordered love, and in particular, as disorder with respect to what we "use" and what we "enjoy."[6] At any rate, for Luther, the ultimate "viciousness of original sin" manifests itself precisely in a self-serving form of seeking God: fallen human nature "seeks God for its own sake." It is not as if sinners merely hoard divine gifts and then flee or reject God and Christianity, leading bluntly profane lives of wickedness or debauchery. On the contrary, Luther contends, the depths of sin are evident precisely in

---

5. *LW* 25:291; *WA* 56:304.

6. Augustine, *On Christian Teaching*, trans. R. P. H. Green (Oxford: Oxford University Press, 1997), esp. 9-29.

so-called sacred precincts. There sinners, far from fleeing or rejecting Christianity, set about the task of achieving self-serving aims in and through Christian life. There sinners, far from fleeing or rejecting God, set about the task of "seeking God for their own sake." Sin may and does take other forms, of course, but for Luther the tragedy of sin is finally and preeminently a Christian tragedy. It is, in a word, the tragedy of idolatry, not overt atheism or sacrilege.

An idol never announces itself as such, but on the contrary always presents itself as the genuine article. In Exodus 32, to cite the *locus classicus*, at the foot of the mountain of God, the golden calf (or "the golden young bull," a much better translation) is worshiped not according to some new ceremony or breakaway sect, but expressly *as* the God of Israel, the very one, the Israelites proclaim, who brought them up out of the land of Egypt—and so is worshiped precisely in what Aaron calls "a feast to the LORD" (Exodus 32:5). The form of the idol is the form of the original, and the form of worshiping the idol is thus the form of worshiping the original. Sorting out the difference, then, between the original and the counterfeit, between true worship and idolatry, is a fraught, elusive business. Where God builds a church, the devil builds a chapel. The devil comes disguised—all too well disguised—as an angel of light.

Indeed, this fraught, elusive business is the proper context within which to understand Luther's well-known doctrine of justification. So *incurvata* is fallen human nature, Luther insists, that it attempts to coopt even and especially the good gifts of God and claim them as our own meritorious achievements, and in so doing forfeits those very gifts. This simultaneous lunge and loss is a trope to which Luther repeatedly returns: in *The Freedom of a Christian*, for example, he refers to Aesop's fable of the dog carrying meat in his mouth who sees his own reflection in a river, snaps at the meat in the reflection—and so both snaps at nothingness and loses the meat in the process.[7] For Luther, this is a "permanent temptation," to borrow Kierkegaard's phrase, that persistently attends the visible, tangible forms of Christian life, and preeminently so with respect to the most exalted of those forms, including hierarchies, good works, ceremonies ("that is, dangers"), and the like. The temptation is this: to move to appropriate and arrogate and, in effect, thereby to reverse into self-serving counterfeits what ought to be God-and-neighbor-serving gifts. Or, expressed in gestural terms (which is to more closely approach the heart of the matter, since human life so often has to do with gestures, patterns of action, and modes of life): the temptation is to twist or confound or misrecognize what ought to be occasions for *receiving* gifts and celebrating the giver into occasions for *seizing* goods as our own achievements, and thereby celebrating ourselves.

"What must I do," asks the lawyer in Luke's Gospel, "to inherit eternal life?" (Luke 10:25). What must *I do?* Luther's doctrine of justification, at its core, is an answer to this question that goes something like this: *Nothing. You can do nothing. Your salvation is not a task for you to accomplish. You have much to do—but none of your works justify you, and therefore all of your works can be done for other reasons, on other grounds, in other ways. They should not be works performed by one* incurvatus in se, *deeply curved inward in self-serving solipsism, narcissism, and loneliness. God has saved you—so by all means, open out toward God and into God and with God, with gratitude and joy. All of your works, insofar as they are works consistent with genuine Christian discipleship, can only take place on the basis of that gratitude and joy.* In other words, at its heart Luther's doctrine of justification is a bulwark against the idea—permanently tempting as it is in Christian life—that our actions, and in particular our exalted, holy, honorable, *Christian* actions, contribute to our justification. For

7. *LW* 31:356; *WA* 7:58.

conceiving and carrying out our work in this way, Luther insists, amounts to a disastrous idolatry: we use God's name and perform inspiring ceremonies and proclaim "a feast to the LORD," but in truth we worship an impressive product of our own making, a golden bull, and in that sense, on an even deeper level, we worship ourselves—the ultimate form of being *incurvatus in se*: self-worshiping-self.

This is the battleground, the proper context for understanding Luther on justification. This is the arena within which he vowed to "constantly cry out" against the idea that "we have forgiveness of sins and eternal life...through the observance of [Christian] traditions" rather than strictly "through [Jesus Christ's] death and resurrection." Precisely because of its deeply curved, self-serving character, such Christianity, Luther declared, is anti-Christianity, the domain of "the Antichrist," and "I shall announce that all your ceremonies and religion are not only a denial of God but supreme blasphemy and idolatry."[8] Yes, justification through faith alone—but what is at stake for Luther in his doctrine of justification is providing what he understood to be key intellectual conditions for instilling and supporting a certain kind of resistance among Christian disciples. Resistance to what? To the persistently alluring idea that there is something we can do to inherit eternal life, some excellent, holy action or set of actions we can take "to obtain righteousness in the sight of God."[9] This temptation is only heightened in the midst of prestigious ceremonies, that is, in the midst of dangers (and by the way, the danger does not decrease, and in some respects may increase, if we shift from one ceremonial form to another, say, "high-church" to "low-church"). If we fall for this temptation—and here is what is finally at stake in all of this for Luther—we fall away

---

8. *Lectures on Galatians* (1535); *LW* 26:224; *WA* 40I:357.
9. *LW* 26:231; *WA* 40I:366.

from our own full and genuine humanity. For we are not made to justify ourselves, to coopt and consume our own actions into alleged occasions for acquiring righteousness. Genuine humanity is violated by this attempt, this bid to self-justify and thereby to worship ourselves, to adore ourselves, to praise ourselves, *incurvati in se*.

Part III: *Homo Laudans*

No doubt Luther was interested in orthodoxy in the sense of "right opinion" (*ortho doxa*), about justification no less than any number of other theological topics. But he was even more deeply interested in orthodoxy in the sense of "right praise" (*ortho doxa*, "doxa" as in "doxology"), a fundamental theme he understood as having to do with the proper stance and bearing for human beings throughout their lives as pilgrims and children of God. For Luther, the genuine human being is by no means *incurvatus in se*—but rather the opposite. Call it *excurvatus ad alios*, "curved outward toward others," and in particular, toward God and toward neighbor: toward God, in the sense of trust and doxology; toward neighbor, in the sense of love and care. Accordingly, Luther insists that disciples continually credit God with every good work, and attribute to God "truthfulness, righteousness, and whatever else should be ascribed to one who is trusted"; Luther identifies this attribution as nothing less than "the very highest worship of God."[10] For we are constantly tempted, as Luther has it, to misdirect this attribution of blessing and truth and righteousness away from God and toward ourselves—to "kiss our own hand," as Luther puts it, quoting the Book of Job (Job 31:27).[11]

There is a kind of doxological zero-sum-game in Luther's thinking here, a devotional either/or, a fundamental premise that human

10. *LW* 31:350; *WA* 7:54.
11. *LW* 31:346; *WA* 7:51.

beings are praising beings—*homo laudans*, we might say, "human praising"—and that in practice we cannot praise two masters. We cannot simultaneously kiss God's hand and kiss our own. For example, in the *Heidelberg Disputation* of 1518, under Luther's seventh thesis we find the following: "To trust in works...is equivalent to giving oneself the honor and taking it from God, to whom fear is due in connection with every work. But this is completely wrong, namely to please oneself, to enjoy oneself in one's works, and to adore oneself as an idol." Likewise, in the 1519 *Lectures on Galatians*, Luther frames the point this way, speaking to God: "man will praise, glorify, and love Thee when he realizes the goodness of Thy mercy and does not, in his self-righteousness, praise himself. For those who [claim to be] righteous . . . do not praise Thee, but praise themselves."[12]

Luther often figures in the popular Christian imagination as in the first place the brash and angry man, nailing some theses on some door somewhere, or in any case raising the prophet's fist of indignation against Christendom's abominations—and then, as a kind of second movement, after the prophetic sermon has been delivered, more pastorally assuring us that, while works and ceremonies and so on are indeed "dangers," he has no intention of doing away with them. He is very much in favor of works and ceremonies, but just wants to be sure that they take place on the right footing and in the right spirit.

But we do well to turn this rhetorical sequence around and consider Luther's work from the other direction, that is, as beginning not with the prophetic objections, but rather with the human life in and with God on behalf of which he raises those objections in the first place. To wit, for Luther, human beings are made—and remade, through the Spirit's restorative work in and through the church—to

12. *LW* 27:185; *WA* 2:466–67.

be *excurvati ad alios*, "curved outward toward others," toward God in faith and praise, and toward neighbors in love and care. Humanity is fundamentally *homo laudans*, "human praising," such that everything we do, all our works of every sort, we properly do as a way of praising God, explicitly and implicitly, thanking God freely out of a felt sense of surplus and joy, our cups running over, celebrating what God has done. We are not, by contrast, fundamentally *homo operans*, "human working," such that our praise is carried out, explicitly or implicitly, as a form of self-serving work. The shape of our life and being is at stake here, the choreography or performance of our humanity—and for this reason, Luther thinks in liturgical terms, precisely because the rhythms and choreographies of liturgy are meant to be epitomes or types for the proper rhythms and choreographies of life. Luther writes that the role of the "priest," for example, is to function as a "visible type" for the priesthood to which all Christians are ordained through baptism[13]—and this basic approach is characteristic of his thinking about particular liturgical actions: the particular actions are microcosmic icons or types of the larger liturgical patterns through which we live our lives. The *Ninety-Five Theses*, for example, open with the practice of penitence, and frame that practice as an ongoing, comprehensive mode of Christian life.[14] Likewise, in *The Babylonian Captivity* (1520), Luther spells out baptism as a lifelong penitential path, culminating only in the eschaton.[15] Luther thinks through liturgy, and he envisions human life as lived through liturgies writ large, *excurvatus ad alios*, loving neighbors and praising God.

In this liturgical anthropology, Luther conceives human being as *homo laudans*, praising God above all, and serving neighbors as itself a mode of doxological life. As such, we are *excurvati ad alios*, and as

13. *LW* 31:354; *WA* 7:56.
14. *LW* 31:25; *WA* 1:233.
15. *LW* 36:57ff, esp. 69.

such, we are genuine human beings in the image of God—or more specifically, in the image of Christ, the One for others, even to the point of each disciple becoming "as it were a Christ to the other that we may be Christs to one another and Christ may be the same in all, that is, that we may be truly Christians."[16] What counts is not merely thinking correctly about Christ, but being Christ; not merely Christocentrism, or even Christomorphism, but living in and through and as Christ in our daily lives and work. Gestures and modes of life that contradict this Christological existence, and that aim to replace it with its opposite (*incurvatus in se*), are antihuman and anti-Christ—and so Luther mounts his attack.

From this angle, we can see how Luther's signature idea of "justification through faith" is ultimately a doctrine rooted in theological anthropology; it belongs to a spirited defense of humanity as created by God to be *excurvatus ad alios*. For Luther, the attempt to self-justify is fundamentally inhumane. This anthropology is in important respects liturgical not only because Luther frames his case in gestural, finally doxological terms, but also because he so vividly draws the dilemma in the first place as one already manifesting as a reality—and as a permanent, dangerous temptation, a reality constantly threatening to break forth—not outside the Christian sanctuary, but squarely and gloriously within it. The dilemma manifests not as "the Turk" or "the Jew," then, but preeminently as "the Christian," as Christendom, triumphant and resplendent, regaled by angels of light.

One concluding word about why I think these aspects of Luther's work are so potentially fruitful for constructive theological development today. First, these ideas are quite vividly and powerfully drawn in their own right. Second, the fact that Luther so often puts

16. *LW* 31:367–8; *WA* 7:66.

them in liturgical terms means that they are already gestural and dispositional from the outset, not merely cerebral or conceptual, and this makes these ways of thinking especially given to theological development in terms of patterns of action and modes of life. And third, I take it that religious triumphalism—and tradition-based triumphalism more generally—is a deeply troubling, pressing problem in the twenty-first century, both within and without Christianity, and each tradition does well to seek out, identify, renovate, and develop resources within it that might help articulate strong, humble forms of human life. Luther's attack on Christendom holds the promise of a thoroughly penitential, baptismal, doxological way of being Christian, and way of being human, that is at once bold and humble, ambitious and modest, free and compassionate—or, as Luther himself might put it, subject to none, and subject to all.[17]

---

17. Cf. the lines near the opening of *The Freedom of a Christian*: "A Christian is a perfectly free lord of all, subject to none. / A Christian is a perfectly dutiful servant of all, subject to all." *LW* 31:344; *WA* 7:49.

5

Exocentric Ministry and Worship: A Response to Brian Brewer and Matthew Boulton

Derek R. Nelson

Quite by accident, Professors Brewer's and Boulton's essays take as a presupposition the same, familiar theme of Luther's theology—namely, the sinful human tendency toward selfishness and self-centeredness. Yet each begins from a very different point of departure and takes this key insight in a surprising, provocative direction. Each also uses it to address a quite different problem in contemporary Christianity and Christian theology. Brewer's deft history tells the migration of Luther's concept of the common priesthood from one of accountability one-to-another to a kind of self-centered, atomistic view where the Christian says to himself, "No priest is going to tell *me* what to believe." And Boulton's essay shows how quickly a well-intentioned worship of God can become a kind of dry formalism. Even worse, the gestures and orientation of our worshipping lives easily shift shapes to self-justifying and God-negating forms of life as *homo operans*, or as Alexander Schmemann aptly called it decades ago, *homo faber*.[1]

In responding to these fine essays, I want in both cases to offer something like a supplement to their analyses, and then to push their lines of thinking further, to see what kind of assistance to ecumenical life in the Christian churches today their proposals might yield. In both cases, I wish to highlight what Wolfhart Pannenberg characterized as *exocentricity*, the finding of one's true center outside of oneself.[2] For Pannenberg, as well as for contemporary theology's most insightful theorist of human nature, David Kelsey, exocentricity names that paradoxical dynamic wherein attempts at securing the integrity of the self by insulating it from others do precisely the opposite.[3] And self-discovery and self-security also paradoxically emerge in moments of self-donation and "eccentric existence," wherein the human's true identity comes from without—notably, but not only, from God.[4] One looks outward, relating to others, and thereby becomes oneself. This, it seems to me, is what ministry is all about, and therefore the central meaning of the priesthood of all believers, and also of worship, and therefore *homo laudans*.

Let us consider first the nature of the relationship of ordained to

---

1. Alexander Schmemann, *For the Life of the World: Sacraments and Orthodoxy* (Crestwood, NY: St. Vladimir's Press, 1973), 15. Schmemann, to be sure, is not alone in using this designation.

2. *Anthropology in Theological Perspective*, trans. M. J. O'Connell (London: Bloomsbury/T&T Clark, 1999), 37-83.

3. David H. Kelsey, *Eccentric Existence: A Theological Anthropology* (Louisville: Westminster John Knox, 2009).

4. See Kelsey, *Eccentric Existence*, Chapter 22.

lay ministry. What do the two have in common, and what is the difference—and the basis for the difference—between them? This is a pressing question for Lutherans, and not just Lutherans. In a synod (diocese) of the Evangelical Lutheran Church in America (ELCA) where I once served, nearly one third of the congregations were unable for a variety of reasons (including economic and geographic ones) to be served by ordained pastors. So congregations had to make do. Bi-vocational ministry was normal, and the bishop and lay leadership exercised great creativity in responding to the crisis. Talented and willing laypersons preached week after week to their congregations. Many laypersons received training in worship leadership. It is natural to ask the question: were those people pastors? Especially when one considers their serving in this way for ten, or in some cases, twenty years. The line between ordained and lay, never especially clear in my mind, grew blurry. Thinking about it in terms of lines drawn is probably not especially helpful, anyway.

When the ELCA was formed in 1988 one of the major doctrinal disputes was about this very issue. One of its predecessor bodies insisted on congregationalism and a definition of ministry wide enough to include parochial elementary school teachers. Another, largely influenced by immigrants from the Church of Sweden (which retained apostolic succession through the Reformation and beyond), had been moving for decades toward an apostolic vision of the office of bishop. The decision during the merger process was, basically, not to decide.[5] And the ELCA has still not made a decisive determination on this issue. Because the issue is still very much on the table, then, Lutherans ought to be especially attentive to what new voices, such

---

5. For one version of the story, see Edgar Trexler, *Anatomy of a Merger* (Minneapolis: Augsburg Fortress Press, 1991). A perceptive, even if withering, critique can be found in Carl E. Braaten, "The Special Ministry of the Ordained," in *Marks of the Body of Christ* ed. Carl E. Braaten and Robert W. Jenson (Grand Rapids, MI: Eerdmans, 1999), 123-36.

as Brian Brewer's, celebrate as the signal contribution of Luther's understanding of the common priesthood.

At this point it is necessary to repeat an often-observed point that might seem pedantic, but I hope will not be. Some people are surprised to hear that the phrase "priesthood of all believers" never appears in Luther's writings, either in German or Latin (*das allgemeine Priestertum aller Gläubigen* or *sacerdotium commune fidelium*).[6] Perhaps its first appearance in print is the 1675 manifesto of Pietism, the *Pia Desideria* of Philipp Jakob Spener. Some have thought that Spener used his idiosyncratic rendering of the concept, but not the term itself, in his preface to the sermons of the proto-Pietist Johann Arndt.[7] His idea, which is actually quite unlike Luther's, is that the "spiritual priesthood" refers to the laity, who ought to take charge of their spiritual lives.

The absence of the term is not in itself necessarily problematic for me. After all, the word "Trinity" is not present in the Bible, yet the concept appears throughout. But that does mean that later generations, such as Spener and Arndt, will have an easier time superimposing their concerns and contexts over Luther's writings, because the term and its meaning are not spelled out in a way that resists eisegesis. This is precisely what we see when Spener calls the common priesthood the laity. In contrast, Luther's intention in his influential writings is very different—he wants to deal with an *emergency* in the church. He is not trying to come up with a theory

---

6. This is how *Lumen Gentium* 10.2 refers to what it supposes is the Lutheran position. See also Wolfhart Pannenberg, *Systematic Theology*, trans. Geoffrey Bromiley (Grand Rapids, MI: Eerdmans, 1997), 3:124-8.

7. See Timothy J. Wengert, *Priesthood, Pastors and Bishops: Public Ministry for the Reformation and Today* (Minneapolis: Fortress Press, 2008), 1-2. I am also grateful to Professor Wengert for developing a similar line of thought to mine in his lecture, "Servants of the Crucified: The Office of Bishop in the Lutheran Confessions," Berkeley, California, October 19, 2005.

of the laity, but rather finds himself in need of a plan for ministry, at least for a while.

Brewer's essay deals relatively little with the usual suspect for a discussion of the common priesthood, which is the 1520 *Address to the Christian Nobility*. There Luther discusses 2 Peter 2 and Revelation 5 about as extensively as he does anywhere else. But the issue at stake is not the relationship of laypersons to ordained clergy. Rather, Luther is trying to demolish the late medieval notion, prevalent especially in the beleaguered territories of the Holy Roman Empire, of "*Stand.*" This German word is not easily rendered into English. "Estate" would be close, but few understand what that means today. The newer translation of the *Book of Concord* renders it "walk of life," which sounds a bit clunky, perhaps, but comes close to the meaning. Everyone in German-speaking lands assumed that there were two *Stände* in the church itself: the secular and the spiritual (including priests, bishops and monastics). The point Luther is trying thereby to make is to affirm the baptismal calling of certain officeholders, especially the nobility and princes, by saying there is in reality only one *Stand*, the Christian one.

Ordinarily, bishops exercise the duties of ordaining, priests exercise the duties of sacraments and preaching, sextons take care of the grounds of the church, and so on. But emergencies render these offices moot. If there were to be a fire in town, then someone needs to sound the alarm, find some pails and get to work. It would be foolish to the point of ridicule to say, "Boy, I wish the mayor had delegated responsibility for firefighting to me. That would be really convenient, as this fire is right in front of me." No—it does not matter what office you normally hold; by virtue of your citizenship in that town, or simply by virtue of being a sensible human being, you respond to the fire. By analogy the same thing is true in an ecclesial emergency: if the gospel is at stake, the priesthood common to all by virtue of their baptism justifies, even mandates, taking action.

I think that issue is still in the background for Luther's 1523 treatise, *On the Institution of the Ministries of the Church* (*De instituendis ministris Ecclesiae*), which Brewer's essay engages in a significant way.[8] The occasion for that writing, incidentally, was a request from a man named Gallus Cahera. Cahera was a pastor in the Hussite Utraquist church in Bohemia. Their church was in crisis because it was sending its ordinands to Rome to pledge loyalty to the pope in order to receive ordination, after which they came home and renounced the papacy and gave communion in both kinds at their first mass. The situation sounds like a man who goes off to his job delivering Coca-Cola, and comes home and cracks open a Pepsi.

That particular writing of Luther's does not, in my judgment, endorse anything like a priesthood of all believers that would justify viewing an ordained minister as a functionary, or one "option" among many for organizing the ministry of the church. Cahera told Luther that the situation in Bohemia was dire (he also misled Luther about how ready they were to accept the Reformation), and Luther responded accordingly. The key to his argument is that there is one priesthood, common to all who have been baptized. So if you happen to be on the battlefield and your friend is dying and he wants to be baptized, you do it—you do not wait for the chaplain. If you move to a town where the gospel is not being preached, you teach your family the best you can from the Bible and catechism and whatever other means you have. These are emergency measures, but they are nonetheless valid.

In light of these considerations, we have to raise the question of whether Luther even has a meaningful notion of "the priesthood

---

8. *Concerning the Ministry, LW* 40:iii–44; *WA* 12:169–95.

of all believers" that would speak to a church centuries after the Reformation, with enough stability to obviate "emergency" measures. In response to Brewer's argument that there is such a notion, I want to make two short affirmations and raise two questions. First, I think the way Brewer has cast the need for mutuality among Christians is done very beautifully. It is clear to me that Brewer has his finger on the pulse of Luther's insight that ministry happens not when an office is filled, but when a need is met. One of the Lutheran confessional writings, the *Smalcald Articles*, describes the church as the place where "mutual conversation and consolation" of the brothers and sisters takes place. As a pastor I was amazed at how open my (Protestant) parishioners were to practicing confession and forgiveness not just with me, but with each other. It is a powerful thing, one the Protestant churches ought to do more of. Brewer is to be thanked for describing that dynamic so well.

Secondly, I think the analysis followed in Brewer's essay could extend even further to tie the common priesthood to Luther's theology of *vocation*. It is not just our participation in Christ's priesthood by faith in the Gospel, but also the Christian freedom to follow the Law in a concrete way that would cause us to share in this mutuality that Brewer articulates. I happen to be a partisan of Gustaf Wingren's notion that vocation is primarily about the personal and personalized response to the law, for Luther, even though that view seems out of favor at present. I think Luther had a Torah-like view of the law, one which understood the generativity for positive human relationships that just, law-ordained social structures could have. As Brewer points out, Luther thought that "If you are a manual laborer, you find that the Bible has been put into your workshop, into your hand, into your heart. It teaches and preaches how you should treat your neighbor. . . . Indeed, there is no shortage of preaching. You have as many preachers as you have transactions, goods, tools, and other equipment in your house and home."[9] The common priesthood is not just for "churchy" things like confession of sins, but for Christians trying to understand their quotidian, everyday lives as occasions of the sacred.

The first question I pose for Brewer's essay would be this: if, as I have been arguing, the main reason for the development of Luther's understanding of the public office of ministry is the increasing *stability* of the Reformation in Saxony, Scandinavia and elsewhere, and not a panicked turning away caused by the Peasants' War, would that make a difference to a Baptist understanding of ministry? In other words, would a Baptist appropriation of Luther's view of the common priesthood have to be different if it accepted that Luther was developing it in the crucible of a crisis in the catholic church, rather than assuming it was a once-for-all teaching that the priesthood of all the believers necessarily implied a functional view of ordained ministry?

The second question for Brewer's essay deals with the matter of whether the common priesthood necessarily invites the problems of private interpretation. Brewer points out ways that a retrieval of Luther's thought on the matter of the common priesthood could minimize the dangers associated with people feeling free to make the Bible mean whatever it is most convenient for them to have it mean. But a number of recent authors say that very thing is absolutely inevitable in Protestantism. Brad Gregory, for example, claims just such a *Wirkungsgeschichte* in his book *The Unintended Reformation*,[10] as do any number of John Milbank's books.[11] And there are views, rarely

---

9. *LW* 21:237; *WA* 32:495, 19-21, 36-38.

10. Brad Gregory, *The Unintended Reformation: How a Religious Revolution Secularized Society* (Cambridge, MA: Harvard University Press, 2012).

11. In *Theology and Social Theory: Beyond Secular Reason* (Oxford: Blackwell, 1990), 94-100, Milbank develops his understanding of the devolution of religion from authority to individualism as "the liberal Protestant metanarrative."

spoken in polite ecumenical conversation, like those of the Roman Catholic theologian Massimo Salani, who recently traced the current woes of fast food—as individualized eating, or "McEucharist"—all the way back to Protestantism's mistaken priesthood of all believers.[12] Clearly one of the benefits of the Roman Catholic view of the teaching authority of the ordained ministry is that private interpretations are forbidden in theory and minimized in practice. One wonders whether similar results would be seen if Protestant churches understood the common priesthood as Brewer hopes they will: not as invitations to individualism, but as mutually-conditioning correctives among *all* the faithful. Christians are to be reminded that the integrity of their ministry comes from authentically serving *other people*; their personal integrity and justification come *extra nos*, too.

Of course, the main site of encounter with the justifying God comes in the proclamation of the Word and reception of sacraments, and therefore exocentricity is fashioned and reinforced in worship. Boulton's essay takes our understanding of Luther's account of human nature, sinful and redeemed, in intriguing new directions by arranging his analysis under the rubric of worship. Reading Luther as a kind of forerunner to Calvin on human nature (the latter wrote that "man's nature, so to speak, is a perpetual factory of idols"[13]), Boulton appreciates how quickly worship of the Triune God, as Luther understood it, degrades itself into base idolatry. The idolatry is all the worse for the fact that as sin, its object, *appears* to be holy and righteous. It is actually a *chapel* that the devil builds next to God's church.

Everyone knows that Luther spoke frequently and forcefully about

---

12. See Bruce Johnston, " 'Protestant' McDonald's Attacked by Theologian," *Telegraph*, November 10, 2000.
13. John Calvin, *Institutes of the Christian Religion*, trans. and ed. L. F. Battles and J. T. McNeill (Louisville: Westminster John Knox, 2006), I:108 [I.xi.8].

sin. But it often is missed how fundamentally Luther's hamartiology differs from the ones he inherited. And Boulton is right to point this out. When teaching undergraduates about this idea, I use the image of a menu. The theology in which Luther was trained had vice on one side of the menu, virtue on the other. The point was to have one's desires and will shaped in such a way that one would choose the low-fat, virtuous options. Luther conceives of sin differently. Our virtues are as sinful as our vices, one Luther interpreter put it.[14] Everything on the menu is made with some trans-fat, too much sugar, or by the hands of underpaid workers in factories far away. Sin is more a dimension of all actions than it is the object of some acts and not others. But if we do not act, if we do not order something from the menu, we will surely starve. So order boldly.[15]

Linking worship to sin reminds us of the—obvious but often forgotten—point that sin is against God. It is not simply mistreating other people, or abusing creation, or disobeying rules. It might be those things, too, but it not therefore sinful. Sin is sin because it offends God, whose beloved those creations are.

It seems to me the crux of Boulton's argument comes in his conception of a worship service as a parable for life. As he puts it, "the rhythms and choreographies of liturgy are meant to be epitomes or types for the proper rhythms and choreographies of life."[16] That is exactly right. And it is in this direction that I think Boulton's analysis can be most helpfully extended. The possibilities for liturgy shaping life have been long undersold in Christianity. One thinks, for instance, of Marva Dawn's work in arguing for worship as a "subversive act."[17] There are precious few contexts in contemporary

---

14. Gerhard Forde, "Christian Life," in *Christian Dogmatics*, ed. Carl E. Braaten and Robert W. Jenson (Minneapolis: Fortress Press, 1984), II:449.
15. I develop this line of thinking in "Justification, Self-Justification and Forgiveness: Ted Peters on Sin and Its Overcoming," in a forthcoming *Festschrift* for Ted Peters.
16. Boulton, "Angels of Light," 89.

life where one's age, race, socio-economic status, IQ or beauty matter less than at the communion table. Worship is therefore profoundly *political*, because it interrupts and relativizes the many hierarchies and exclusionary arrangements upon which our political life seem to depend.[18]

Extending Boulton's analysis along these lines risks something, however. There is a threat latent in emphases of the political and ethical "payoffs" of worship. To put the risk as pointedly as possible: Is ethical action a *telos* of worship or a salutary byproduct? The danger seems to me an instrumentalization of worship, such that church becomes reduced to a kind of fueling station on the pilgrim road. Praising God is an end in itself. Of course Boulton sees this, and development of the distinction between *homo laudans* and *homo operans* would surely help to resist a co-opting of worship for purely political ends. But the threat is a real one, it seems to me, lest the church become merely yet another social agent in the world.

I note in passing that Reformed admirers of Alexander Schmemann seem frequently to overstate the case here. Nicholas Wolterstorff, for example, praises the ethical and justice-yielding payoff of Schmemann's understanding of the world as sacrament. He writes, "Work and worship are fundamentally connected. Both are expressions of gratitude; together they constitute the two phases of the manifestation of devotion."[19] To take just one more example, Presbyterian theologian John Burgess reads Schmemann as a kind of Orthodox version of Karl Barth, helping Christianity resist the temptation to mere formalism and "religion" by driving worshipers

---

17. Marva Dawn, *Reaching out without Dumbing Down* (Grand Rapids, MI: Eerdmans, 1995), 57-73.
18. Samuel Torvend's book *Luther and the Hungry Poor: Gathered Fragments* (Minneapolis: Fortress Press, 2008) nicely illustrates the connection between worship and ethics for Luther. Leaving the communion table frequently meant actually going to those who hunger for bread and taking it to them.
19. Nicholas Wolterstorff, *Until Justice and Peace Embrace* (Grand Rapids, MI: Eerdmans, 1983), 151. Chapter VII is called, "Justice and Worship: The Tragedy of Liturgy in Protestantism."

into the world to change it.[20] Theologies construed under a "Christ transforming culture" ideal type perhaps inevitably tend in this direction.

One final caution for the insistence on human exocentricity, the worship-shaped human being as radically *excurvatus ad alios*, a predictable one, perhaps: feminist and womanist theologians have helped Christians everywhere criticize the asymmetrical demands that an outwardly-directed anthropology can place on women, especially those whose selfhood is already diminished by outrageous demands placed upon them.[21] I do not think Boulton's suggestions in his essay are vulnerable to this kind of critique, because his understanding of the church is that it does, in fact, fund its mandate that its members turn toward others. That is, the one whose attention and adoration are turned to the Triune God have their selves filled by such love and, to put it oddly, *being*, that there is enough selfhood in the bank to share with others. And in Boulton's understanding, the kind of other-directedness he seeks paradoxically repays the giver even as their gift of service is rendered. Others less careful than Boulton, however, run the risk that comes with walking the razor's edge at the frontier of manipulation: all too quickly an invitation to exocentricity can become a demand unfairly shared.

---

20. John P. Burgess, *Encounters with Orthodoxy: How Protestant Churches Can Reform Themselves Again* (Louisville: Westminster John Knox, 2013), 187.
21. For a recent analysis, from a Lutheran perspective, see Mary Gaebler, *The Courage of Faith: Martin Luther and the Theonomous Self* (Minneapolis: Fortress Press, 2013).

6

———

Martin Luther's *Deus Theologicus*

David Tracy

Introduction

With riveting intensity and characteristic honesty, Martin Luther insisted that every aspect of theology is a desperate attempt, always inadequate, always necessary, to understand some aspect of the Unfathomable Mystery of God. Luther always held that theology is an analysis of relationship between the Justifying God and the human sinner—above all the relationship of the sinner now justified by faith alone through the grace of the gospel promise: that divine promise which imputes Christ's righteousness as forgiveness to any sinner justified by grace through faith alone. The sinner thus becomes *simul iustus et peccator*: not *partim/partim* but *totus/totus*.

The central Christic understanding of the justifying God who is

Love is Luther's foundational insight into God's reality as narrated and proclaimed in the New Testament itself, most clearly in the first letter of John: God is love. For Luther, the understanding of the divine fullness revealed in Jesus Christ includes three principal dimensions. First, the fundamental insight into *Deus theologicus* for Luther was a glimpse of the reality of God as both revealed and hidden: revealed *sub contrario*, i.e., in negativity, suffering, abjection, abandonment in the cross of Jesus Christ which paradoxically manifests God's loving promise of forgiveness. Christ's active righteousness is imputed as alien righteousness to us, Christ's righteousness experienced as our passive righteousness in faith alone. Hence, Section I analyzes Luther's first and central understanding of God's self-revelation in the cross of Jesus Christ as the revealed and hidden God of the gospel.

At the same time, there is a second dimension to Luther's *Deus theologicus* and, therefore, another distinct section (Section II) in this article. Martin Luther, in an uncanny existentially fraught theological move, articulated a frightening experience of the utter majesty of God (*Deus nudus*) to *homo nudus* exposed by means of *Anfechtungen* (physical, psychological, spiritual and satanic assaults upon the individual). These assaults occur both before and even, at times, after justification. At sinister moments the Christian experiences the radical hiddenness of God beyond even the word of forgiveness. In revelation, this experience of the inscrutable will of God is exposed and declared in the doctrine of double predestination.

Luther holds that the fact of predestination is revealed in scripture (e.g., in the unnerving story of Jacob and Esau) but the why of predestination (indeed, as we shall see below, double predestination) is not revealed. The why of predestination is forever hidden in the inscrutable will of God whose awesome majesty should be worshipped but not futilely speculated upon by a reason hopelessly beyond its limits. All the Christian can do in experiencing this second terrifying form of divine hiddenness is to flee back to the cross of Jesus Christ where God's revelation of Godself as Love heals.

A third dimension (Section III) of God's reality, so the new Finnish School of Luther research maintains, had emerged in Luther's infrequent but pronounced appeals to justification as *theosis*—a category of divine union which is beyond the "marvelous exchange" of forensic righteousness and beyond even most understandings of Luther's life-long appeals to "*unio Christi.*" The third dimension is further clarified by another non-Finnish contribution to Luther research: the recent scholarship on Luther' semantic, logical and semiotic clarifications of such categories as relation, person, eternity in the traditional Trinitarian understanding of God's nature. In his last dialogical, non-polemical *disputationes* (formulated for the examinations of his doctoral students at Wittenberg), Luther analyzed with philosophical and theological finesse some central traditional Trinitarian concepts for understanding God. Each of the major sections of this article, therefore, will analyze one of the three major dimensions of Martin Luther's complex *Deus theologicus.*

How these three major dimensions of Luther's theological understanding of God may correlate, one with another, is a task which this essay does not address explicitly save for some brief christological suggestions near the end. My major aim in this article is simply to demonstrate three dimensions of Luther's *Deus theologicus.* An attempt to show a complex theological unity of these three dimensions is for another time. This is also true for any critical assessment of Luther's rejection of a fully philosophical (i.e., metaphysical and/or contemplative, not only semantic and logical) approach to God's reality.[1] In sum, before any constructive critique of

---

1. On Luther on reason, see B. A. Gerrish, *Grace and Reason: A Study in the Theology of Martin Luther* (Oxford: Clarendon, 1962); Jennifer Hockenberry Dragseth ed., *The Devil's Whore:*

Luther's theology of God can be launched, it is first necessary to offer an interpretation of the three basic dimensions of Luther's complex *Deus theologicus*. Hence this essay.

I. God Hidden in Revelation: Luther's Theology of the Cross

Truth about the true God is not a human work or achievement. True knowledge of God comes only through faith which is a divine, not a human work. Grace though faith alone[2] is both God's *favor* through the righteousness of Christ imputed to us as forgiveness and *donum* (pure gift, i.e., passive incipient righteousness, which, through the Holy Spirit, can increase until the ultimate *donum* of our graced glory after this life). The righteousness we receive is Christ's own active righteousness that endows upon us passive righteousness. We are reckoned righteous through Christ; his righteousness is now imputed to us. We are now totally justified since God's imputation covers over the many sins remaining. We are, therefore, *simul iustus et peccator*, totally just and totally sinful. Through faith we have become an entirely new creature formed not by any personal work or achievement, even works of love, but formed solely by Christ's grace through faith. The logic of justification is clear: *sola fides* made possible through *sola gratia*, made possible through *solus Christus*. Faith alone is the form of our passive righteousness not, as for most of Luther's medieval predecessors, faith formed by our deeds of love (*fides caritate formata*). Jesus Christ alone is the form of our faith which then entails a faith active in the works of love. Works of love are the result, not the presupposition of faith.

Reason and Philosophy in the Lutheran Tradition (Minneapolis: Fortress Press, 2011), esp. the essays by Oswald Bayer (13-22); Denis R. Janz (47-52); Paul R. Hinlicky (53-60); and Dennis Bielfeldt (61-68).

2. This most important of Luther's theological insights is expressed everywhere in his work, most eloquently and fully, perhaps, in his magisterial *Lectures on Galatians* (1535); *LW* 26—27; *WA* 40I and 40II, 1-184.

Before the grace of faith, we were trapped in self-bondage. We struggle ever more desperately to escape from ourselves, but our deeply damaged selves are curved in upon themselves (*incurvatus in se*) with no exit. Faith grants God's unconditioned forgiveness. Faith exposes the failures of all works-righteousness: in all law, all ritual ceremonies, all penitential acts, all indulgences, and above all, all those products of speculative reason which presume to describe the divine reality. The most basic framework for Luther's understanding of justification by faith alone is the dialectic of law and gospel: the dialectical conflict of these mutually implying opposites lays bare the radicality of the conflict between works-righteousness and faith. The most basic role of law is to make us face our sinfulness, i.e., our inability to keep the law, much less to find forgiveness through it. In contrast, the divine promise of gospel, grasped through Christ's grace by faith, is forgiveness.[3]

Luther's notion of dialectic, unlike Plato's or Aristotle's and far more like Heraclitus's and Hegel's, is structured as a conflict of opposites that not only clash but imply and need each other. The gospel rejects all works-righteousness—and yet at the same time implies the need of the work of law to force the sinner to face his/her sinfulness. On the other side of faith, moreover, the law returns in a valuable new function to order our political and ecclesial lives.

As Jaroslav Pelikan once observed, Western theology is a series of footnotes to Augustine: Catholic theologies, with their analogical language, are heirs to Augustine's nature-grace dialectic especially in Augustine's early and middle works, but even in such relatively late texts as *De Trinitate* and *The City of God*. It is important to understand

---

3. *Promise* (of forgiveness) is persuasively considered the central category in Luther's theology in Oswald Bayer, *Martin Luther's Theology: A Contemporary Interpretation*, trans. T. H. Trapp (Grand Rapids: Eerdmans, 2008), esp. 50–58, and in Bayer's companion work, *Theology: the Lutheran Way*, trans. and ed. J. G. Silcock and M. C. Mattes (Grand Rapids, MI: Eerdmans, 2007), esp. 125–39.

that an analogical imagination is not a non-dialectical method, as it is sometimes interpreted (e.g., by Karl Barth who bizarrely named it an invention of the "Anti-Christ"!). True theological analogy always includes negative dialectical moments. As the Fourth Lateran Council (1215) made clear, negative moments are intrinsic to all properly analogical language in theology: for every positive statement of similarity an even greater negative statement of dissimilarity must be articulated in order to assure the proper use of analogical language in theology.[4]

Luther's fundamental understanding of *Deus theologicus*—from 1514 to 1546—is the God revealed by grace through faith in Jesus Christ. The Gracious, Infinitely Loving God of Jesus Christ is both manifested and hidden in the revelation of the cross of Jesus Christ. Once the favor and gift of true faith happens, authentic *sub contrario* saving knowledge of God as Gracious simultaneously occurs. For Luther, any philosophical notions of God (natural knowledge of God) are now shattered by the revelation of the saving God revealed in the cross. Reason's presuppositions are now reason's self-exposure as deeply damaged. The bondage of the intellect, Susan Schreiner argues,[5] is even deeper for Luther than the bondage of the will. For Luther, the Fall's damage to reason is far deeper than that imagined in Thomas Aquinas's notion of the Fall's resulting in a *"vulnus ignorantiae."* Reason's wound for Luther, like the wound of Amfortas in *Parsifal*, is an open wound healed only from without.

Nor is it the case, as Luther's later debates with John Agricola and the Antinomians clarified, that once faith takes over through a

---

4. For an analysis of the importance of negative dissimilarities in theological analogy, see the classical twentieth century work, Erich Przywara, *Analogia Entis: Metaphysics, Original Structure and Universal Rhythm*, trans. J. R. Betz and D. B. Hart (Grand Rapids: Eerdmans, 2014). See esp. on the Fourth Lateran Council, 349-72 and 506-31.

5. Susan E. Schreiner, *Are You Alone Wise? The Search for Certainty in the Early Modern Era* (Oxford: Oxford University Press, 2011), 324-32.

believer's faith as fundamentally trust (*fiducia*), indeed heartful trust (*fides cordis*), we no longer need the law in either state or church. On the contrary, Luther, in *Against the Antinomians*,[6] held that the earthly kingdom and the heavenly kingdom alike need laws for ordering life rightly. So much was this the case that the "early Luther" could even allow for the possibility that the institution of the church could, for purposes of order, continue with an external head—the pope—as long as the papacy was understood to be of a human, not a divine institution (law not gospel) and as long as the pope preached the gospel.

Martin Luther's fundamental *Deus theologicus* is God's Hiddenness in revelation affirmed by the gift of faith in Christ's cross. Luther's *sola gratia* and *sola fides* are both grounded in *solus Christus*. Without faith in Jesus Christ as the God-man incarnate, the death of Jesus on the cross is yet another tragic murder of an innocent human being—tragic like the crucifixion of Spartacus and countless others in the ancient world.

As early as his first *Commentary on the Psalms* (1515-16), and decisively in the *Heidelberg Disputation* of 1518 (especially Thesis 20),[7] which was contemporary with his second *Commentary on the Psalms* (1518-19), Luther's theology of salvation by faith alone was a theology of the cross. Through the scandal and stumbling block of the theology of the cross, Luther theologically explained that the *Deus theologicus* revealed to faith is paradoxically revealed *sub contrario* in Christ's cross. The God who is Love is the Crucified God. God is revealed in the cross as hidden in folly, godforsakenness: God is hidden both in the disgusting physical sufferings of Jesus, as well as in the devastating spiritual *Anfechtungen* undergone by Jesus in

6. *LW* 47:107-19; *WA* 50:468-77.
7. *LW* 31:52-53; *WA* 1:362.

his desperate prayer for release at Gethsemane, in his humiliating public trial, his abandonment by his friends, his brutal scourging, the mocking of onlookers, his cruel death—a death by crucifixion, a death reserved for the worst criminals. Luther sharply highlights the gospel accent that the crucified Jesus on the cross is abandoned, godforsaken—"My God, my God, why have you abandoned me?"—in both Mark and Matthew. In one of Luther's most profound theological moves, he states that Jesus Christ has taken on our sin and has become sin himself. Christ has taken on our cursed status to become the accursed one himself. Our godforsakenness has become Christ's own on the cross as he cries out into the thundering silence of his Father. Faith as divine favor happens through the cross of Jesus Christ, the crucified Jesus the Christ, i.e., the unique one who alone is both true God and true human. The revelation by faith in the promises of God's mercy enacted in the cross is the revelation of a true knowledge of the true God: God is Godself the Infinitely Loving, forgiving, gracious God, the Hidden Crucified God revealed in the cross of Jesus the Christ. That philosophically and commonsensically unthinkable thought about the crucified God is the true scandal of Christianity.

It is difficult to imagine a more *sub contrario* (in fact, *sub contradictario*) way to describe Luther's *Deus theologicus* than to speak of the Hidden, Crucified God revealed to faith in the cross of Jesus Christ. Here we do not find the Incomprehensible Infinite God of the classical Greek contemplative theologians, such as Gregory of Nyssa.[8] In fact, Luther's theology of the cross is even beyond the medieval Franciscan emphasis on the humanity of the suffering Jesus. Luther did, in fact, have predecessors for several elements in his theology

8. I have analyzed this concept of Infinity in Gregory of Nyssa in, "God as Infinite: Ethical Implications," forthcoming in *God: Theological Accounts and Ethical Possibilities*, ed. Myriam Renaud and Joshua Daniel.

of the cross: above all, of course, Paul's insistence on Jesus Christ and Him crucified; second, Augustine who did also speak of "the Crucified God," although neither as frequently nor as foundationally as Luther did. Further influences on Luther's theology of the cross include the German mystical text *Theologica Germanica*, which the early Luther translated and the older Luther always honored, as well as Johannes Tauler.[9] In sum, in articulating the God revealed *sub contrario* on the cross, Luther did find some predecessors to lead him in that direction (above all else, of course, Paul in Romans and Galatians). But no Christian theologian since Paul himself has possessed the spiritual and the theological as well as the rhetorical, indeed poetic power of Martin Luther to help all Christians, whatever their other theological and spiritual insights, to view God's Infinitely Loving nature as revealed counter-intuitively in the cross, to understand that God is not only Incomprehensible but also Hidden (*absconditus*). For Martin Luther, as later for Blaise Pascal, a treasured biblical text was Isaiah 45:15: "God is truly a Hidden God" ['How canst thou be a God that hidest thyself...?" (Oxford New English Bible)]. The Hidden and Revealed God is Martin Luther's singular contribution to all Christian theological understanding of God. Other theologians have more refined Trinitarian theologies, deeper philosophical theologies, more profound mystical theologies, but no other theologian—not even the more orderly and lucid John Calvin nor the more deeply mystical John of the Cross in his brilliant analysis of "the dark night of the soul"—have the theological power of Luther's theology of the cross revealing *sub contrario* the God who

---

9. On Luther's relationship to the German mystical traditions, see the judicious comment of Bernard McGinn, in his magisterial history of Western Christian mysticism, that to understand Luther one must also interpret mystical elements in his theology without necessarily naming him a mystic. See also *The Theologica Germanica of Martin Luther*, trans., introd., and commentary by B. Hoffman (New York: Paulist, 1980).

reveals Godself not by means of speculative or mystical wisdom but by means of the weakness and folly, the scandal of the cross.

Folly not wisdom: against the humanist and philosophical expectation of his contemporaries, for Luther true knowledge of God is not to be found in speculative wisdom nor in humanist rhetorical theologies. Centuries later Hegel, who claimed to be an orthodox Lutheran, used his own triumphal, unstoppable dialectical method to turn Luther's Hidden God into Hegel's own utterly manifest Absolute God. What Hegel turned into an abstract speculative once-and-for-all Good Friday was, for Luther, the all too concrete Good Friday of the crucified Jesus scandalously revealing the Hidden Crucified God. Most first-century Greek philosophers were already shocked by the outrageous Christian claim that God in Godself became incarnate—much less incarnate in the person of an insignificant Jewish provincial who died the disgraceful death of a criminal. That such a repellant death by crucifixion of an unknown Jewish colonial should be the revelation of God was too absurd to be considered as a serious option for knowledge of God. In Acts, the Athenians listened to Paul on the Unknown God for a while until they politely and somewhat contemptuously turned away. Celsus did the same against Origen; Porphyry considered the very thought of a crucified God an intellectual, moral, and religious insult. Centuries later Friedrich Nietzsche intensified and ironized the charges of the two Platonists (Celsus and Porphyry) by famously describing Christianity as "Platonism for the masses"!

God's naked majesty (*Deus nudus*) informed philosophy at its speculative and dialectical best (Plato, Aristotle, Plotinus, Celsus, Proclus): the thought (almost blasphemous for Porphyry) that the Glory of God—the Plotinian One and the Good—was to be found in the cross of Jesus was as outrageous to the Greek philosophers as it is today to their many now far more secular modern successors. What artist or philosopher would dare this unnerving radical thought: the true God is the Crucified God of Infinite Love; the true knowledge of this God is only to be found revealed as hidden, *sub contrario*, in the cross of Jesus Christ?

Almost any philosophically-inflected theology cannot but find Luther's theology of God hidden *sub contrario* in the cross of Jesus Christ exactly what Paul stated it would be: a scandal, a stumbling block, a foolishness, a weakness of mind and spirit, at the limit an insult to mind and imagination alike. It is not surprising, therefore, that although Christians of course always proclaimed and depicted the cross in images, for the first four centuries the image of the cross was not the shocking central symbol of Christianity as it became and remains, as much as the star of David is for Judaism, or the seated serene Buddha is for Buddhism. In fact, in the hundreds of underground miles of early Christian tombs in the Roman catacombs, one finds far more images of the Good Shepherd or fish (*ichthus*) as symbols of Christianity than an image of the cross, much less a crucifix. The cross—however familiar the image has become—is a scandal.

More than any theologian before or since, Martin Luther is *the* theologian of the cross.[10] For Luther, the Gracious forgiving, Infinitely Loving God—the true nature of the Christian God for all Christans is revealed at its deepest in the hiddenness—the folly, scandal, stumbling block of the cross. Any interpreter who, attending only to other authentie but relatively marginal aspects of Luther's

---

10. See Walther von Loewenich, *Luther's Theology of the Cross*, trans. H. Bowman (Minneapolis: Augsburg, 1976); Alister E. McGrath, *Luther's Theology of the Cross: Martin Luther's Breakthrough* (Oxford: Basil Blackwell, 1985); Gerhard O. Forde, *On Being a Theologian of the Cross: Reflections on Luther's Heidelberg Disputation, 1518* (Grand Rapids: Eerdmans, 1997); Vitor Westhalle, *The Scandalous God: The Use and Abuse of the Cross* (Minneapolis: Fortress Press, 2006)—a particularly valuable book on modern theology's temptations to evade the scandal of the cross.

understanding of God (e.g., through *theosis*) is in danger of missing Luther's most singular contribution to a Christian theology of God: God's deepest self-revelation is the deeply unsettling uncannily disorienting Hiddenness of the Crucified Gracious God, hidden as Infinite Love in the cross of Jesus Christ. As we shall see below there are, to be sure, other important elements in Luther's *Deus theologicus*. But without the God Hidden in the revelation of the cross of Jesus Christ as the central focus for any further insights into God's Reality for Luther, one is in danger of turning Luther's theology of the cross into yet another theology of Glory. Luther cannot be read otherwise anymore than Dostoevsky can be read as Jane Austen.

II. The Hidden God beyond Revelation

Luther never abandoned his primordial insight into the God Hidden in revelation.[11] However, in his later theology after 1525, Luther moved into yet deeper theological waters with strange, disturbing insights into another dimension of the *Deus theologicus*. Especially but almost only in his classic text *De servo arbitrio* (1525), Luther contended, beyond the already sharp paradoxes of God's self revelation *sub contrario* in the hiddenness of the cross, that there exists another frightening revelation of God's Hiddenness beyond, before, and behind the revelation of the Hidden, Crucified God of Jesus Christ. This form of divine Hiddenness was theologically caused by Luther's closer attention to the implications for divine Hiddenness in the sometime Augustinian and Pauline doctrine of

---

11. See B. A. Gerrish, "To the Unknown God': Luther and Calvin on the Hiddenness of God," *The Old Protestantism and the New: Essays on the Reformation Heritage* (Chicago: University of Chicago Press, 1982), 131–50; John Dillenberger, *God Hidden and Revealed: The Interpretation of Luther's Deus Absconditus and its Significance for Religious Thought* (Philadelphia: Muhlenberg, 1953); Hellmut Bandt, *Luthers Lehre vom verborgenen Gott: Eine Untersuchung zu dem Offenbarungsgeschichtlichen Ansatz Seiner Theologie*, Theologische Arbeiten Band VIII (Berlin: Evangelische Verlagsanstalt, 1958); Susan E. Schreiner, *Are You Alone Wise?* 293-96 (on satanic hiddenness *sub contrario* as an "angel of light").

double predestination, "the horrible decree" as Calvin rightly named it. This frightening insight into God's Hiddenness was a matter of biblical revelation for Luther, as well as a matter of his intense personal experience of spiritual temptations, assaults, *Anfechtungen*.[12] This second sense of divine hiddenness assaulted Luther with doubt and sometimes despair with the thought that he might not be among the elect. These *Anfechtungen* (assaults and temptations) were, for Luther, not only subjective but objectively satanic and even ultimately divine (since Satan's actions—as a creature—were finally under the final control of the Creator). And with these assaults came a new experience, *coram Deo*, that brought terror.

Anfechtung (Latin: *temptatio* or *tentatio*) is a central category for Luther. *Anfechtung* is both a subjective and objective reality. As a subjective experience *Anfechtung* is the experience of a spiritual assault on an individual producing fear, even terror in the face of the unfathomable majesty of God. *Anfechtung* is also an objective theological reality since for Luther its objective origin is a satanic

---

12. Luther's friends report his observing in a collegial double-conversation: "If I would live long enough I would like to write a book on *Anfechtung*, for without this nobody can understand the holy Scriptures or faith, or know the faith and love of God, indeed he or she cannot know what hope is" (*WATR*, nr. 4777; 4:490, 24-491, 1). A grave error of some Luther interpretation is to read Luther's *Anfechtungen* as solely a matter of Luther's uniquely sensitive and often depressed temperament as distinct from a reality more theologically objective than psychologically subjective. The subjectivist reading of Luther covers a large spectrum of interpretations from Friedrich Nietzsche's through Erik Erikson's and some Catholic interpreters, such as Heinrich Denifle and Hartmann Grisar. On Luther's life and character, the classic works on certain crucial years in Luther's life remain Heinrich Bornkamm, esp. *Luther in Mid-career, 1521-1530* (Philadelphia: Fortress Press, 1969), and Martin Brecht, *Martin Luther: His Road to Reformation, 1483-1521* (Philadelphia: Fortress Press, 1985). For the importance of Luther's belief in the *temptatio* placed in his mind and life by a fully objective Satan, read the fascinating study of Luther's life and thought by Heiko A. Oberman, *Luther: Man Between God and the Devil* (New Haven: Yale University Press, 1989). For a deliberately short and moving life of Luther which, among several salient points, fruitfully emphasizes Luther's fleshly joy in life: marriage, eating, drinking beer, singing, composing his splendid hymns, laughing, joking, enjoying sex, etc. These life-affirming dimensions of the man Luther are too easily lost by a temptation (like my own) to emphasize almost exclusively Martin Luther's profound subjective experiences of and objective understandings of *Anfechtung*. See Martin Marty, *Martin Luther: A Life* (London: Penguin, 2008).

reality (and therefore also an objectively divine reality since God controls all and therefore permits satan to tempt-assault an individual (e.g., Job). Philosophically, Rudolf Otto (a Lutheran and a proto-phenomenologist) provided a phenomenological description of the holy as a combination of both subjective and objective phenomena in *The Idea of the Holy* (1917): every authentic experience of the uncanny holy is *mysterium tremendum et fascinans*. In his *Table Talk* Luther once said that he wished, one day, to write a treatise on *Anfechtung*. Would that he had!

Theologically, Luther's concept of *Anfechtung* is likewise related to his unnerving sense that an apocalyptic battle always rages throughout history as well as in the heart of every individual. Part of Luther's attraction for many post-modern thinkers is Luther's honest and profound sense of God experienced at times as the Void through experiences of *Anfechtungen*. Luther's influence on post-modernity is more often indirect than direct (i.e., Heidegger, Sartre, Camus et al.) by means of Søren Kierkegaard's notion of Angst, the major influence in both mid-century existentialist thought and post-modern fragmentary thought. A sense of the Void, whether as pure negativity (Sartre's *nausea*; Camus's "the absurd") is also an aspect of Nietzsche's tragic yes to reality as sheer Will to Power without purpose, without beginning, and without end.

On the other hand, the Void can be, for the enlightened Buddhist, an experience of a positive ultimate reality if one can learn to stop grasping at false ultimacies and stop clinging to the ego and let go into the Void. Then the Void is experienced as ultimately trustworthy. For Buddhists, the Void is experienced as pure negation only for those grasping egotists unable to let go to the Void as embracing, enhancing ultimate emptiness. Buddhists (especially Mahayana) and Martin Luther agree on our fundamental dilemma: our inability to escape our clinging egos (Luther's description of the ego as *incurvatus in se*). Moreover, Pure Land Japanese Mahayana Buddhists, unlike Zen Buddhists, believe, with Luther, that our situation (personal-existential and social-historical) is so bleak that only Other-Power can emancipate us; Zen Self-Power will fail. Analogously, Martin Luther fiercely rejected all Pelagian, neo-Stoic and humanist claims to sufficient self-powers through moral and religious self-discipline. Luther insisted that all such claims were ultimately pathetic exercises in self-delusion: only God through the grace of Jesus Christ received as salvific in faith alone can save us.

Luther's sense of the Void is the hiddenness of God experienced *sub contrario* in the Word of the cross and even, at times, beyond the Word in the terror of hiddenness experienced in *Anfechtungen*. It is healed with joy by God's gracious forgiveness paradoxically disclosed by God's gift of faith in the justifying cross of Jesus Christ.

Luther's category of *Anfechtungen* is indeed important for understanding him. However, Oswald Bayer exaggerates when he claims that *all* Lutheran theology finds its touchstone in an experience of *Anfechtung*.[13] Clearly that is the case with Luther's theology of the hidden God revealed *sub contrario* in the paradox of the cross. It is even more the case, of course, with Luther's concept of the radical hiddenness of God, beyond the Word. Nevertheless *Anfechtung-temptatio* is not the touchstone of the theological *oratio* and *meditatio* traditions present in Luther's theology of the full *Deus theologicus*—as, for example, in the distinct *oratio-meditatio* in Luther's theology of God as Incomprehensible Love experienced by the justified one in *theosis*. For that matter, neither is *temptatio* present in Luther's late dialectical disputations in which, as we shall see below, Luther

---

13. Oswad Bayer, *Theology the Lutheran Way*, trans. J. G. Silcock and M. C. Mattes (Grand Rapids, MI: Eerdmans, 2007), 57-65.

developed semiotic and semantic concepts (relation, person, eternity, etc.) for clarifying the traditional Trinitarian understanding of God.

Perhaps *Anfechtungen* did drive Luther's earlier more polemical disputations such as his *Disputation against Scholastic Theology* (1517) or his fierce polemical disputes with Eck, Cajetan, Latomus, Karlstadt, Müntzer, Zwingli, and others. Admittedly, even in his later Wittenberg period—the period of his brilliant meditative *disputationes* on the Trinity and christology—Luther at times seemed driven (through *Anfechtungen*) to lash out against his adversaries, not only polemically but virulently, in his two notorious late treatises against the Jews and against the popes: *On the Jews and Their Lies* (1543) and *Against the Roman Papacy, an Institution of the Devil* (1545).

In my judgment these late outbursts are unworthy of so great a human being and so profound a theologian as Martin Luther. Anyone who admires Luther as much as I do as that rarest of human phenomena—both a religious and a theological genius—cannot but deeply regret these such violent outbursts along with his earlier voracious outbursts against the peasants. Of course, Luther lived in a polemical age as well as an age where anti-Semitism was widely practiced by Christians (including Erasmus). The fact of the usually taken-for-granted fact of polemical debates, not dialogical nor meditative exchanges between intellectual adversaries (including humanists like Lorenzo Valla or Pietro Arentino), contextualizes but does not excuse Luther's sometimes beyond-the-limit polemical violence. Among his many talents Martin Luther, like Jonathan Swift in a later age, had a natural talent for polemic. Luther's polemic sometimes nicely illuminates a complex issue (e.g., on the Eucharist versus Zwingli; on the centrality of the Word versus the Zwickau prophets; on indulgences versus Eck and Cajetan). At other times Luther's polemics—like all polemics (e.g., Eck, Thomas More,

Müntzer with their increasingly violent *ad hominem* attacks on Luther's person culminating in Müntzer's infamous 1524 pamphlet, *Speech against the Mindless, Soft-living Flesh in Wittenberg*)—clouds rather than illuminates. In our own age characterized, at its rare best, by a turn to the other and a turn to language culminating in what Charles Taylor has rightly named "the dialogical turn" of much contemporary historically conscious thought, the most important necessity—in radical distinction from Luther's polemically charged sixteenth century and the four centuries of polemical intra-Christian polemical confessional strife that followed—is for a dialogical turn: dialogical ecumenism within Christianity and the gradual emergence of inter-cultural and inter-religious dialogues globally. Polemics, to be sure, are sometimes necessary (e.g., against Nazism) and often very funny. Dialogue is ordinarily emancipatory if sometimes slightly boring. The real difference between the two genres is their conflicting attitudes to the other: genuine dialogue always listens to the other as other; polemics ignores the other—save as a contemptible target for its attacks and insults. There must be an other for dialogue; there is no real other for polemics. The turn to the other is a dialogical, not polemical turn.

The doctrine of double predestination, unlike the doctrine of the theology of the cross with its *sub contrario* revelation of God's Infinite Graciousness, exposed Luther to new experiences of doubt and despair. Even after justification, Luther still found himself at times in desperation. At those times he seemed to live at the very edge of the abyss with that relentless question: is God ultimately gracious *pro me*?

Nowhere else does Luther so clearly exist in the cusp between the medieval world and the early modern world. On the medieval side, Luther maintained an unusually strong belief in Satan as a person, a personal force of evil with whom he struggled constantly.[14] For Erasmus, on the contrary, Satan had become largely a powerful metaphor for objective evil but no longer an actual person. On both the medieval and early modern sides of Luther's sensibility—certainly before and not infrequently even after his reformatory insight—there always breathed his peculiarly intense *Anfechtung*-experiences occasioned by satanic assault. Those manifested themselves as temptations to disbelieve that God had elected Martin Luther to be one of the saved (a minority of humankind for Luther as for Augustine in any event).

Luther, perhaps like Paul in Romans and Augustine in his anti-Pelagian works, held to the doctrine of double predestination. The doctrine, for Luther as for Calvin, was in the Bible: God's hardening of Pharaoh's heart, God's election (in Rebekah's womb) of the younger son Jacob over the elder son Esau; above all, in the intractable Pauline metaphor of the potter and the clay.

Erasmus' attempts in his *De libero arbitrio* to remove the sting of these scriptural statements of predestination seem as strained and implausible as Augustine's earlier attempt[15] to explain away the directly opposite yet equally clear biblical passages on God's universal will for the salvation of all, as in First Timothy—"This is right and acceptable in the sight of God our Savior who desires everyone to be saved and to come to a knowledge of the truth" (1 Tim. 2:3). First Timothy has often served as the *magna carta* text for all those theologians who argue for a biblically based hope (not, of course, Origenist knowledge) for universal salvation—Gregory of Nyssa, Scotus Eriugena, Karl Rahner, Karl Barth, Hans Urs von Balthasar, Paul Tillich and many other contemporary Christian theologians. On no other central soteriological issue is a christological

---

14. See Oberman, *Luther*, esp. 209-26.
15. Augustine, *On Rebuke and Grace* (*De correptione et gratia*), Chapter 44: 'In What Way God Wills All Men to be Saved'; in *A Select Library of the Nicene and Post-Nicene Fathers of the Christian Church*, ed. Philip Schaff, 5:489.

reading more needed than on the doctrine of predestination (e.g., as in Karl Barth) if one is to challenge the traditional understanding (Augustine, Luther, Calvin et al.) of divine predestination as double predestination. Erasmus's evasiveness will not do. However, closer attention to the biblical message of hope for a universal salvation allied with a fuller christology and pneumatology can, I believe, allow for the hope (not knowledge) of universal salvation that is neither Pelagian nor semi-Pelagian nor Origenist.

Luther's other warrant for the second form of God's terrifying Hiddenness not in but beyond the revelation of God's graciousness hidden *sub contratrio* in the cross of Jesus Christ is the phenomenon he appealed to so often—*Anfechtung* both subjectively and objectively affirmed by Luther as bearing great theological import. This second sense of God's radical, frightening Hiddenness has, in the contemporary period, paradoxically proved one of Luther's most compelling insights not only for Christians but also for all those many persons who experience the Void, i.e, those of the edge of an abyss of the seeming meaninglessness of life. This peculiarly modern form of *Anfechtung* has occurred to many—whether Christian (Pascal's '"Le silence éternel des ces éspaces infinis m'effraye";[16] Kierkegaard's probable translation of Luther's *Anfechtung* into modern *Angst*),[17] or non-Christian (all the secular existentialists, e.g., Sartre with his concept of "nausea" or Camus's "the absurd"). A sense of contemporary *Anfechtung* can also be found in many post-moderns who, through irony, parody, and pastiche, refuse not only Christian faith-hope but also any Romantic or modernist hopeful epiphanies, along with the post-modernist embrace of chance, not fate or

16. *Pascal's Pensées*, #313; bilingual ed., trans., notes and introd. H. F. Stewart (New York: Random House, 1965), 172 (French), 173 (English).

17. Søren Kierkegaard, *The Concept of Anxiety*, trans. and ed. R. Thomte (Princeton: Princeton University Press, 1980).

providence, much less divine predestination. For secular post-modernity, pure chance is the final truth of reality; we live in an indifferent purposeless, meaningless universe of pure chance: in science, Steven Weinberg (the meaningless Void) versus Albert Einstein (the impersonal Spinozist God). Post-modern *Anfechtungen* often take the form of either radical irony or an experience of excess, beginning with Georges Bataille, post-modernity's failed prophet. Post-modernity's response to Blaise Pascal's wager on faith in the face of the eternal silence of an indifferent universe was nowhere more sharply stated than in the very title of post-modernity's charter poem, Mallarme's "Un coup de dès jamais n'abolira le hazard."[18] Luther, who in *De servo arbitrio* expressed his respect for the ancients' obsession with fate, would have understood the new post-modern *Anfechtung* evoked by chance. He would, of course, have rejected with all the rhetorical force at his command what he would name a delusional post-modern evasion through irony and parody as well as any excess-laden form (or formlessness) of any aggressive nihilism.

So powerful are Martin Luther's acute phenomenological descriptions of his various experiences of *Anfechtung* that many readers (late medieval, early modern, late modern or post-modern) can come to acknowledge such experiences as one's own (John Calvin, John of the Cross, Søren Kierkegaard, Fyodor Dostoevsky, Emily Dickinson, Simone Weil, Dietrich Bonhoeffer, Ingmar Bergman, David Foster Wallace, and countless others). As Luther acknowledged, not all human beings experience the unnerving *Anfechtungen* that he himself endured. Melanchthon did not; Erasmus, often melancholic, prayed for divine release from his experiences of weakness, lethargy, weakness of heart—not *Anfechtung* but *pusillanimitas*, a word Erasmus borrowed from Jean Gerson's tract *De*

---

18. Stéphen Mallarmé, *Poems*, bilingual ed., trans. and ed. A. Hartley (Hammondsworth, England: Penguin, 1965), 200-33.

Remediis Contra Pusillanimitatem.[19] The Latin word does not translate well into the English since "pusillanimity" in English usually implies a weakness of character whereas for Gerson, *pusillanimitas* is defined in almost *Anfechtung* terms as *maximum timor* (maximal fear) and *desperatio* (desperation). William James famously distinguished between two basic human types,[20] "the sick souls" who breathe *Anfechtung* and "the healthy-minded" who do not. These contrasting types tend not to understand one another—witness Pelagius and Augustine, Eriugena and Gottschalk, Arminius and the Synod of Dort, Erasmus and Luther, D. F. Strauss and Nietzsche, Turgenev and Dostoevsky, Jane Austen and Emily Bronte. The list could easily be extended.

The Christian theological debate on predestination has proved itself an important topic in Christian theology since Paul in Corinthians, Romans and Galatians and, in Western theology, since Augustine.[21] Some version of the doctrine of predestination especially one explicitly related to the doctrine of providence is a central Christian biblical belief. However, the doctrine of double predestination, affirmed at times in Augustine, was insisted upon in *De servo arbitrio* by Martin Luther but not much dwelt upon after that: never denied but rarely expounded upon. Double predestination was far more strongly affirmed and developed by John Calvin but

---

19. See the discussions in Marc Vial, *Jean Gerson, Theoricien de la théologie mystique* (Paris: Le Cerf, 2006) and in Steven E. Ozment, *Homo Spiritualis: A Comparative Study of the Anthropology of Johannes Tauler, Jean Gerson and Martin Luther (1509-1516) in the Context of Their Theological Thought* (Leiden: Brill, 1969).

20. William James, *The Varieties of Religious Experience* (Garden City: Doubleday, 1978), 138-96.

21. See the excellent article in the history of the reception of Augustine's understanding of predestination: Susan E. Schreiner and Jeremy C. Thompson, "Predestination," *The Oxford Guide to the Historical Reception of Augustine*, ed. Karla Pollman et al. (Oxford: Oxford University Press, 2013), 3:1591-9; on Luther's complex and changing relationships to Augustine, see David C. Steinmetz, "Luther and Augustine on Romans 9," in *Luther in Context* (Grand Rapids, MI: Baker, 1995), 12-23; Denis R. Janz, "Predestination," in *The Westminster Handbook to Martin Luther* (Louisville, KY: Westminster John Knox, 2010), 110-12.

even there not a central doctrine about God. God's sovereignty and God's gracious mercy were the principal theological understanding of God for Calvin. The classical Calvinism defined in the Synod of Dort against Arminius is not the heart of Calvin's own theology, much less Luther's, even though both did hold to double predestination as implicit in the belief in the omnipotence of God.

Like probably most contemporary Christian theologians I do not affirm Luther's doctrine of double predestination since it seems to me inevitably to imply theological and philosophical determinism, which the alternative doctrine of providence need not. Luther's *Anfechtung*, like the salvific faith to which it can point as the only hope for release, is both subjective ("the sick soul") and objective (Satan is a symbol of the objective power of radical evil).

However powerful Luther's notion of the second form of God's Hiddenness is today in different Christian and secular forms, one must analyze further Luther's own account of God's Hiddenness behind or beyond revelation. Luther expressed this idea in several texts—for example, in his biblical commentaries on Isaiah and Genesis and classically in his response to Erasmus, *De servo arbitrio*.[22]

Never in Christian history, save in the original conflict of Augustine and Pelagius, did such an influential and somewhat unfocussed theological debate occur as that between the volcanic Luther and the moderate, tolerant Erasmus. The temperaments of Luther and Erasmus were undoubtedly opposed, but their strong theological differences were more important in the debate. A conflict on the theology on God, not merely a conflict of temperament, caused the Erasmus-Luther debate—a debate ultimately on the very reality of God, i.e., the fuller meaning of the *Deus theologicus*. Their

---

22. See Martin Luther, *De servo arbitrio*, *LW* 33; *WA* 18 600-787. Both Erasmus' and Luther's treatises can also be found, in English, in *Luther and Erasmus: Free Will and Salvation*, ed. E. G. Rupp, The Library of Christian Classics, vol. 17 (Philadelphia: Westminster, 1969).

conflicting treatises—Erasmus' *De libero arbitrio* and Luther's *De servo arbitrio*—could more accurately be named *De Deo*.

Erasmus, one of the greatest historical-philological scholars of his period and the prime promoter of a Christian humanist theology of reform depicted, in his many writings, including *De libero arbitrio*, a gracious portrait of a gracious God. An analysis of Erasmus' too seldom honored theology of God must await some other occasion.[23] Luther's far richer, deeper, and more complex *Deus theologicus* is my present focus. *De servo arbitrio* is unique in its systematic theological power combined with its deeply disturbing insights into this new, sinister form of God's hiddenness beyond or behind the always fundamental revelation of God's graciousness hidden in the cross of Jesus Christ.

Luther's more strictly philosophical (i.e., logical and semantic, not metaphysical) arguments in *De servo arbitrio* are mostly on the logic of

---

23. See B. A. Gerrish, *The Old Protestantism and the New: Essays on the Reformation Heritage* (Chicago: University of Chicago Press, 1982), 11-27; Marjorie O'Rourke Boyle, *Erasmus on Language and Method in Theology* (Toronto: University of Toronto Press, 1977) and *Rhetoric and Reform: Erasmus' Civil Dispute with Luther* (Cambridge: Harvard University Press, 1983); Georges Chantraine, *Mystère et Philosophie de Christ selon Erasme* (Gemblou: Duilot, 1971). Erasmus's use of a more dialogical notion of *collatio* was intended to contrast with Luther's non-dialogical notion of *assertio*. To understand Erasmus's position more fully, one should also consult his post-Luther debate work where Erasmus argues (against Luther's accusations) that his position is not in any way Pelagian, in *Desiderie Eramie Hyperaspistes Diatribae adversus servum arbitrium Martini Luther*. *Liberium arbitrium* and *servum arbitrium* are more accurately translated as "freedom of choice" and "enslavement of choice" rather than as simply "free will" and "servile will" to emphasize that the issue is about freedom of choice solely in matters of salvation. Luther held that in other matters (e.g., everyday choices) the will is free; only in matters pertaining to salvation is there no freedom; i.e., the "chief article" of Luther always was justification through grace by faith alone without any works-righteousness whatsoever: no merits whether condign or congruent. Erasmus, whose knowledge of Scholastic philosophical theology was as unsure as his usual contempt for it was sure, nevertheless appealed in the controversy to Thomas Aquinas's distinction between *necessitas consequentiae and necessitas consequens*. For Thomas's own slowly developed position, see Bernard Lonergan, *Grace and Freedom: Operative Grace in the Thought of St. Thomas Aquinas*, ed. J. Patout Burns (New York: Herder and Herder, 1971), and Michał Paluch, *La Profondeur de l'amour divin. Évolution de la doctrine de la prédestination dans l'oeuvre de Saint Thomas d'Aquin* (Paris: Vrin, 2004). For the Carolingian debate, see D. Ganz, ed., *Charles the Bald, Court and Kingdom* (Oxford: Oxford University Press, 1981), 353-73.

the notions of divine "omniscience" and "omnipotence," along with a notion of non-compulsory divine necessity in human wills, to deny 'freedom of choice"—which Erasmus defended and Luther rejected as self-delusion. It is intriguing to wonder what difference, if any, the logically acute Luther would have found in some modern analyses of what divine "omniscience" and "omnipotence" can and cannot logically mean—as in Charles Hartshorne's logical analyses of these classical concepts.[24]

This famous debate between Luther and Erasmus is ultimately disappointing partly because Erasmus, unlike Luther, did not really know much contemporary late-medieval scholastic logical and semantic nominalist philosophy, which Luther knew very well indeed.[25] The debate was at least as dependent on philosophical argumentation as on biblical hermeneutics (in which Erasmus held his own in his defense of several biblical texts on free choice). Luther's cry was "Let God be God." Erasmus's suggestion was "Let God be Good."

By any fair assessment, I think, Luther's theological position on the two forms of God's Hiddenness, even for those who reject his position on double predestination, is far more compelling.[26] Perhaps

---

24. Charles Hartshorne, *inter alia*, see *The Logic of Perfection* (LaSalle: Open Court, 1973), esp. 118–91.

25. Graham White, *Luther as Nominalist: A Study of the Logical Methods used in Martin Luther's disputations in the Light of their Medieval Background* (Helsinki: Luther Agricola Society, 1994); Heiko A. Oberman, *Forerunners of the Reformation: The Shape of Late Medieval Thought* (New York: Holt, Reinhart and Winston, 1966).

26. Although, as I argued earlier in the text, Luther's theological account of the experience of *Anfechtung* is both a subjective-experiential and objective-theological. This dual concept is one of Luther's signal contributions in his understanding of *Deus theologicus*. However, to make an experience of *Anfechtung* necessary for every theologian, as Luther sometimes did and as Oswald Bayer always does, is exaggerated. Luther himself realized that some theologians he admired did not seem to experience *Anfechtungen* including his admired mentor Johann von Staupitz and his Wittenberg younger colleague, Philip Melanchthon. On Staupitz, see David Steinmetz, *Luther and Staupitz: An Essay in the Intellectual Origins of the Protestant Reformation* (Durham: Duke University Press, 1986); on Melanchthon, see Sachiko Kusukawa, *The Case of Phillip Melanchthon* (Cambridge: Cambridge University Press, 1995).

this famous debate was less a debate (it was certainly not a dialogue) but more like two ships passing in the night: one large, heavily-armed destroyer—Martin Luther—filled the horizon with fire and light; the other ship—Desiderius Erasmus—was more like an elegant, very well crafted, smoothly sailing humanist skiff that, after a few well-aimed shots, spent the rest of its brief sailing time heading for the nearest safe port.

If Martin Luther could have found a way—inevitably for him a way paradoxical in language and dialectical in method—he might have contrived another brilliant dialectic to depict how the hiddenness beyond revelation described in *De servo arbitrio* dialectically implied the need (the christological need) for God's Hiddenness in revelation. To my knowledge he never did. Perhaps it cannot be done and one must either choose only the Gracious God hidden in revelation (as Karl Barth and several other interpreters of Luther suggest) or be content simply to juxtapose these two very different, even conflictual theological insights into two irresolvably conflicting aspects of God's Hiddenness—in revelation and beyond revelation.

For my part, those Christians who, at one time or another, have experienced themselves at the edge of a Void of seeming meaninglessness cannot but be deeply thankful to Martin Luther: first and above all, for his incomparable theology of the cross to which theology, in such situations, one must flee—that cross which does disclose God's Hiddenness in negativity, i.e., *sub contrario* in the suffering, weakness and folly of the crucified Jesus Christ revealing the Gracious, Crucified God; second, for Luther's brilliant and enduring phenomenology of *Anfechtung* to expose the human experience of a second terrifying form of a divine hiddenness whose only solution, as Luther himself maintained, is to flee back to the cross: *ad deum ex deo*. We should admit, but not attempt to explain *Deus nudus*.

III. Luther's Incomprehensible God of Infinite Trinitarian Love

Luther's two accounts of God's Hiddenness—in revelation and beyond revelation—are in their theological depth and existential power a singular indeed uniquely profound contribution to a Christian theological understanding of God. However, there is a further richness and complexity in Luther's depictions of *Deus theologicus* still to be addressed. In the final case—God's Incomprehensible Trinitarian mystery—it is less a matter of originality than of Luther's continuity with the classical tradition: first, the medieval tradition of the disputation which Luther reinstituted at the University of Wittenberg in his last years in order to address the classical christological and Trinitarian questions anew with the sharpened semantic and logical tools he had learned in his youth; second, his continuity with the tradition of various forms of mystical theology on the Trinitarian God not as the Hidden God but as the Incomprehensible God of theologies (largely Eastern) of justification as *theosis*. These two recent scholarly emphases are clearly different but, at times, seem sufficiently akin to treat them in the same section since together they provide further components constituting Martin Luther's labyrinthine *Deus theologicus*.

In addition to the two forms of God's Hiddenness constituting Luther's *Deus theologicus*, are his Trinitarian reflections—his logical and semantic late disputations on the Trinity as well as his life-long reflection on the many dimensions to Christ's presence to the justified.[27] For Luther, Christ is first present *to* the justified in a marvelous exchange: Christ's imputed forgiving presence *pro me* (God's favor through Christ); second, Christ is present *in me*, i.e., Christ is also present *in us* through the sanctifying power of the

---

27. Christine Helmer, *The Trinity and Martin Luther: A Study of the Relationship between Genre, Language and the Trinity in Luther's Works (1523-46)* (Mainz: Philipp von Zabern, 1999).

Holy Spirit. In other words, often but admittedly not always in the case of Luther himself, if not in the case of the later Melanchthon, justification not only imputes Christ's active righteousness to us by the *favor* of the forgiveness of sins but Christ is also present *in me* (*donum*).[28] The Christic presence in the justified finds different denominations in Luther beginning with his rethinking of the traditional image of the *commercium admirabilem*—i.e., that exchange whereby Christ on the cross takes on our sin, our accursedness, our godforsakenness while, in the same wondrous exchange, the justified take on Christ's strength, Christ's wisdom. Additionally, Luther articulates a *commercium admirabilem* of Christ in the souls of the justified in other images and metaphors especially, throughout his life, *unio Christi*. At the limit, in several texts (thirty-seven to be exact, the Finnish theologians claim) Luther's concept of *unio Christi* may also be daringly read, in its final form, as *theosis*. The Orthodox tradition's concept of justification as deification was strongly held among the Greeks, including by Luther's most admired of the Greek Fathers, Athanasius of Alexandria in his *On the Incarnation*, "The Logos was made human so that we might be made God."[29] *Theosis* was also adopted, but less frequently and more tentatively, by Western theology as in Augustine.

Prior to further reflection on this now famous and controversial recent Finnish Lutheran reading of Luther's "justification" as *theosis*, I will first briefly describe another recent and significant related but distinct scholarly development in Luther's Trinitarian *Deus theologicus*: namely, a renewed scholarly attention into Luther's late disputations on the Trinity by Luther's use of late medieval logical,

---

28. *Inter alia*, see Tuomo Mannermaa, *Christ Present in Faith: Luther's View of Justification*, ed. and introd. K. I. Stjerna (Minneapolis: Fortress Press, 2005), 13-37, esp. 31 on *favor* and *donum*.

29. *De Incarnatione*, 54; in *Patrologia Graeca* XXV, 192B; see Saint Athanasius, *On the Incarnation*, trans. John Behr (Yonkers, N.Y.: St. Vladimir's Seminary Press, 2011), 167.

semiotic and semantic philosophy. By such means, Luther clarified certain complex logical issues for understanding the classical doctrines of the Trinity such as the concepts relation, infinity, essence, person, and eternity.

In re-reading for this assignment several excellent earlier modern works on Luther's theology (Rupp, Watson, Althaus, Ebeling, et al.[30]), I was surprised to notice (which I had not in earlier readings years ago) that these now almost classical studies of Luther's theology give very little attention, if any, to these later Trinitarian disputations of Luther, despite their obvious value for any full-fledged description of Luther's *Deus theologicus*. This lack has now been repaired by several scholars, especially Christine Helmer's study of Luther's developed Trinitarian *Deus theologicus* in hymns, sermons and late disputations.

Furthermore, one can claim that Luther's late disputations illustrate how his theological analysis of *Deus theologicus* was enriched by observing how faith does not merely, as in his earlier disputations (for example, the *Disputations in Scholastic Theology*), shatter reason's vain

---

30. Gerhard Ebeling, *Luther: An Introduction to His Thought*, trans. R. A. Wilson (Philadelphia: Fortress Press, 1970); Paul Althaus, *The Theology of Martin Luther*, trans. R. C. Schultz (Philadelphia: Fortress Press, 1966); Gordon Rupp, *The Righteousness of God: Luther Studies* (London: Hodder and Stoughton, 1953); Philip S. Watson, *Let God Be God: An Interpretation of the Theology of Martin Luther* (London: The Epworth Press, 1954). It is no disparagement of these important, indeed classical works of Luther which educated so many of us so well, to observe that, faithful to their period (1950s and 1960s), they mention but do not really analyze Luther's Trinitarian theology. On the other hand, Karl Barth's suggestion in *Church Dogmatics* II/2:76, despite his earlier over-criticism of Luther's two forms of divine hiddenness (*Church Dogmatics* I/1:479) argues that christological theology of election is a promising key to a possible theological resolution: viz. that from all eternity God was the electing God of Jesus Christ. Indeed, for Barth, election is the very essence of God. Moreover, as God-man Jesus Christ is both the electing God and the elect human being: the election of Jesus is the election of humanity. Barth's christological route is surely a valuable one—especially if, as I suggest in the text, the full range of christological symbols (incarnation-cross-resurrection-elevation-sending of the Spirit-promised second coming) were taken into account. On Barth on election, see Bruce McCormack, "Grace and Being. The Role of God's Gracious Election in Karl Barth's Theological Ontology," in *The Cambridge Companion to Karl Barth*, ed. John Webster (Cambridge: Cambridge University Press, 2000), 92-100.

and self-deluding attempts to move beyond its own limits. Faith also paradoxically redeems reason for newly illuminated theological use. It is not merely that Luther always affirmed the classical doctrines of christology and Trinity, as every interpreter would admit. Luther in these late disputations used all his considerable semantic and logical skills to help further understand the mystery of the Incomprehensible Trinitarian God *as* mystery. Here Luther used all the late medieval logical tools at his disposal to do what the Scholastics of both the *via antiqua* (e.g., Thomas Aquinas and Scotus) and the *via moderna* (e.g., William of Ockham and Gabriel Biel) always had as one of their principal goals: to make as precise as possible exactly where the mystery of the Trinity lies. Luther makes exactly the same kind of clarifying logical moves in his late disputations on the Trinity. As a result, the Trinitarian mystery becomes not merely affirmed but now serves theologically as an integral dimension in Luther's *Deus theologicus.*

In my judgment, the central encompassing affirmation of any genuinely Christian articulation of God is the Trinitarian affirmation: any method (whether mystical *theosis*, neo-Platonic metaphysics, or nominalist logic and semantics, or, in contemporary thought, both analytic philosophy and phenomenological, hermeneutical, metaphysical or contemplative philosophies) that can help Christians understand better (though always incompletely) the Trinitarian mystery should always be risked. Martin Luther, in continuity with the classical Trinitarian tradition, did not hesitate to use all the many analytical philosophical aids at his disposal to help formulate the central Trinitarian character of his portrait with ever greater depth and complexity. Luther's *Deus theologicus* was firmly a *Deus Trinitas.*

Recent scholarly studies of late-medieval nominalist semantics and logic have greatly clarified Luther's expertise. Luther reintroduced the medieval *disputatio*[31] (a genre he always liked but now used less polemically) as a test of a doctoral student's theological knowledge and skill. Luther, as professor, wrote the theses; the students (and, at the limit, the professors including Luther) played the necessary roles of *opponens* and *respondens*. *Disputatio* as a genre was an impressive medieval transformation of ancient dialogue and dialectical arguments alike. Moreover, the late medieval (especially Ockham) developed technical developments in logic and semantics beyond Aristotle[32] which provided Luther with even more precise technical tools than the technical uses of Aristotelian logic (especially the syllogism) in the theology of the high medieval Scholasticism of Thomas Aquinas, Bonaventure and others as well as the almost all-encompassing use of logic in the theology of Duns Scotus, Doctor Subtilis. When one reads Luther's later *disputationes*, Erasmus' earlier, not entirely unjust ironic title for Luther, Doctor Hyperbolicus, evaporates. The late Luther, the university professor at Wittenberg, with the rigorous technical, logical and semantic skills honed in his youth as a student at Erfurt, by no means rejected paradox as an important language for theology. However, Luther will now clarify, rather than polemically and hyperbolically intensify, his portrait of *Deus theologicus*, by analyzing conceptual terms (especially relation and person) in classical Trinitarian theology.

Through the influential scholarship of Heiko Oberman[33] on late medieval theology followed by the more recent scholarship of

---

31. Paul R. Hinlicky, ed., *The Substance of the Faith: Luther's Doctrinal Theology for Today* (Minneapolis: Fortress Press, 2008), which contains three substantive essays, with some important differences of interpretation of the later Luther's semantic and logical analyses of Trinitarian theology, by Micky L. Mattox (11-57), Dennis Bielfeldt (59-131), and Paul R. Hinlicky (131-73). For a good example of Luther's later *disputatio*, see *Die Promotionsdisputation von Georg Major und Johannes Faber 12. Dezember, 1544* in *WA* 39II:284-386.

32. On the nature of the medieval genre of *disputatio* in the University of Wittenberg from 1535-45 (approximately), see Christine Helmer, *The Trinity and Martin Luther*, 41-57.

33. See Graham White, *Luther as Nominalist*, esp. 144-220.

Graham White, Dennis Bielfeldt, Paul R. Hinlicky, and Christine Helmer, one can understand the basic contours of Luther's Trinitarian *Deus theologicus* far better than earlier accounts were able to do. These new welcome scholarly works have educated us all to see how important the Trinitarian doctrine of God was for Luther. Indeed, Luther articulated, in his Trinitarian work, a new Word-Spirit dialectic that may well prove his most profound theological dialectic for understanding both God-in-Godself in and through our relationships through the Word in the Spirit to the very inner relationships of Father, Son and Holy Spirit in the Trinity.

Therefore, in the later Luther, reason—once illuminated and redeemed by faith—could have a new life in theology. For Luther, reason (here logic, semantics and semiotics) is no longer turned in upon itself with confusion about its own limits allied to a fatal blindness to its own self-bondage in its deeply wounded noetic state after the Fall. Philosophy was now freed by salvific faith to play what Luther considered a transformed (because redeemed) role, especially through a rigorous logical use of reason in the disputations. In his later years at Wittenberg, Luther used the genre of *disputatio* in a far more traditional way than in his early work—as a rational means to clarify theological truths logically and to argue for them non-polemically.

The second recent scholarly innovation is the claim about *theosis* by the now famous Finnish School of Lutheran research. The Finnish scholars, beginning with Tuomo Mannermaa,[34] have been strongly

---

34. *Inter alia*, Carl E. Braaten and Robert W. Jenson, eds., *Union with Christ: The New Finnish Interpretation of Luther* (Grand Rapids, MI: Eerdmans, 1998); Tuomo Mannermaa, *Two Kinds of Love*; Simo Peura, *Mehr als im Mensch? Der Vergöttlichung als Thema der Theologie Martin Luthers von 1513-19* (Stuttgart: Philipp von Zabern, 1994). An especially valuable work for comparative and possibly constructive theological purposes to relate the Finnish School to the more traditional interpretations of God's Hiddenness may be found in Sammeli Juntunen, *Der Begriff des Nichts bei Luther in den Jahren 1510 bis 1532* (Helsinki: Luther-Agricola-Gesellschaft, 1996), which provides resources that could be employed in future work (preferably by the

influenced by their decades-old long dialogue with theologians of the Russian Orthodox Church. As a result of the new research on Luther occasioned by these dialogues, the Finnish Lutheran theologians and Luther researchers have paid theological notice to those texts of Luther on *theosis* previously either ignored or under-interpreted. Many modern interpreters of Luther—neo-Kantians, like Ritschl, and the existentialist hermeneutical thinkers, like Ebeling—did always allow that, for Luther, justification meant that not only our sins were forgiven (*favor*) and no longer reckoned to us but that justification also included a *commercium admirabile* between Christ and the believer as well as a *unio Christi* whereby Christ was also present to us as pure gift (*donum*). However, until fairly recently, most Lutheran theologians except those in the Osiander tradition thought that any participation language to explicate that *unio* was too Platonic for understanding the non-Platonic Luther.

So strong was the hold of the later Melanchthon's idea of a strictly forensic justification—a position codified in the *Formula of Concord* and so strong (so the Finns claim) was the neo-Kantian paradigm among many modern Luther interpreters that any ontological reading of Christ's presence, especially any participation language, was disallowed. For example, even those Protestant thinkers, like Albert Schweitzer, who argued for a Christ-mysticism in Paul would not allow for a God-mysticism in either Paul or Luther. For Schweitzer as for the Swedish Lutheran Anders Nygren, *unio mystica* was not appropriate to describe Luther's *unio Christi*. For them a love-mysticism was too Catholic and too neo-Platonic-participatory (*eros*) to interpret Luther.

---

author Professor Juntunen himself); Graham White, *Luther as Nominalist*, 27-32, 81-124, as well as the older classic work, Martin Grabmann, *Die Geschichte der scholastischen Methode: Nach den gedruckten und ungedruckten Quellen*, 2 vols. (Freiburg: Herder, 1909-11); Heiko A. Oberman, *Harvest of Medieval Theology* (Cambridge: Harvard University Press, 1963).

I must leave to experts the further discussion of the many further controversial claims of the Finnish theologians and researchers. However, one claim seems secure—at least to this non-expert. The texts on *theosis* clearly exist in Luther's voluminous texts and therefore should command hermeneutical attention either to disown them as not really representative of Luther's basic theological position or to incorporate them into the singular, perhaps heterogenous and more capacious complexity of Luther's theology of God, his *Deus theologicus*. These texts, although not prominent, are one of Luther's ways of articulating the *Christus praesens* to and in the justified—not only as *commercium admirabile*, not only as *unio Christi* but also, however infrequently, as *theosis*, i.e., *unio mystica*. Why were these texts so long ignored and why are the Finnish readings so quickly dismissed especially by many German scholars? Perhaps for the reason cited above: a Melanchthonian, purely forensic notion of justification is considered necessary by many Lutheran theologians to prevent a new Osiander-like reading from resurfacing. It is also possible that the Finnish interpreters may be exaggerating the importance of their genuine discovery of *theosis*, over-emphasizing the importance of the *theosis* texts, even over-systematizing the many-faceted excess of texts by Martin Luther under what seems to function for the Finns as a "new main article" to understand all of Luther: justification as *theosis*. As far as I can see, the many-faceted debate on the new Finnish interpretation of Luther has just begun. Like many non-experts I look on the debate with an interest bordering on fascination.

In the meantime, this much is clear: Luther is undoubtedly original in his model for *Deus theologicus*, i.e., in his unique and epoch-making description of the two forms of God's Hiddenness. By that double move, Luther does interrupt and, to a certain extent, disrupt the earlier traditions on adequate God-language by his singular—and, in my judgment, persuasive— concept of the double Hiddenness of God both in and beyond revelation. At the same time, Luther's logically developed Trinitarian theology is not discontinuous at all with classical Trinitarian theology. In sum, Martin Luther is like any original mind—both deeply innovative and therefore discontinuous with dimensions of prior traditions and at the same time, unmistakably continuous with the classical tradition.

In the meantime, however, the classical understanding of God's Incomprehensibility in the *theosis* texts of Luther possesses a mystical undertone that seems to me a promising component in any adequate contemporary full description of God. If these many faces of Luther's *Deus theologicus* could one day be correlated one to the other into some theological unity without the loss of any of these vital components, it would be a major theological contribution for all Christian theology, not only Lutheran theology. Otherwise, we are left—or, at least, I am left—with affirming each of these components as genuine dimensions of Luther's *Deus theologicus* without being able to correlate them into a single clear unity.

My own belief is that Luther's diverse elements for his portrait are less likely, in a final estimate, to prove mutually contradictory as distinct from uneasily and paradoxically mutually enriching through a christology that would expand Luther's emphasis on the cross to the fuller range of the central christological and pneumatological symbols which can also be found in his work: incarnation-cross-resurrection-elevation-the sending of the Spirit, and the eschatological reality of the Second Coming. Some future attempt to coordinate these christological symbols in Luther may prove the way forward to correlate his twofold Hiddenness of God with his Incomprehensible Trinitarian God. Perhaps.

A concluding suggestion: Luther's unique notion of the Hidden God should be brought into direct contact with Gregory of Nyssa's

Infinite-Incomprehensible Trinitarian God.[35] Rethinking Luther's relationship to the early Greek theologians and not only to Augustine could, I believe, be a breakthrough encouraging further theological reflections on the issue on God as both Incomprehensible and Hidden, an ideal that is, for me at least, a central focus of the issue of an adequate model of *Deus theologicus* today: how can we best correlate the Incomprehensible God tradition with the Hidden God tradition and both as related to the Trinitarian God. If we could, there can be no doubt that Martin Luther must be a major voice in any such conversation. Martin Luther is one of those very rare Christian theologians who belong to all Christian theology.

---

35. It would prove more fruitful first to relate Martin Luther's Hidden God tradition to Gregory of Nyssa's Infinite-Incomprehensible God tradition, rather than immediately comparing, as I once thought, Luther's Hidden God tradition and Dionysius the Aereopagite's In-comprehensible God tradition, especially given Luther's fierce turn against Dionysius. The rich Dionysius tradition itself, moreover, is presently having a major revival—all to the better, in my judgment. However, a comparison between the Hidden (*absconditus*) and Incomprehensible (*incomprehensibilis*) theologies of God would probably be best undertaken first (not last!) by comparing Luther to the relatively non-controversial Gregory of Nyssa in God's Infinity and Incomprehensibility. On Gregory, see David Tracy, "God's Infinity: Ethical Implications," in *Theism and Ethics*, ed. Miriam Renaud and Joshua Daniels, forthcoming.

7

———

Much Ado about Nothing: The Necessary Non-Sufficiency of Faith

Matt Jenson

I used to be afraid to go to the beach by myself. I remember the pit in my stomach, considering a trip to La Jolla Shores, thirty minutes from my parents' home in San Diego. It was neither a fear of drowning nor the insecurity that comes with being paler and scrawnier than the next guy. No, my anxiety stemmed from a pious root. I just *knew* that, were I to arrive at the beach alone, I would feel an inner compulsion to share the gospel with someone.

I am an evangelical—proudly so, I might add. I was born and bred among evangelicals, was nurtured in evangelical institutions and forms of piety. Furthermore, I encountered the good far more than the bad and the ugly of evangelicalism. I saw evangelicals' resolute commitment to publish the good news that Jesus Christ died for the sins of the whole world, such that no sin can outpace the grace of God in the cross of Christ. This is the heart of Scripture, and its announcement is the heart of the evangelical *modus vivendi*. We are witnesses.

Still, it is one thing to identify, rather vaguely, as witnesses; it is quite another to have to go about the work of witnessing. My parents were on the staff of Campus Crusade for Christ (now, Cru), one of the most evangelistic of evangelical para-church ministries. Before I reached adolescence, I had memorized the Four Spiritual Laws, perhaps the most oft-used tract of the mid-twentieth century. We were sent out in pairs, like Jesus' disciples, to announce good news, stopping people on the streets of Ft. Collins, Colorado, with an arresting question—*If you died tonight, do you know where you would go?*—meant to carve space for an evangelistic conversation. (We had no idea what to say to the man who quickly replied, "To the morgue!") So I was used to witnessing; still, it petrified me. But, in the midst of my fear, I knew the eternal consequences of rebuffing the divine condescension, of rejecting Jesus Christ.

Hence my dilemma at water's edge. I could not, in good faith, ignore the languishing souls at La Jolla Shores. Sometimes I would attempt to witness to someone just to ease my anxious conscience.

***

I begin with this memory for a number of reasons. To begin with, first-person narrative—in the form of testimony—is the evangelical genre.[1] Our theology does not usually develop through engaging catechisms and confessions or reading authoritative interpreters of the

---

1. The other genre which suggests itself as particularly fitting for evangelicalism is the hymn. As others have suggested, evangelical theology is best sung.

biblical texts, and many of us scorn creeds as impediments to the reading of Scripture. In the absence of a strong formal theological tradition—and in the presence of the ongoing work of the Spirit—evangelicals turn to experiences of God, chiefly our own, patterned on and mediated by Scripture, to make sense of God and his world.[2] But if evangelicals eschew formal theologizing at times, it is not because we lack theological commitments. Our theological reflection tends toward the *ad hoc,* listening day in and day out to the Word of God in the context of our life together. We do this for our own sakes, encouraging one another in the church with stories of God's mercies, colossal and quotidian. We do this, too, for the sake of the world, telling how the story of Scripture is our story, is *my* story, and how it can be yours, too.

My memory of anxious witness also gathers together the strands of what remains an apt character sketch of evangelicalism. David Bebbington names four qualities

> that have been the special marks of Evangelical religion: *conversionism,* the belief that lives need to be changed; *activism,* the expression of the gospel in effort; *biblicism,* a particular regard for the Bible; and what may be called *crucicentrism,* a stress on the sacrifice of Christ on the cross. Together they form a quadrilateral of priorities that is the basis of Evangelicalism.[3]

The conversion of a sinner has been the "goal" and "theme" of Evangelicalism; and conversions "could seem a panacea."[4] Conversion, whether gradual or sudden, is what makes a Christian.

---

2. Alan Jacobs expresses surprise at the absence of personal narratives in the recent recovery of narrative theology and seeks to fill the gap in his *Looking Before and After: Testimony and the Christian Life* (Grand Rapids: Eerdmans, 2008).

3. D. W. Bebbington, *Evangelicalism in Modern Britain: A History from the 1730s to the 1980s* (Grand Rapids: Baker Book House, 1992 [1989]), 2-3 (see the exposition in 2-17).

4. Ibid., 5.

Conversion invites assurance: "Not only is he a Christian; he knows he is a Christian."[5] Bebbington notes a shift here:

> Assurance had been an important theme of pre-Evangelical Protestant spirituality, but the experience had never been regarded as the standard possession of all believers. The novelty of Evangelical religion…lay precisely in claiming that assurance normally accompanies conversion.[6]

Nothing is more natural than for those who have been born again to tell others the good news. Jonathan Edwards reported that "[p]ersons after their own conversion have commonly expressed an exceeding great desire for the conversion of others. Some have thought that they should be willing to die for the conversion of any soul."[7] Activism, beginning with evangelism but extending more broadly to an "imperative to be up and doing," marks evangelicals, for good or ill.[8] Witness the extraordinary missionary effort over the last two centuries by evangelicals as well as the common complaints of burnout, which seem to have marked the movement from its beginnings.[9] "Biblicism" describes the evangelical veneration of Scripture; it also can name a common sense interpretation that eschews self-conscious hermeneutical frameworks and engagement with the history of interpretation. Bebbington notes that early evangelicals were less interested in developing a doctrine of Scripture than they were in the Bible's role as a means of grace, though that changed with the rise of historical criticism and the modernist controversy.[10]

---

5. Ibid., 6.
6. Ibid., 7.
7. Quoted in Bebbington, *Evangelicalism in Modern Britain,* 10.
8. Bebbington, *Evangelicalism in Modern Britain,* 12. One of the deleterious effects of such an active orientation is that "[l]earning…could be disregarded as a dispensable luxury. At the beginning of the nineteenth century Independent ministers were trained not in theology or Greek, but simply in preaching."
9. "A working week of between 90 and 100 hours was expected of men in the nineteenth-century Wesleyan ministry" (Bebbington, *Evangelicalism in Modern Britain,* 11).

Finally, evangelicals have long held that the heart of the Christian faith is the cross of Christ; "nothing but the blood of Jesus" is necessary for salvation, and nothing else will avail for salvation. Evangelicals have long held that God became man to die on the cross in our place.[11] "To make any theme other than the cross the fulcrum of a theological system was to take a step away from Evangelicalism."[12]

Bebbington's interest in evangelical "religion" rather than evangelical theology matches evangelicals' primary concern with the new birth and a life of active witness. What matters is that those who are dead in their sins become alive in Christ, having heard the good news about Jesus proclaimed in Scripture; everything else serves this end.

That such a joyful vocation should issue in such a tortured conscience as mine should, then, give us pause. And this is a final reason I began with my memory of witnessing on the beach—to suggest something of the disproportion and distortion that can mark evangelicals' understanding of faith, making a renewed attention to the doctrine of faith vital for an evangelical movement whose vocation in the church catholic is to champion the clarity and simplicity of the biblical gospel of grace revealed in the cross of Christ.

Of course, as many compassionate evangelicals might say, maybe I'm just thinking too much. In one sense, this is exactly right. And yet, I suspect that evangelical confusion about faith derives less from too-careful examination than it does from a hastiness and immaturity of thought. Twenty years ago, in his "epistle from a wounded lover," Mark Noll wrote:

10. Ibid., 13–14.
11. On the emphasis on substitutionary atonement, see Bebbington, *Evangelicalism in Modern Britain*, 15–16.
12. Bebbington, *Evangelicalism in Modern Britain*, 15.

The scandal of the evangelical mind is that there is not much of an evangelical mind. An extraordinary range of virtues is found among the sprawling throngs of evangelical Protestants in North America. . . . Notwithstanding all their other virtues, however, American evangelicals are not exemplary for their thinking, and they have not been so for several generations.[13]

While much has changed since Noll first wrote, we evangelicals still need to think more and better rather than less. In a recent progress report on the evangelical mind, Noll spots several "built-in barriers to productive thinking" that remain.

These barriers include an immediatism that insists on action, decision, and even perfection *right now*; a populism that confuses winning supporters with mastering actually existing situations; and an antitraditionalism that privileges current judgments on biblical, theological, and ethical issues (however hastily formed) over insight from the past (however hard won and carefully stated).[14]

In contrast to such intellectual bad habits, evangelicals need to learn to think interdependently, listening together to the Word of God in the church catholic—beginning with its local expression and extending to its global and historical expressions. We also need to think discursively, preferring long thoughts and nuanced analyses over slogans and shibboleths.[15]

Consider what follows an exercise in habit formation, as we seek to listen to Luther's witness to the Word and carefully examine his understanding of the nature and dynamics of faith. First, I will outline Luther's well-developed teaching on faith in his second lectures on Galatians, published in 1535. These lectures feature Luther in a

---

13. Mark A. Noll, *The Scandal of the Evangelical Mind* (Grand Rapids: Eerdmans, 1994), 3. The line about an "epistle from a wounded lover" is found on p. ix.
14. Noll, *Jesus Christ and the Life of the Mind*, 152. He is also concerned about a "nearly gnostic dualism."
15. See Noll's six goals for deepening the evangelical life of the mind in Noll, *Jesus Christ and the Life of the Mind*, 167.

mature setting, assailed by those without (in Rome) and those within (the sacramentarians, some of whom had shared Luther's roof and table); he keeps his eye on the legalism of the former and the libertinism of the latter. In a final section, I will consider three besetting evangelical temptations regarding faith and the way in which an appropriation of Luther's teaching might bolster evangelical thought and life.

The Faith of Galatians

Galatians takes us to the heart of Luther's own project. "The Epistle to the Galatians is my dear epistle," he once said. "I have put my confidence in it. It is my Katy von Bora [that is, his wife]."[16] We do well, then, to turn to these lectures on the epistle in which Luther has put his faith in order to discern the contours of faith itself.

In the preface to the publication of the 1535 lectures, Luther prizes faith:

> For in my heart there rules this one doctrine, namely, faith in Christ. From it, through it, and to it all my theological thought flows and returns, day and night; yet I am aware that all I have grasped of this wisdom in its height, width, and depth are a few poor and insignificant firstfruits and fragments.[17]

This can serve as a cautionary note to evangelicals, whose easy familiarity with the language of faith can turn lackadaisical. "To the growing son of an Evangelical Anglican home in the mid-nineteenth century it seemed that the clergy taught nothing else but justification by faith."[18] So it is today in many churches. And yet, Luther insists:

> [T]his doctrine can never be discussed and taught enough. If it is

---

16. *LW* 54:20; *WATR* 1:69.
17. *LW* 27:145; *WA* 40/I:33.
18. Bebbington, *Evangelicalism in Modern Britain*, 6.

lost and perishes, the whole knowledge of truth, life, and salvation is lost and perishes at the same time. But if it flourishes, everything good flourishes—religion, true worship, the glory of God, and the right knowledge of all things and of all social conditions.[19]

G. K. Chesterton once wrote that Luther "had a single and special talent for emphasis; for emphasis and nothing except emphasis; for emphasis with the quality of earthquake."[20] Luther's claim that "the whole knowledge of truth, life, and salvation" hinges on the doctrine of faith displays just such an emphasis; and it does so for two reasons.

First, as Matthew Boulton argues elsewhere in this volume, Luther discerns in the doctrine of faith the division between true worship and idolatry, the salvation and damnation of humanity. "The one who has faith is a completely divine man, a son of God, the inheritor of the universe. He is the victor over the world, sin, death, and the devil."[21] "This faith is our victory (1 John 5:4); with it we conquer the terrors of the Law, of sin, death, and every evil, though not without a great struggle."[22] Luther can even write that faith "consummates the Deity; and, if I may put it this way, it is the creator of the Deity, not in the substance of God but in us."[23]

Luther urges the ongoing teaching of the doctrine of faith for another reason—because of how very vulnerable it is. Faith suffers the slings and arrows of sin, the flesh, and the devil; and "cross and conflict follow immediately upon the knowledge of Christ."[24] It is attacked from without, and "there is a clear and present danger that the devil may take away from us the pure doctrine of faith and may substitute for it the doctrines of works and of human traditions. It

---

19. *LW* 26:3; *WA* 40/I:39.
20. G. K. Chesterton, *St. Thomas Aquinas* (London: Hodder & Stoughton, 1933), 231-32.
21. *LW* 26:247; *WA* 40/I:39.
22. *LW* 26:369; *WA* 40/I:564.
23. *LW* 26:227; *WA* 40/I:360.
24. *LW* 27:25; *WA* 40/II:29-30.

is very necessary, therefore, that this doctrine of faith be continually read and heard in public."[25]

Faith is also attacked from within, in the conspiracy of reason and the flesh. These two "simply want to work together. . . . [C]onscience is always murmuring and thinking that when righteousness, the Holy Spirit, and eternal salvation are promised solely on the basis of hearing with faith, this is too easy a way."[26] Reason knows that the way of the world is *quid pro quo,* and the flesh seeks and glories in its own achievement. Neither is content with the simple receptivity of faith, and so they seek to destabilize it by troubling the conscience.

Of course, "so far as the words are concerned, this doctrine of faith is very easy, and everyone can easily understand the distinction between the Law and grace; but so far as practice, life, and application are concerned, it is the most difficult thing there is."[27]

The Law: The Need for Faith

We typically think of laws as guidelines for our common life, or as boundaries that mark the limits of proper behavior. Luther acknowledges such a political use for the law, though his pessimism (or realism, if you will) moves him to speak of it as a restraint on sinners, "just as a rope holds a furious and untamed beast and keeps it from attacking whatever it meets," rather than a blueprint for society.[28] In the life of the church, however, "the proper use and aim of the Law is to make guilty those who are smug and at peace, so that they may see that they are in danger of sin, wrath, and death, so that they may be terrified and despairing, blanching and quaking at the rustling of a leaf (Lev. 26:36)."[29] The law makes sinners; that

---

25. *LW* 26:3; *WA* 40/I:39.
26. *LW* 26:215; *WA* 40/I:345–46.
27. *LW* 26:144; *WA* 40/I:251.
28. *LW* 26:308; *WA* 40/I:479.
29. *LW* 26:148; *WA* 40/I:257.

is, it indicts the complacent, exposing and exacerbating their sin, demanding justice. It "make[s] men not better but worse"; "it does nothing but reveal sin, work wrath, accuse, terrify, and reduce the minds of men to the point of despair. And that is as far as the Law goes."[30] "For the Law demands: 'Do this!' "[31] But we cannot, and will not. Even when we attempt to comply, "the Law always terrifies and accuses, saying: 'But you have not done enough!'"[32]

Still, Luther knows that the law is God's creation, his gift to his people. It is "the best thing that the world has on earth . . . which, like a sun, is added to feeble reason, the earthly light or human flame, to illumine and direct it" and is, "except for faith . . . the best, the greatest, and the loveliest among the physical blessings of the world."[33] "The Law is good (1 Tim. 1:8), holy, and useful; but it does not justify."[34]

What role does it play in the Christian life, then? It leads the sinner (for every Christian is still a sinner) to say, with Paul, "Wretched man that I am! Who will deliver me from this body of death?" (Rom. 7:24) By virtue of "this humiliation, this wounding and crushing by the hammer," the law serves as "a minister and a preparation for grace. For God is the God of the humble, the miserable, the afflicted, the oppressed, the desperate, and of those who have been brought down to nothing at all."[35] The law strips the sinner who then longs to be clothed with Christ. The law starves the sinner who then hungers for Christ.[36] "As the dry earth thirsts for rain, so the Law makes the troubled heart thirst for Christ. . . . He gladly soaks and irrigates this dry ground."[37]

30. *LW* 26:327, 313; *WA* 40/I:506, 486.
31. *LW* 26:303; *WA* 40/I:472.
32. *LW* 26:149; *WA* 40/I:258.
33. *LW* 26:184, 251; *WA* 40/I:306, 396.
34. *LW* 26:180; *WA* 40/I:301.
35. *LW* 26:314; *WA* 40/I:488.
36. *LW* 26:345; *WA* 40/I:529.

The Gospel: The Object of Faith

With its demands, the law brings us to the end of ourselves. Demands cease with the gospel, "which does not teach me what I should do—for that is the proper function of the law—but what someone else has done for me, namely, that Jesus Christ, the Son of God, has suffered and died to deliver me from sin and death."[38] The gospel changes the subject.

Luther recalls the anxious scrupulosity of his monastic years, in which he curved in on himself in a sincere—and sinful—attempt to please God and assuage his conscience:

> When I was a monk, I made a great effort to live according to the requirements of the monastic rule. I made a practice of confessing and reciting all my sins, but always with prior contrition; I went to confession frequently, and I performed the assigned penances faithfully. Nevertheless, my conscience could never achieve certainty but was always in doubt and said: "You have not done this correctly. You were not contrite enough. You omitted this in your confession."[39]

When Luther discovered the Pauline "not I, but Christ" (Gal. 2:20), he realized that the gospel "commands us to look, not at our own good deeds or perfection but at God Himself as He promises, and at Christ Himself, the Mediator."[40] The good news is that our faithful God keeps his promises and has fulfilled them in Christ. Thus our attention is turned from our impoverished selves to Christ and his riches. Faith is "a constant gaze that looks at nothing except Christ, the Victor over sin and death and the Dispenser of righteousness, salvation, and eternal life."[41] Like the Israelites in the wilderness, who

---

37. *LW* 26:329; *WA* 40/I:509.
38. *LW* 26:91; *WA* 40/I:168. "For the Law demands: 'Do this!' The promise grants: 'Accept this!' " (*LW* 26:303; *WA* 40/I:472).
39. *LW* 27:13; *WA* 40/II:15.
40. *LW* 26:387; *WA* 40/I:589.
41. *LW* 26:356; *WA* 40/I:545.

had only to look at the bronze serpent to be healed, sinners need only fix their eyes on Christ to be delivered from sin, death, and the devil.[42] Faith's only proper object is Christ, and the one who "diverts his gaze from this object does not have true faith."[43]

Faith gazes at Christ; it also grasps Christ. Luther describes Christ as a jewel that a believer possesses by faith.[44] So closely united are Christ and the one who trusts in him that they become one flesh.

> [B]y [faith] you are so cemented to Christ that He and you are as one person, which cannot be separated but remains attached to Him forever and declares: "I am as Christ." And Christ, in turn, says: "I am as that sinner who is attached to Me, and I to him. For by faith we are joined together into one flesh and one bone." Thus Eph. 5:30 says: "We are members of the body of Christ, of His flesh and of His bones," in such a way that this faith couples Christ and me more intimately than a husband is coupled to his wife.[45]

As a result, "what is ours becomes His and what is His becomes ours."[46] At the cross, this perfectly righteous One took on himself the sin of the world, becoming "the highest, the greatest, and the only sinner."[47] So fully has he appropriated our sin that Paul can teach that "there is no more sin, no more death, and no more curse in the world, but only in Christ."[48] As Christ takes on my sin and death, through faith I receive his righteousness and life. The gospel testifies to Christ's righteousness and invites people to place their trust in him, such that "Christ is our principal, complete, and perfect righteousness."[49] Luther means much the same thing in writing that

---

42. *LW* 26:356-57; *WA* 40/I:545-46.
43. *LW* 26:88; *WA* 40/I:164.
44. *LW* 26:89; *WA* 40/I:165.
45. *LW* 26:168; *WA* 40/I:285-86.
46. *LW* 26:292; *WA* 40/I:454.
47. *LW* 26:281; *WA* 40/I:439.
48. *LW* 26:285; *WA* 40/I:445.
49. *LW* 27:71; *WA* 40/II:90.

"faith is our righteousness in this present life,"[50] because faith is nothing other than a confident repose in Christ the Righteous. Because Christian righteousness changes the subject, to speak of "my righteousness" is to speak of the One who is righteous for me. "[T]his is the righteousness of Christ and of the Holy Spirit, which we do not perform but receive, which we do not have but accept, when God the Father grants it to us through Jesus Christ."[51]

This is the doctrine of justification, "that we are pronounced righteous and are saved solely by faith in Christ, and without works."[52] Luther praises

> that single solid rock which we call the doctrine of justification, namely, that we are redeemed from sin, death, and the devil and endowed with eternal life, not through ourselves and certainly not through our works, which are even less than we are ourselves, but through the help of Another, the only Son of God, Jesus Christ.[53]

Fides sola means *solus Christus,* understood with reference to the human role in salvation.[54] What is our role? Faith alone. That is, we are to trust in "the help of Another" and never in ourselves. Faith is thus never alone, insofar as it grasps Christ; faith praises the believer's insufficiency and thereby glorifies the sufficiency of Christ.

Faith Comes by Hearing

How does one come to have faith? "But if they hear His Word and believe, Christ becomes present to them, justifies and saves them."[55]

---

50. *LW* 27:64; *WA* 40/II:80.
51. *LW* 26:6; *WA* 40/I:43.
52. *LW* 26:223; *WA* 40/I:355.
53. *LW* 27:145; *WA* 40/I:33.
54. Luther can attribute our justification to "God alone" working "solely by His grace through Christ" (*LW* 26:99; *WA* 40/I:181), to "faith in Christ" alone (*LW* 26:223; *WA* 40/I:355), and to "Christ alone" (*LW* 27:17; *WA* 40/II:20).
55. *LW* 26:240; *WA* 40/I:379.

Luther's answer is Paul's: "So faith comes from hearing, and hearing through the word of Christ" (Rom. 10:17). Significantly, according to Luther's translation, faith comes from *preaching,* a testament to the centrality of the public ministry of the Word in the gathered assembly. "Therefore a man becomes a Christian, not by working but by listening."[56]

> For the Word proceeds from the mouth of the apostle and reaches the heart of the hearer; there the Holy Spirit is present and impresses that Word on the heart, so that it is heard. In this way every preacher is a parent, who produces and forms the true shape of the Christian mind through the ministry of the Word.[57]

Believers have preachers for parents and the Word for a womb. Luther expands on this with reference to Paul's description of Christians as sons and heirs of God. An heir

> obtains the inheritance in a purely passive, not in an active way; that is, just his being born, not his producing or working or worrying, makes him an heir. He does not do anything toward his being born but merely lets it happen. . . . Therefore just as in society a son becomes an heir merely by being born, so here faith alone makes men sons of God, born of the Word, which is the divine womb in which we are conceived, carried, born, reared, etc.[58]

The Word is a womb we never leave, though, being "born, reared, etc." "Thus everything happens through the ministry of the Word."[59] The church has only one task, which is to "preach the Gospel correctly and purely and thus give birth to children."[60]

Not all have ears to hear, however. While one need only "let it happen," need only listen to become a Christian, the Spirit must

56. *LW* 26:214; *WA* 40/I:345.
57. *LW* 26:430; *WA* 40/I:649.
58. *LW* 26:392; *WA* 40/I:597.
59. *LW* 26:442; *WA* 40/I:665.
60. *LW* 26:441; *WA* 40/I:664.

"impress that Word on the heart, *so that it is heard.*" Such spiritual hearing is a gift and signals the divine presence surrounding faith. Faith trusts in the Word of God, which publishes the good news about Christ, and is received as the Spirit enables a person to hear it as good news *for her.*

Luther stresses that faith is a divine gift mediated through the Word. Faith is not a human accomplishment, something to be mustered; it is given to us by God as he nourishes us with his Word throughout our lives.

> This is why we continually teach that the knowledge of Christ and of faith is not a human work but utterly a divine gift; as God creates faith, so he preserves us in it. And just as He initially gives us faith through the Word, so later on He exercises, increases, strengthens, and perfects it in us by that Word. Therefore the supreme worship of God that a man can offer, the Sabbath of Sabbaths, is to practice true godliness, to hear and read the Word. On the other hand, nothing is more dangerous than to become tired of the Word.[61]

The Word stabilizes and strengthens believers by instructing them and reminding them of the promises of God. It tethers faith to its object. Despite common usage, "faith" cannot name a posture or attitude devoid of an object. One cannot have faith *per se*; one must have faith in someone or something. In the womb of the Word, faith clings to its object, being nourished by Christ.

The Ground of Assurance

Ever alert to the reality of *Anfechtungen,* Luther confesses that "reason is easily offended by the ugly shape of the cross."[62] Reason and the flesh recoil at faith and protest that "this is too easy a way."[63] But God

---

61. *LW* 26:64; *WA* 40/I:130.
62. *LW* 26:421; *WA* 40/I:638.
63. *LW* 26:215; *WA* 40/I:346.

himself promised to "destroy the wisdom of the wise," and the faith that listens to the word of the cross likewise "slaughters reason."[64] Faith turns a deaf ear to reason and listens only to the Word of God, which reassures us.

> This Word makes us certain that God cast away all His wrath and hatred toward us when He gave His only Son for our sins. The sacraments, the power of the keys, etc., also make us certain; for if God did not love us, He would never have given us these. Thus we are overwhelmed with endless evidence of the favor of God toward us.[65]

The Word of God and the other means of grace give us certainty, a strong and stable confidence grounded outside of us in the One who created out of nothing and gave us his Son for our sins.

> And this is the reason why our theology is certain: it snatches us away from ourselves and places us outside ourselves, so that we do not depend on our own strength, conscience, experience, person, or works but depend on that which is outside ourselves, that is, on the promise and truth of God, which cannot deceive.[66]

Cartesian certainty interrogates the subject of faith, looking for weaknesses, questions, quiet doubts. Lutheran certainty looks to the object of faith in the Word of promise. Where the former is subject to all the horrors of the funhouse of the human psyche, the latter trusts in "the help of Another."

> [T]he chief point of all Scripture is that we should not doubt but hope, trust, and believe for a certainty that God is merciful, kind, and patient, that He does not lie and deceive but is faithful and true. He keeps His promises and has now accomplished what He had promised, handing over His only Son into death for our sins, so that everyone who believes in the Son should not perish but have eternal life (John 3:16).[67]

64. 1 Cor. 1:18-19; *LW* 26:228; *WA* 40/I:362.

65. *LW* 26:388; *WA* 40/I:592.

66. *LW* 26:387; *WA* 40/I:589. In his writings on the sacraments, Luther develops an extensive account of the sacramental mediation of the Word and promise of God.

And "there is no comfort of conscience so solid and certain as is this passive righteousness."[68] Nor is this solely an assurance based on past divine action. We have a trinitarian witness to the trustworthiness of God's continuing favor, as "Christ, that mighty giant" confidently intercedes at the Father's right hand and the Spirit of Christ indwells us.[69]

Faith or Love

Two millennia of violence in the name of Jesus demand that questions be put to faith. What difference does it make? Does the simple fact that one professes a belief in a series of claims about Christ entail a life lived in his light? What about the hypocrisy? What about the compromises which even the well-intentioned make, quiet treacheries of the One they name as Lord? In a society in which baptism made the citizen, how could one see the sheep for the goats? Questions like these, already voiced in the epistle of James (see 2:14-17), prompted a scholastic distinction between unformed and formed faith. The latter faith was "formed by love," and it was this that justified.

Despite the respectable tone of the distinction, Luther detected in it the bankruptcy of faith and a collapse back into justification by works. "Just as our opponents refuse to concede to us the freedom that faith in Christ alone justifies, so we refuse to concede to them, in turn, that faith formed by love justifies."[70] For his opponents, "faith is the body, the shell, or the color; but love is the life, the kernel, or the form."[71] It is the form that makes a thing what it is, and so the scholastics implicitly deny that faith is anything apart from love. If

67. *LW* 26:386; *WA* 40/I:588.
68. *LW* 26:5; *WA* 40/I:41.
69. *LW* 26:378-79; *WA* 40/I:577.
70. *LW* 26:90; *WA* 40/I:167.
71. *LW* 26:129; *WA* 40/I:228.

this superficially resembles James' claim that faith without works is dead, it conceals a subterranean assault on the proper sufficiency of the faith in Christ which alone justifies sinners. Luther follows this through in insisting that, rather than love, it is *Christ* who forms faith. Indeed, Luther can even claim that "Christ is my 'form,' which adorns my faith as color or light adorns a wall."[72] Here again, we see Luther's defense of *sola fide* as a way to underscore *solus Christus*. Faith needs no adornment by love but is sufficient to itself precisely because it is adorned by Christ, who is present in faith.

> Christian faith is not an idle quality or an empty husk in the heart, which may exist in a state of mortal sin until love comes along to make it alive. But if it is true faith, it is a sure trust and firm acceptance in the heart. It takes hold of Christ in such a way that Christ is the object of faith, or rather not the object but, so to speak, the One who is present in the faith itself.[73]

Christ, not love, makes faith what it is—and what it is is this "sure trust and firm acceptance in the heart" that grasps Christ and brings him near. Here Luther approaches Paul's gnomic statement in Gal. 2:20: "It is no longer I who live, but Christ lives in me." As the object of faith, Christ becomes the reigning subject of the Christian's life.

Perhaps it is Christ's presence to and in faith that gives Paul—and Luther—such confidence in speaking of it. An example is Paul's hypostasizing of faith "working through love" in Gal. 5:6, which Luther picks up on in describing a robust faith whose instrument is love.

> Paul does not make faith unformed here, as though it were a shapeless chaos without the power to be or to do anything; but he attributes the working itself to faith rather than to love. . . . He makes love the tool through which faith works. Now who does not know that a tool has its

72. *LW* 26:167; *WA* 40/I:283.
73. *LW* 26:129; *WA* 40/I:228-29.

power, movement, and action, not from itself but from the artisan who works with it or uses it?[74]

Faith and Love

Faith is not formed by love; love is formed by faith.[75] This never implies love's denigration, in Luther's mind; rather, it puts love in its place and frees it from the burden of the law. If Luther appears at times to dismiss works, closer examination reveals that his vitriol is reserved for works considered as a basis for justification.[76] He remains adamant that faith alone, apart from works, justifies us before God; "and yet it does not remain alone, that is, idle. Not that it does not remain alone on its own level and in its own function, for it always justifies alone. But it is incarnate and becomes man; that is, it neither is nor remains idle or without love."[77] The allusion is deliberate.[78] Just as Christ, "though he was in the form of God, did not count equality with God a thing to be grasped, but emptied himself, by taking the form of a servant, being born in the likeness of men," so faith, which has ascended to the heights with Christ, descends in humble love to its neighbor.[79]

> Because you have taken hold of Christ by faith, through whom you are righteous, you should now go and love God and your neighbor. … These are truly good works, which flow from this faith and joy conceived in the heart because we have the forgiveness of sins freely through Christ.[80]

74. *LW* 27:29; *WA* 40/II:36.
75. See *LW* 26:161; *WA* 40/I:275.
76. Likewise, Luther does not reject the law *per se*, but rather its trespassing into the territory of the gospel. As a salve for consciences, the law has no place; that does not mean it has no place at all.
77. *LW* 26:272; *WA* 40/I:427.
78. Faith should be "diffused" throughout love in the same way that Christ's divinity was diffused through his humanity. (*LW* 26:266; *WA* 40/I:417).
79. Phil. 2:6–7. This Christological analogy frames Luther's *Freedom of a Christian* (*LW* 31:333–77; *WA* 7:1–38).
80. *LW* 26:133; *WA* 40/I:234.

Works of love are entirely necessary, just not necessary for justification. We love not in order that we might be loved, but "because he first loved us" (1 John 4:19). The Holy Spirit, who indwells us by faith as we are united to Christ, agitates us to love. "He does not permit a man to be idle but drives him to all the exercises of devotion, to the love of God, to patience in affliction, to prayer, to thanksgiving, and to the practice of love toward all men."[81]

The "whole of the Christian life" is faith and love or works.[82] "Both topics, faith and works, must be carefully taught and emphasized, but in such a way that they both remain within their limits."[83] Luther even shares his opponents' disdain for faith without works, a faith which is "worthless and useless," "a fantastic idea and mere vanity and a dream of the heart"—and therefore no faith at all.[84] The champion of *sola fide* thus can write that, "[i]f faith alone is taught, unspiritual men will immediately suppose that works are not necessary."[85]

Tempting Faith

In light of Luther's exposition of faith, I conclude with three temptations evangelicals face in living by faith in Christ.

Easy-believism

Somewhere along the line, the spartan Lutheran slogan of *sola fide* became warped into a cognitive, contractual soteriology in which all I have to do is assent to a small set of beliefs about the death of Jesus for me and God will be obliged to grant me entrance into heaven. Evangelicals, perhaps more than anyone, are guilty of turning *sola*

---

81. *LW* 26:155; *WA* 40/I:265.
82. *LW* 27:30; *WA* 40/II:37.
83. *LW* 27:63; *WA* 40/II:78.
84. *LW* 26:155; *WA* 40/I:266.
85. *LW* 27:63; *WA* 40/II:78.

fide into a one-time technique for getting saved, which guarantees eternal life and then allows people to get on with their lives.

It is the great merit of Luther's account of faith that he refuses to compromise its simplicity. Nothing else is needed for us to be justified in the sight of God. Faith itself, as I have written elsewhere, "is nothing," and lives like the moon on borrowed light. "Faith is a negative concept that opens up space to speak about something else." By "faith alone," Luther means to speak not of "this human action, not that," but instead "God's action, not ours."[86] It is Christ alone who saves me. Thus, the response to easy-believism cannot be to demand more and better of the believer.

Rather, the response to easy-believism requires a re-conception of belief itself. What is faith? Faith is "the trust of the heart, which takes hold of Christ, clings only to Him and to nothing else besides."[87] The only demand of faith is that we "believe in Jesus Christ."[88] But no matter how simple faith is, and no matter how splendid Christ is, faith is nonsense to reason, an offense to the flesh, and a threat to the devil. Nor do we merely believe once, at conversion; we must believe again and again, daily hearing the gospel anew and trusting in Christ. Thus, faith is a "difficult" thing; and "a fall from faith is as grave as it is easy."[89]

> I have often experienced, and still do every day, how difficult it is to believe, especially amid struggles of conscience, that Christ was given, not for the holy, righteous, and deserving, or for those who were His friends, but for the godless, sinful, and undeserving, for those who were His enemies, who deserved the wrath of God and eternal death.[90]

---

86. Matt Jenson and David Wilhite, *The Church: A Guide for the Perplexed* (New York: T&T Clark, 2010), 113.
87. *LW* 26:430; *WA* 40/I:649.
88. *LW* 26:86; *WA* 40/I:160.
89. *LW* 26:393, 414; *WA* 40/I:599, 628.
90. *LW* 26:36; *WA* 40/I:89.

Despite the goodness of the gospel, sinful humanity resists an account of the world in which God loves sinners. What's more, "there is a clear and present danger that the devil may take away from us the pure doctrine of faith and may substitute for it the doctrines of works and of human traditions."[91] All one has to do is believe—but "how difficult it is to believe." Luther calls evangelicals to the difficult simplicity of faith.

A Faith without Distinctions

Luther wrote that the one who knows how to distinguish law from gospel is "a real theologian."[92] The distinction "is necessary to the highest degree; for it contains a summary of all Christian doctrine."

> Therefore let everyone learn diligently how to distinguish the Law from the Gospel, not only in words but in feeling and in experience. ... For so far as the words are concerned, the distinction is easy. But when it comes to experience, you will find the Gospel a rare guest but the Law a constant guest in your conscience, which is habituated to the Law and the sense of sin; reason, too, supports this sense.[93]

Without both law and gospel, as well as their proper application, one loses the Christian faith. Evangelicals, often enough, neglect one or the other, or misapply them.

On the one hand, many have succumbed to what Philip Rieff calls "the triumph of the therapeutic."[94] Therapy in itself is good; the gospel is a divine therapy by which the Son takes on our humanity and heals it and the Spirit unites us to the crucified and risen Jesus and, healing us, conforms us to his image. But Rieff discerns in contemporary society an unheard of triumph of the therapeutic in

---

91. *LW* 26:3; *WA* 40/I:39.
92. *LW* 26:115; *WA* 40/I:207.
93. *LW* 26:117; *WA* 40/I:209.
94. Philip Rieff, *The Triumph of the Therapeutic: Uses of Faith After Freud* (Chicago: University of Chicago Press, 1987 [1966]).

which individual emotions float free from the demands of a community, such that feeling good is itself the end of life rather than one feeling good *insofar* as one has come into step with the way of the world. Similarly, a therapeutic gospel, all-too-commonly adhered to by evangelicals and others, tells its adherents that God loves them (which makes them feel good) without telling them of their sin and the ensuing cost of God's love in the gift of his Son (which would not make them feel good). God loves me, and I should love myself. But here, the accusing law, whose ministry is to drive us to Christ, is absent; and, eventually, Christ is rendered redundant. I am perfect just the way I am, and I have no need for another's intercession. (That such a therapeutic gospel would have little resources for responding to affliction is patent.)[95]

On the other hand, many evangelicals begin with the gospel only to settle into a toilsome life under the law. My anxious excursions to the beach capture this inconsistency perfectly. Even as I went out to tell people of the surprising mercy and grace of God, I found my conscience wracked with guilt and buckling under pressure. No matter my theological convictions, my functional theology demonstrated how crippling the law can be when misapplied—and how quickly one can forget the gospel. The law was "a constant guest in [my] conscience." Even though it "is the best of all things in the world, it still cannot bring peace to a terrified conscience but makes it even sadder and drives it to despair."[96] Of course, my terrified conscience, earnest though it was, could hardly serve as an apt witness to the grace and peace that "embrace the whole of Christianity."[97]

95. For another recent critique of a therapeutic gospel, see J. Todd Billings, "Catholic and Reformed: Rediscovering a Tradition," *Pro Ecclesia* 23:2 (Spring 2014): 132-46.

96. *LW* 26:5; *WA* 40/I:42.

97. "[T]hese two words embrace the whole of Christianity. Grace forgives sin, and peace stills the conscience" (*LW* 26:26; *WA* 40/I:72-73).

A Faith Curved Inward

Faith can become fascinated with itself. A faith that attends to itself is a faith curved inward. Luther's image for the sinner perfectly contrasts with the life of the righteous person. The former is curved in on himself; the latter finds her life outside herself, in Christ.

This can happen when, bizarrely, faith prides itself on its great feats, trumpeting its accomplishments. The wide variety of prosperity gospels trades on stories of Herculean faith, calling people to "just have a little more faith" and their (American) dreams will come true. Such faith demands; it doesn't receive. It tells God how it is, rather than listening to the Shepherd's voice.

For one example, consider a common occurrence—the evangelical altar call. A significant portion—perhaps up to half—of the time in an altar call is dedicated to pleading with sinners to repent and believe the gospel. Compare this with the first speeches in Acts. On the day of Pentecost, Peter takes as his text the prophecy of the Spirit's outpouring in Joel 2, describes the death and vindication of Jesus by the Father, and then concludes with the announcement that "God has made him both Lord and Christ, this Jesus whom you crucified" (Acts 2:36). The evangelical altar call involves a fatal error of proportion in which we place far more emphasis, and give far more time, to the rhetoric of persuasion. This suggests a lack of confidence in the preached Word to be the Spirit's means of conversion, and it likewise suggests an implicit belief that faith is a human work rather than a divine gift. As Randall Balmer noted, fresh off a tour through the subculture of evangelical America, "Ostensibly at least, modern-day evangelicals still subscribe to the rudiments of Luther's theology, although . . . their theology emphasizes human volition in salvation far more than Luther would have countenanced."[98]

Faith can also worry about itself. It can turn the joyful call to trust in Christ into a legal demand for action. In these moments, faith grows introspective, and this reflexivity throws it into despair: Have I believed enough? Did I really mean it? While faith does work, evangelicals do well to join Luther's consistent call to locate our lives outside ourselves in Christ, and thus to meet the law's insidious questions about the adequacy of our faith with the gospel's insistence on the adequacy of Christ's faithfulness.[99]

> But if Christ is put aside and I look only at myself, then I am done for. . . . By paying attention to myself and considering what my condition is or should be, and what I am supposed to be doing, I lose sight of Christ, who alone is my Righteousness and Life . . .'[100]

Luther helps re-center faith as trust in the alien promise of God. Luther's *pro me* is exactly right, but evangelicals often lose the center of its gravity in the *Christ* who is *pro me*. The interest of evangelicals should be in the One believed, not the one who believes. Rather than being distracted by either the thrill of faith's victories or the agonies of its defeats, evangelicals do well to stress "the life-altering glories of Jesus Christ, rather than the whims of private eurekas."[101] Luther picks up on an image from Israel's wilderness wandering that Christ applied to himself to make his point:

> The Jews, who were being bitten by the fiery serpents, were commanded by Moses to do nothing but look at that bronze serpent with a fixed gaze. Those who did so were healed merely by their fixed gaze at the serpent. But the others, who did not listen to Moses, looked at their wounds rather than at the serpent and died. Thus if I am to gain comfort in a struggle of conscience or in the agony of death, I must take hold of nothing except Christ alone by faith, and I must say: "I believe

98. Randall Balmer, *Mine Eyes Have Seen the Glory: A Journey into the Evangelical Subculture in America* (New York: Oxford University Press, 1989), x.
99. Even Luther on occasion fell into locating assurance in the believing subject, albeit derivatively. See *LW* 26:379; *WA* 40/I:578.
100. *LW* 26:166; *WA* 40/I:282.
101. Noll, *Jesus Christ and the Life of the Mind*, 167.

in Jesus Christ, the Son of God, who suffered, was crucified, and died
for me. In His wounds and death I see my sin; and in His resurrection I
see victory over sin, death, and the devil, and my righteousness and life.
I neither hear nor see anything but Him. . . ." Therefore in Him we live
and move and have our being (Acts 17:28).[102]

***

Luther offers a vision of faith as the church's embattled, but
conquering, repose in the faithfulness of Christ, whose living, dying,
and rising are for us and our salvation. If evangelicals have admirably
appealed to the sufficiency, even simplicity, of faith in Jesus, we have
too often failed to notice the subtle, insidious migration of emphasis
from the trusted object of faith to faith's believing subject. This
makes faith a work and finds us back in Egypt, seeking to justify
ourselves, ironically, on the basis of our own merits. Coupled with
this migration is our paradoxical neglect of the Word in which Christ
clothes himself and offers himself to us—a neglect whose paradox lies
in the ubiquity of a Bible that we leave to gather dust.

It need not be so. I remember standing with tens of thousands
of men at Folsom Field at the University of Colorado in 1993. The
PromiseKeepers men's movement had gathered momentum, calling
Christian men to repentance, reconciliation, and responsibility as
men of God. Rev. E. V. Hill, pastor of Mt. Zion Missionary Baptist
Church in Los Angeles, preached a sermon on "How to Make the
Enemy Run," brandishing his Bible and reaching a crescendo as he
recounted Jesus' temptation and defeat of Satan in the wilderness:

Jesus said, "Devil, it is written! It is written!" That's what he said. . . .
And every time the devil opened his mouth, Jesus threw Scripture in
his mouth! . . . He hit 'im, over and over and over, with the Scripture.
And guess what happened? The devil raaannn! And guess what you can
do, beginning tonight? You don't have to take it. . . . Hit 'im! "It is

102. *LW* 26:357; *WA* 40/I:546.

written!" When the devil comes up and says, "How do you know you've been saved? You're not saved!" "Yes, I *am* saved!" Hit 'im! "If thou shalt confess with thy mouth the Lord Jesus, and believe in thine heart, that God hath raised him from the dead, thou shalt be saved!" Hit 'im! Hit 'im! Hit 'im! "Whosoever shall call upon the name of the Lord shall be saved!" Hit 'im! "There is therefore now no condemnation to them that are in Christ Jesus." Hit 'im! . . . All you have to do is take out your Bible and say, "Where are you, devil? Come on, devil! Let's get it on! Let's get it on!" Hit 'im! Hit 'im! Hit 'im! "Let's get it on!" He's defeated! Our Lord is King of Kings and Lord of Lords. Hit that devil with the Word! Hit 'im! Hit 'im! Hit 'im![103]

The emboldened, exultant crowd took up the chant, filling the stadium with shouts of "Hit 'im!" And Rev. Hill walked off the stage, a fit witness to Luther's trust in the Word of God in the face of the devil.

---

103. It is far better to listen to Hill's words than read them. See https://www.youtube.com/watch?v=5YDSgZ5c3iw.

8

———

Is Faith Really a Gift? A Response to David Tracy and Matt Jenson

Ted Peters

It is a scholar's delight to read and respond to two such fine treatments of the "Ecumenical Luther," one by my beloved *Doktorvater*, David Tracy, and the other by an insightful disciple and critic of American Evangelicalism, Matt Jenson. It is my plan here to reiterate briefly the distinctive ways these two scholars find Martin Luther to be ecumenical; and, then, I will turn to an ecumenical or philosophical issue and ask: is justifying faith really a gift? Our theological question will be: does the gift of grace come with strings attached? If so, do the strings disqualify it as a gift?

David Tracy's "Martin Luther's *Deus Theolgicus*" provides a marvelously comprehensive and penetrating review of Luther's understanding of the gracious God who is both revealed and hidden. On the one hand, Luther's reliance on a theology of the cross leads to a God revealed yet still mysterious, revealed under the opposite (*sub contrario*) and even under a contradictory opposite (*sub contradictario*). The theology of the cross nullifies knowledge of any deity gained at the conclusion of a rational argument. Here revelation and faith are pitted against reason. Yet, on the other hand, when by heartfelt faith (*fides cordis*) we become grounded in the hidden God, reason as faith-seeking-further-understanding is unleashed anew. "Faith also paradoxically redeems reason for newly illuminated theological use," observes Tracy.

> This much is clear: Luther is undoubtedly original in his model for *Deus theologicus*, i.e., in his unique and epoch-making description of the two forms of God's Hiddenness. By that double move, Luther does interrupt and, to a certain extent, disrupt the earlier traditions on adequate God-language by his singular—and, in my judgment, persuasive—concept of the double Hiddenness of God both in and beyond revelation. At the same time, Luther's logically developed Trinitarian theology is not discontinuous at all with classical Trinitarian theology.[1]

In sum, the ecumenical Luther both innovates and recalibrates the Latin tradition regarding our knowledge of God.

In Matt Jenson's paper, "Much Ado about Nothing: The Necessary Non-Sufficiency of Faith," he lifts up three weaknesses in American Evangelicalism: (1) easy-believism; (2) faith without distinctions; and (3) faith curved inward. Within this framework, Jenson reminds us how "Luther stresses that faith is a divine gift mediated through the Word. Faith is not a human accomplishment, something to be mustered; it is given to us by God as he nourishes us on his Word throughout our lives."[2] Faith is a gift; but for a gift to be a gift it must

---

1. Tracy, 137-38.

be received, opened, and used. With our reception of God's gift in mind, Jenson appeals to the rigor of Luther's more athletic analysis of faith and prescribes exercises to strengthen Evangelical faith. I would like to extend this analysis of faith: from faith "curved inward" to "faith active in love" (Gal. 5:6).

Tracy, too, recognizes in Luther's treatment of faith its gift character: "Grace though faith is both God's *favor* through the righteousness of Christ imputed to us as forgiveness and *donum* (pure gift, i.e., passive incipient righteousness, which, through the Holy Spirit can increase until the ultimate *donum* of our graced glory after this life). The righteousness we receive is Christ's own active righteousness which endows upon us passive righteousness." If the retired Pope Benedict XVI would join our conversation, he might say that we Christians have come to know "the astonishing experience of gift."[3]

What is that gift? According to Luther, our justification and hence our salvation are gifts we receive from a gracious God in faith; they are not the product of human efforts, works, merits, or achievements. To stress that faith and the salvation that comes with faith are gifts from a gracious God is much more than a distinctively Lutheran insight; it is a shared ecumenical treasure.

In what comes next, I would like to shift our agenda slightly away from the ecumenical Luther toward the ecumenic Luther. By the commonly employed term *ecumenical,* I along with most scholars refer to the healthy attachment all Christian members share with the one Body of Christ. Like heads and hearts and hands, Christian members should work with one another for the good health of the entire body.

---

2. Jenson, 155.
3. Pope Benedict XVI, *Caritas in Veritate* (2009), 34; http://www.vatican.va/holy_father/benedict_xvi/encyclicals/documents/hf_ben-xvi_enc_20090629_caritas-in-veritate_en.html.

But, each of our bodies lives in a context, a neighborhood. So also does the One, Holy, Catholic, and Apostolic Body of Christ live in a broader cultural context. Borrowing from philosopher Eric Voegelin, I refer to the broader world context as the *ecumené* or, adjectively, *ecumenic*.[4] The ecumenic task of the theologian is to engage critically with disciplines outside the ecclesial domain such as philosophy, non-Christian religions, culture, and the natural sciences. In order to deal with the concept of the gift theologically, I would like to pause and review what is being said these days about the concept of gift phenomenologically. Might an ecumenic Luther result?

Is a Gift really a Gift?

Because gifts commonly come with strings attached, many who analyze gifting phenomenologically conclude that no gift is free. Every gift requires reciprocity, response, indirect payment. We will look at the gift as phenomenon in a moment. But, first, let's remind ourselves of what Luther thinks about the gift of grace in faith. Our theological question will be: does the gift of grace come with strings attached? If so, do the strings disqualify it as a gift?

The work of British evangelical Alister E. McGrath illustrates the problem. He writes, "The *gift* of justification lays upon us the *obligation* to live in accordance with our new status."[5] If he would be a German, he might say the gift (*Gabe*) comes with a duty (*Aufgabe*). What McGrath fails to recognize is that Luther and his disciples would not want to say such a thing, because they believe that the gift of justification is just that, a gift, and not an obligation. Yet, we ask: can the Lutherans get away with this? If the concept of grace (*gratia*)

---

4. Eric Voegelin, *Order and History*, 5 vols. (Baton Rouge, LA: Louisiana State University Press, 1956-1987), Volume V: *The Ecumenic Age.*

5. Alister E. McGrath, *Justification by Faith: What It Means To Us Today* (Grand Rapids MI: Zondervan, 1988), 117.

refers to God's disposition of mercy toward us, and if the concept of gift (*donum*) refers to what is given to us, we must ask: are there any strings attached? Conditions? Obligations? If the gift comes with obligations, as McGrath thinks, does this make it a conditional gift and, thereby, a non-gift?

As background, we note how Luther seems to distinguish grace from gift. "Grace must be sharply distinguished from gifts," he writes. "A righteous and faithful man doubtless has both grace and the gift . . . but the gift heals from sin and from all his corruption of body and soul . . . Everything is forgiven through grace, but as yet not everything is healed through the gift . . . for with the gift there is sin which it purges away and overcomes." Because God's justification declares a person just while still in a state of sin, the person of faith begins the arduous process of overcoming that sin. The sin prior to and following justification is the same, argues Luther; but our status before God is different. Prior to justification sin warrants wrath, condemnation, death. Subsequent to justification, sin is not counted, so to speak. While we strive to purge sin from our daily life, "it is called sin, and is truly such in its nature; but now it is sin without wrath, without the law, dead sin, harmless sin, as long as one perseveres in grace and gift."[6] Note how this applies "as long as one perseveres in grace and gift."

Elsewhere Luther equates grace and gift. "But 'the grace of God' (*gratia Dei*) and 'the gift' (*donum*) are the same thing, namely, the very

---

6. *Against Latomus* (1521); *LW* 32:229; *WA* 8:107. Gift with response seems to be the structure of grace and reconciliation in the work of Karl Rahner. "For God's salvific action on man is not merely a forensic imputation of the justice of Christ. And it is not merely the announcement of a purely future act of God. Nor is it constituted merely by man's faith, however this is to be further interpreted. It is a true, real, creative action of God in grace, which renews man interiorly by making him participate in the divine nature—all of which, being the condition of possibility of a salutary action on the part of man, is prior, at least logically, to such *action* of man." Karl Rahner, "The Word and the Eucharist," *Theological Investigations* (New York: Crossroad, 1973), 4:257. Is the renewal a human response to the divine gift or is it the gift itself?

righteousness (*iustitia*) which is freely given to us through Christ."[7] In our justification, grace and gift are the same thing, he says. It appears that Luther is not consistent on his use of terms.

Whether grace and gift are identical or different is not an issue that bothers contemporary theologians. What has become an issue, however, is the question: does the gift of grace come with strings attached? Does it necessarily imply reciprocity? Does the declaration of forgiveness in justification-by-faith necessarily imply effective transformation in the sinner? Does justification require sanctification before reconciliation?

I recommend that we use the term *grace* to refer to the divine disposition to give. "Grace is the favor, mercy, and gratuitous goodwill of God toward us,"[8] says Philip Melanchthon, suggesting that *grace* belongs to the divine disposition. With this in mind, I recommend that we use the term *gift* to refer to what God gives and we receive. I further recommend that we use the term *agape* to refer to gracious love—that is, love that asks for nothing reciprocal in return. These belong together, as Tracy suggests when writing, "Grace, therefore, is that gift; it is most clearly experienced in what Christians name radical faith, authentic hope, and agapic love."[9] Our theological question will be: does the gift of grace come with strings attached? If so, do the strings disqualify it as a gift?[10]

---

7. *Lectures on Romans* (1515–16); *LW* 25:306; *WA* 56:318.

8. Philip Melanchthon, *Loci Communes* (1521); in *Melanchthon and Bucer*, ed. Wilhelm Pauck, Library of Christian Classics, vol. 19 (Philadelphia: Westminster, 1969), 88. "The fundamental meaning of grace is the goodness and loving kindness of God and the activity of this goodness in and toward his creation." Joseph Sittler, *Essays on Nature and Grace* (Minneapolis: Fortress Press, 1972), 24.

9. David Tracy, *On Naming the Present: God, Hermeneutics, and Church* (Maryknoll, NY and London, England: Orbis and SCM Press, 1994), 101.

10. Tracy employs the term "pure gift" when he writes, "We know the experience of pure gift by the word 'grace'." *On Naming the Present*, 101.

Altruism and Reciprocity

"In all societies gifts have reciprocal character," Sammeli Juntunen asserts.[11] There is no free lunch. Anthropologists make it clear that reciprocity hangs on to gifts like barnacles to a ship's hull.

The strings attached to a gift may be invisible, at least at first. Hospitality is a form of gift-giving with threads so fine they are invisible, until you bring them into focus under the philosopher's magnifying glass. This leads theologian Risto Saarinen to aver, "there is no free gift. If somebody offers you a gift, this person is increasing his or her social status and putting you in his or her debt. It belongs to the idea of gift that this is not said but, on the contrary, explicitly denied."[12] This turns a gift into a lie. When we give, we deny that strings are attached; yet, our reputation in the eyes of the recipient is enhanced not only by the gift itself but also by our denial of the strings attached. If we are the recipients, we contribute to the self-justification and delusion of magnanimity on the part of the gift-giver.

The phenomenology of gift-giving introduces a dilemma or aporia. The dilemma has been pointed out by philosophers such as Jacques Derrida. The dilemma looks like this: If I give you a gift, then I look good and put you in my debt. But if this is to be a genuine gift, there must be no reciprocity, return, exchange, counter-gift, or

11. Sammeli Juntunen, "The Notion of Gift (*donum*) in Luther's Thinking," in Luther *Between Present and Past: Studies in Luther and Lutheranism*, ed. Ulrik Nissen et al. (Helsinki: Luther-Agricola-Society, 2004), 55. Socio-biologists employ the concept of *reciprocal altruism* in their attempt to explain inclusive fitness in evolution. Gifting is, by definition, reciprocal even when we pretend that it is not. The giver gains through an enhanced reputation, which Harvard's E. O. Wilson calls "indirect reciprocity, by which a reputation for altruism and cooperativeness accrues to an individual, even if the actions that build it are no more than ordinary. A saying in German exemplifies the tactic: *Tue Gutes und rede darüber*. Do good and talk about it. Doors are then opened, and opportunities for friendships and alliances increased." *The Social Conquest of Earth* (New York: W.W. Norton, 2012), 249.

12. Risto Saarinen, *God and the Gift: An Ecumenical Theology of Giving* (Collegeville, MN: Liturgical Press, 2005), 18.

debt.[13] The concept of the gift implies that you return nothing to me. Yet, in giving you the gift, my social standing increases; and you are required to respond with gratitude. The mere recognition of the gift by the receiver nullifies the gift as gift. Within the economy of exchange, the very condition that makes gift-giving what it is includes strings even while, by definition, it denies the strings.

Now we must ask: does this observation regarding gift-giving in the economy of exchange apply to the gift given us in the gospel? No, says German theologian Oswald Bayer. "God's coming into the world and his existence in it is *contrary* to human experience and corresponding expectations" for reciprocity.[14] No strings attached.

Contra Bayer, Danish theologian Bo Holm sees strings when he interprets Luther's understanding of the gospel through an economic lens. What is the economy of justification? It requires a component of reciprocity, mutuality, exchange. In response to God's love, we love. We participate. "Justification is the opening of reciprocity, making realized reciprocity itself the gift of grace."[15] Grace stimulates. We respond. Holm likes the sentence that connotes economic reciprocity: "*Deus dat ut dem, et do ut des* (God gives that I may give, and I give that you may give)."[16]

However, if we look through the lens of new creation rather than today's economy, gift looks different. The indwelling Christ is God's gift to us; and this amounts to a creation, a new creation. It is Christ from within the new creature who motivates our life of loving service. Luther likens the justified person to a tree that sprouts

13. Jacques Derrida, *Given Time 1. Counterfeit Money* (Chicago: University of Chicago Press, 1995); cited by Saarinen, *God and the Gift*, 24.

14. Oswald Bayer, "Gift: Systematic Theology," in *Religion Past and Present*, ed. Hans Dieter Betz et al. [English translation of *Religion in Geschichte und Gegenwart*, 4th ed.], 14 vol. (Leiden and Boston: Brill, 2007-2014), 5:431.

15. Bo Holm, "Luther's Theology of the Gift," Niels Henrik Gregersen et al. (eds.), *The Gift of Grace: The Future of Lutheran Theology* (Minneapolis: Fortress Press, 2005), 85.

16. Holm, "Luther's "Theology of the Gift," 86.

leaves. Is the tree obligated to sprout leaves? No. Sprouting leaves is natural to the tree. Similarly, Luther likens the justified person to the sun. Do we have to demand that the sun shine? No. The sun shines spontaneously. So also does the person of faith who has been given the living Christ spontaneously love the neighbor. In sum, this particular gift does not involve a reciprocal or obligatory character. This leads Juntunen to conclude: "I think that the idea of the *donum* being comparable to creation makes it clear that all reciprocity between the giver and the receiver is excluded."[17]

Even without strings, argues Finnish scholar Simo Peura, the indwelling Christ leads to transformation, to effective justification, and even to deification (*theosis*). Peura believes that Luther in his notion of faith includes "participation, change, and deification. The aim of justification is actually a complete transformation in Christ."[18] This transformation follows from the real presence of Christ in faith. "Luther's understanding that God the Father is favorable to a sinner (*favor Dei*) and that Christ renews a sinner (*donum Dei*) is based on the idea of a *unio cum Christo*. This same idea explains why grace and gift are necessary to each other. Gift is not only a consequence of grace, as is usually emphasized in Lutheran theology, but it is in a certain sense a condition for grace as well."[19] For Peura, we now have a "condition for grace." Does this condition amount to the completion of the gift-giving, a completion that requires our response, participation, and achievement? Are these the strings?

---

17. Juntunen, "Gift," 61.
18. Peura, "Christ as Favor and Gift," in *Union in Christ: The New Finnish Interpretation of Luther*, ed. Carl E. Braaten and Robert W. Jenson (Grand Rapids, MI: Eerdmans, 1998), 60. The key to the New Finnish School of Luther Research is the real presence of the indwelling Christ. "Faith means the presence of Christ and thus participation in the divine life," writes Tuomo Mannermaa. "Christ 'is in us' and 'remains in us.' The life that the Christian now lives is, in an ontologically real manner, Christ himself." *Christ Present in Faith: Luther's View of Justification*, trans. Kirsi Stjerna (Minneapolis MN: Fortress Press, 2005), 39.
19. Peura, "Christ as Favor and Gift," 56.

Might we compare the gift of grace to a Christmas gift, wrapped in such a way that the contents are hidden? We may shake it, but in itself this shaking will not reveal precisely what the contents are. We must open it. Once it is open and we can identify it, then we will put it on or use it or in some way integrate it into our other possessions. The gift may be a stimulus, but it becomes a gift in the full sense only when we respond. No giver would give an expensive gift without expecting it to be enjoyed through usage. This response does not amount to reciprocity, to be sure; yet the gift giver feels a sense of accomplishment only when the gift is opened, used, and appreciated. Does gift analysis help us understand the gospel?

Existence as Gift

According to Martin Heidegger's analysis of human consciousness, we sort of wake up at some point in our life and realize that we are here. We are here. And your or my being-here is not the result of our own decision or action. We are just here in this time and this place. We are *Dasein*, simply being there, anywhere specific. This being-here has the feel of having been thrown. We feel we have been thrown from non-existence into existence. We live with a sense of thrownness, *Geworfenheit*.[20] Might we think of our basic having-been-thrown-into-existence as a gift? Jean-Luc Marion considers this and remarks: "The gift delivers Being/being."[21]

The way our language works on this matter is informative. In English, we simply say "there is" when identifying something that exists. The same in French, *il y a*. But note what happens in German: *es gibt*. To say, "there is," we literally say, "it gives." Marion

---

20. Martin Heidegger, *Being and Time*, trans. J. Macquarrie and E. Robinson (New York: Harper, 1962).

21. Jean-Luc Marion, *God without Being*, trans. T. A. Carlson (Chicago: University of Chicago Press, 1991), 101.

comments, "No one more than Heidegger allowed the thinking of the coincidence of the gift with Being/being, by taking literally the German *es gibt*, wherein we recognize the French *il y a*, there is . . . we would understand the fact that there should be (of course: being) as this fact that *it gives, ça donne*. Being itself is delivered in the mode of giving."[22] *To be is to be gifted*, say philosophers such as Heidegger and Marion. *To be is to be graced*, say theologians.

Now we ask: who threw us into existence? Who is the giver when we say, *es gibt*? Is our very existence best understood as a gift? And, if so, how can we pay back the giver? We cannot. There is no reciprocity possible. No economy of exchange is at work. The basic gift of our existence is radical, brute, impenetrable.[23] The philosophers seem to stop with givenness. Might there be a giver? Is it too soon to say the giver is God?[24]

Another philosopher of Heidegger's ilk, Eric Voegelin, suggests that we are thrown into existence and then retrieved by the same source. While we exist between birth and death, we experience estrangement. If we give attention to the giftedness of our existence, we become attuned to the being—the ground of being—from which our existence is estranged.

---

22. Marion, *God without Being*, 102.

23. Marion places both feet in the pure givenness or pure giftedness of existence without relying on the being of the giver. Thereby Marion can think of God without being. Critics such as John Milbank want to deny this move to Marion. When you and I recognize the givenness and hence giftedness of our very existence and respond in gratitude, this counts as reciprocity. It implies a divine giver. See John Milbank, *Being Reconciled, Ontology and Pardon* (London: Routledge, 2003), and the discussion by Saarinen, *God and the Gift*, 30-33.

24. What we are looking at here is the phenomenology of human experience which raises the question of transcendence and the question of God. "This realization that one's existence is completely dependent upon factors beyond one's control—factors unified by the mind's instinctive drive toward simplicity, coherence, oneness—issues in the theological concept of God's sovereignty. When it is compounded with gratitude for the goodness of this life which God's sovereignty has effected and is continuously sustaining we have the germ of the concept of grace; God's free and unstinted gifts to man which not only have made his life possible but sustain and enable it at every point along the way." Huston Smith, *Religions of Man* (New York: Harper, 1958), 103.

Attunement, therefore, will be the state of existence when it hearkens to that which is lasting in being, when it maintains a tension of awareness for its partial revelations of the order of society and the world, when it listens attentively to the silent voices of conscience and grace in human existence itself. We are thrown into and out of existence without knowing the Why or the How, but while in it we know that we are of the being to which we return.[25]

As a philosopher, Voegelin uses the word *being* where a theologian might use the word *God.* Heidegger and Voegelin both tell us that if we simply stop for a moment to reflect on our thrownness into existence, we will catch the first glimmer of grace in our creation. In, with, and under our very being-here is grace.

Two of Heidegger's disciples—Lutheran philosopher Knud Løgstrup and Jewish philosopher Emmanuel Lévinas—begin their phenomenological analysis of the human condition by looking at the givenness of the basic human situation. According to Løgstrup, "life has been given to us. We have not ourselves created it." When we wake up to realize that we have been given a life which we did not create, we further realize that we are not alone. Someone who is other is present. We find ourselves already in relationship with other persons, persons whom we trust and to whom we owe moral responsibility. The other person is other; and our relationship is already characterized as love for the other. "Man's relationship with the other is *better* as difference than as unity: sociality is better than fusion," writes Lévinas; "The very value of love is the impossibility of reducing the other to myself." In sum, what we have been given is existence, and this is personal existence-in-relationship-to-the-other. This relational existing is basic, fundamental. It is the givenness with which we begin to understand ourselves as individuals.[26] The gift of

---

25. Eric Voegelin, *Order and History,* Volume I: *Israel and Revelation,* 5.
26. See citations and discussion of Løgstrup and Lévinas on gift in Hans S. Reinders, "Donum or Datum? K. E. Løgstrup's Religious Account of the Gift of Life," in *Concern for the Other:*

existence has an obligation to love the other—the neighbor—built into it.

Is identifying our given state of existence sufficient? Not for Luther. Luther would not stop here. He would go on to identify the giver, God, and prompt within us a sense of gratitude for God's gracious gifts. He opens his commentary on the creed in the *Small Catechism* with the lines, "I believe that God has created me together with all that exists. God has given me and still preserves my body and soul: eyes, ears, and all limbs and senses; reason and all mental faculties . . . And all this is done out of pure, fatherly, and divine goodness and mercy, without any merit or worthiness of mine at all! For all this I owe it to God to thank and praise, serve and obey him. This is most certainly true."[27]

What Luther says here deserves special attention. The first thing to note is the priority of you and me as individual persons over the universe and everything that exists. Your and my subjective identity and awareness come first; then everything else that objectively exists. God is personal. Our self or our soul provides the point of orientation from which we look out upon the world.

Second, God's grace in creation comes with strings attached. On the one hand, we are not responsible for our existence. We have been placed here by "divine goodness and mercy, without any merit or worthiness" of our own. On the other hand, we "owe (*schuldig sind*) it to God to thank and praise, serve and obey him." We are obligated to show gratitude for the gift of existence. Whether we show gratitude or not does not change the fact that God is gracious, that God is merciful and good. But, we ask: is it necessary for us to

Perspectives on the Ethics of K. E. Løgstrup, ed. Svend Andersen and Kees van Kooten Niekerk (Notre Dame, IN: University of Notre Dame Press, 2007), 177-206.
27. Martin Luther, *The Small Catechism* (1529); *BC* 354-55.

show gratitude to God if our existence is to be a gift? Is this reciprocal response necessary for this basic gift actually to be a gift?

The reformers left us with an unresolved problem. On the one hand, they stressed that the gifts of God's grace are utterly independent of any merit or worthiness on our part. On the other hand, God's gifts are concrete and specific to us in our daily lives. This specificity implies participation, transformation, and soul-formation. This participation implies a response on our part, an active living out of the gift. Does this amount to merit or worthiness after the fact?

Justifying Faith, Loving Neighbors, and Sinning Boldly

Is justifying faith the same as the gift of being-here? Is the anonymous *es gibt* the model for the divine gift of justification? Are all people of all times and all places automatically justified because of some eternal divine decree? Does justification come automatically with creation?

Not according to Saarinen. Justifying faith is personal, he contends. For any gift to be given there must be a receiver; and the receiver is a participant in the gift-giving interaction. This applies especially to the gifts of God's grace in faith. "Faith does not signalize a cooperative act, but a personal participation in the reciprocity of giving and receiving. A gift cannot be given if the receiver is not there." Saarinen teases out the implications for the means of grace, the sacraments. "At least four requirements can be read from the Lutheran Confessions: (1) that the recipient is alive, (2) is faithful, (3) is a person and (4) is not just anybody, a placeholder or a representative of a larger group, but the very person to whom the sacrament is physically given."[28] Or, to say it another way, reception makes it possible for giving to result in a gift.

Does the very fact that a receiver is present for the gift to be a gift entail reciprocity? Not precisely. At least no reciprocity is required according to the economy of exchange where we would be obligated to pay God back for his gracious gifts. Our gratitude does not accrue directly to God's advantage; rather, our gratitude comes to expression as our love for our neighbor.

This is the point where Saarinen, following Luther, develops the notion of *agape* love in the Christian life. "In Luther's account, Christians are called to imitate the divine love in such a manner that they fulfill the needs and wants of others."[29] *Agape* attends to the needs of the needy, not to your or my needs as the lover of the needy. "A pure love would require a person who is not seeking his own profit but would act altruistically. Giving a completely free gift would be an example of pure love and altruism."[30] Now, to be frank, I need to ask: is it possible that *agape* love defined this way is possible in the human economy of exchange?

The answer is "no" for two reasons. The first is the philosophical reason adumbrated above, namely, all gift-giving in the economy of exchange is a disguised form of reciprocity. There are no gifts without strings attached. Would this apply to a gift God gives us? Let's work with the hypothetical "yes" answer to this to see where it might lead.

The second reason has to do with theological anthropology. According to the Augustinian tradition on human nature—the tradition to which Luther belongs—the human ego cannot in this life be de-centered. Everything that we do—whether we are baptized

---

28. Saarinen, *God and the Gift*, 11.
29. Ibid., 56.
30. Ibid., 52.

or unbaptized—is an expression of the ego for the sake of the ego. There can be no human action which is totally selfless or ego-free. Every one of our attempts to love our neighbor with *agape* love is compromised if not contaminated with a self-serving motive. Even the pursuit of a transformed soul would betray a self-serving motive, thereby disqualifying what action we take as pure *agape*. In sum, pure *agape* is impossible for us.

"Luther shares this skepticism with regard to pure love and genuine altruism. For Luther, human reason is inevitably egoistic and thus incapable of pure giving," comments Saarinen; "Luther is always and tirelessly making the point that all human efforts to do good and to live a good life are contaminated by egoism."[31] If this skepticism obtains, then why ask us to respond to God's grace by graciously loving others? Are we being asked to do the impossible?

Adumbrating all of these strings makes me feel like I've just dumped a bowl of spaghetti over the life of the faithful Christian. To try to unravel it all in order to find a single pure strand of pure self-sacrificial love would be both tedious and unnecessary. Plunge ahead, Luther would say. Sin boldly! Don't let the spiritual spaghetti tie us up and restrict our bold attempts at loving our neighbor.

Resolution: This Is a Pseudo-Problem

It appears that we have a philosophical problem, a dilemma or *aporia*. If we define a gift as what is given without any strings attached, then, in the ordinary economy of human exchange, no pure gift-giving can practically exist. Every gift implies a gain given to the gift-giver, a gain due to the obligation of the receiver to offer thanks and to define the gift-giver as someone who is a gift-giver. To be defined as a gift-giver is to be noble, generous, and good. In short, the act

31. Ibid., 52.

of gift-giving including its reciprocal response serves the function of self-aggrandizement for the gift-giver. If this obtains, God looks less than fully gracious, because God's gift giving becomes an expression of divine narcissism. In addition, the command for us to love God and love our neighbor with *agape* love—to give to God and give to neighbor—becomes a fiction, an incongruent demand. In daily life, loving and gift-giving without strings attached simply does not take place, at least in pure form.

Now, let me suggest the following: this is not a real problem. It is a pseudo-problem. The difficulty arises from the fallacy of misplaced concreteness, to use the term of Alfred North Whitehead.[32] Tracy offers a variant: "though life is reflected upon through general ideas, it is always lived in the details."[33] There is a confusion at work among the philosophers of gift, a confusion between what is abstract and what is concrete, between what is general and what belongs to details. Or, to put it another way, the apparent impossibility of pure reciprocity-less gifting along with pure selfless loving confuses an abstract generality with the concrete details of our daily life. It confuses the dog with the tail.

Recall how I suggested we define our terms: *grace* should refer to the divine disposition to give; *gift* should refer to what God gives and we receive; and *agape* should refer to gracious love. Each of these is an ideal definition, an abstraction, a general idea, a concept. None of these describes with precision what actually happens in your or my daily life. Nor does any of these describe with precision what actually happens in God's relationship to us. We need to begin with what actually happens—*the concrete*—and then reflect theologically—*the*

32. Alfred North Whitehead, *Process and Reality, Corrected Edition,* ed. D. R. Griffin and D. W. Sherburne (New York: Macmillan, Free Press, 1929, 1978), 7.
33. David Tracy, *Plurality and Ambiguity: Hermeneutics, Religion, Hope* (New York: Harper, 1987), 70.

abstract—on what happens. What happens is the dog; and our reflective waggings represent the tail. The tail should point us to the dog, not the reverse.

The dog in this case is the event of Jesus Christ. What does this event mean? It means that God has entered the created order, become present in our souls, forgiven us our sins, justified us by grace; and we have begun to live with faith, hope, and love. An interaction has taken place in the history of the world and in the biography of our individual lives. That's the dog, the concrete dog.

The dog's wagging tail consists of our attempt to understand the dog abstractly by proffering theological ideas and religious descriptions about what the dog means. Theological reflection is second-order discourse, one step removed from concrete experience.[34] Our theological attempt to define terms such as *grace, gift,* and *agape* is tail-wagging. Let's avoid confusing the tail with the dog, confusing the abstract descriptions from the concrete reality toward which they point.

God's interaction with the world and with our individual souls is messy. It's not neat. It's ambiguous. On the one hand, God comes with grace and beauty and glory. God comes in light. On the other hand, the world greets God with selfishness and ugliness and tragedy. The world's darkness snuffs out the light. Where we find ourselves is at the point of collision, experiencing two realities at once. To posit pure concepts such as grace, gift, or *agape* is to posit abstractions, to imagine ideals that simply do not exist in pure form in our everyday world. Such purities do not exist either for us or for God.

Part of the mission of St. Paul's letters to the Romans and Galatians was to persuade us that our justification is the result of God's grace

---

34. "Theology is not the same as faith or belief, but a disciplined and relational reflection upon them." Catherine Keller, *On the Mystery: Discerning God in Process* (Minneapolis: Fortress, 2008), 17.

and not of our works. The Reformation took up the same mission, reiterating that we are saved by God's grace and not by any merit on our part. So far, so good. Once this point has been made, what does it add to speak of a divine gift that is so pure that it avoids contamination by reciprocity? What does it add to speak of *agape* love that is so pure that no ego or self is involved? Speaking this way only *adds abstractions that may become distractions.* We live everyday responding to God's love with our own love; and this takes place in a world already messy with ambiguity. This observation led Luther to throw in the towel on the purity question and simply tell us to "sin boldly."

God as Both Giver and Gift

In order to stress the graciousness of God, Luther generously slathered the concept of gift over many theological expositions. Take the Trinity, for example, which Tracy raises in his essay. The three persons of the Trinity give themselves to one another, making each of them both a giver and a gift within the divine life (*ad intra*). In turn, each person gives to us, making the divine both giver and gift for us (*ad extra*). "The Father gives himself to us," writes Luther. "But," he adds, "this gift has become obscured and useless through Adam's fall. Therefore the Son himself subsequently gave himself." It does not end there. "The Holy Spirit comes and gives himself to us also, wholly and completely."[35] Saarinen comments that this amounts to a specifically Lutheran emphasis: "the trinitarian creed is rewritten from the perspective of God's self-giving."[36]

In parallel fashion, the Mass or the Sacrament of the Altar must be understood as a divine gift to us and for us. The reformers rejected the

---

35. *Confession Concerning Christ's Supper* (1528); *LW*, 37:366; *WA* 26:505-6.
36. Saarinen, *God and the Gift*, 46.

idea that on the church's altar a sacrifice is performed that propitiates God's wrath and renders satisfaction on our behalf. The priest at the altar cannot offer a sacrifice as a gift to God, because Christ's death on the cross has put an end to all human sacrifices. Rather, it is God who renders satisfaction in Christ and offers the benefits to us. "For the passion of Christ was an offering and satisfaction not only for original guilt but for all other remaining sins," we find in the *Augsburg Confession*. "Likewise, Scripture teaches that we are justified before God through faith in Christ. . . . The Mass, therefore, was instituted so that the faith of those who use the sacrament should recall what benefits are received through Christ. . . . For to remember Christ is to remember his benefits and realize that they are truly offered to us."[37] Every leak in the bottom of the spiritual boat is plugged by reference to God's self-giving and our receiving.

When it comes to justification-by-faith, we must avoid seeing faith as an efficacious product of human achievement. I weep when I read Matt Jenson: "many evangelicals begin with the gospel only to settle into a toilsome life under the law."[38] Jenson's description is accurate. The tragedy is that where the gift of faith should liberate, for "many evangelicals" it incarcerates.

For the gospel to liberate we must see faith as a gift. Or, perhaps better said, our faith is our act of unwrapping the gift that the Holy Spirit gives, namely, the presence of Christ. The indwelling Christ is due to both the giving of Christ and Christ as gift. "Through receiving Christ by faith, we have union with Christ. The gift is given for us, but also to us," as Saarinen says.[39]

In sum, the generous use of the language and conceptuality of gift becomes one of the ways we emphasize the priority of God's grace

---

37. *Augsburg Confession*, XXIV; *BC* 71.
38. Jenson, 163.
39. Saarinen, *God and the Gift*, 51.

in our creation, redemption, and daily lives.[40] There is no pill we need to take to relieve the intellectual constipation brought on by the philosophical debate over the nature of gift. Our employment of gift language is an attempt to explicate the significance of the gospel message; we are not trying to shape the gospel to fit a predetermined concept of gift.

Inadvertent Passivity

"Works of love are entirely necessary, just not necessary for justification," writes American evangelical Jenson.[41] Works of love connote a "faith *active* in love." Yet, German evangelical Oswald Bayer stresses passivity, not activity. "When I hear the gospel, that I have been accepted and adopted by God for the sake of Jesus Christ in the Holy Spirit,," exclaims Bayer, "I am radically passive. I receive that which is given to me as a 'categorical gift'."[42]

Lutherans celebrate our passivity. But, is this a good idea? If we overstress the idea of gift to the extent that we inculcate a sense of passivity in the person of faith, we may distort the life of faith. The life of faith is not passive. It is active. The Holy Spirit empowers us to be ourselves, to become ourselves. "The fruit of the Spirit is love, joy, peace, patience, kindness, generosity, faithfulness, gentleness, and self-control" (Gal. 5:22-23). The Holy Spirit forms our soul. If the gift of Christ's presence is a seed, then this seed comes to harvest in our life with these fruits. We would not want the passivity concomitant to the giftedness of justification-by-grace to obviate this spiritual activity.

Overstressing giftedness can blunt a healthy sense of self-worth

---

40. "Grace is the Christian theological word for describing the event, happening, gift of God's self-communication in creation and redemption." Tracy, *On Naming the Present*, 100.
41. Jenson, 160.
42. Oswald Bayer, "With Luther in the Present," *Lutheran Quarterly*, 21:1 (Spring 2007): 11.

and destroy our initiative to pursue social justice. The standard critique for centuries of the Lutheran branch of the Reformation is that the overemphasis on unilateral divine grace has led to quietism, to unresponsiveness in the face of social injustice. In recent times, feminists have criticized the larger atonement tradition for its lack of support for women who, in the face of sexism, need to stand up for their rights. "Jesus' vicarious suffering becomes critiqued as an appropriate theological or anthropological model since it could disable one's own ability or confidence to stand up to oppression," comments Marit Trelstad.[43] If a divine gift disables rather than enables us, we have made a mistake in interpreting it.

Conclusion

Both David Tracy and Matt Jenson are well aware that Martin Luther and his followers emphasize that our justification and hence our salvation is a gift from God, a gift from a gracious God. To tease out what this could mean, we have explored philosophical discussions which take into account the phenomenology of gift giving. For the most part, phenomenologists find that no pure gift giving exists in the human economy because gift givers commonly receive an indirect return in the form of enhanced reputation and even adulation. In addition, for a gift to be a gift it must be received—that is, some level of the recipient's participation in the phenomenon of the gift belongs to the very definition of gift.

---

43. Marit Trelstad, "Introduction," in *Cross Examinations: Readings on the Meaning of the Cross Today* ed. Marit Trelstad (Minneapolis: Augsburg, 2007), 7. Rather than set deification of the believer as the end or goal, most Lutherans see the transformative power of God's grace resulting in ethics and neighbor-love. Lutheran ethicist Cynthia Moe-Lobeda is characteristic. "The centerpiece of Christian moral agency is the crucified and living Christ dwelling in and gradually transforming the community of believers, the form of Jesus Christ taking form in and among those with faith. Christians as objects of Christ's love become subjects of that love. . . . The indwelling Christ, mediated by practices of the Christian community transforms the faithful toward a manner of life that actively loves neighbor." *Healing a Broken World: Globalization and God* (Minneapolis: Fortress Press, 2002), 74.

With this in mind, it would not be prudent for a theologian to overstress the pureness of the divine gift. Nor is it necessary. The actual interaction between our gracious God and our estranged humanity is an ambiguous one, not a pure one. The history of salvation includes the death of Jesus on the cross, an enigmatic yet revelatory moment wherein we see our gracious God at work in, with, and under the darkness of suffering. To talk about a "pure gift" is to postulate an abstraction from the concrete history of grace.

Still, gift language helps us explicate the meaning of our fundamental biblical symbols such as the cross or Pauline affirmations of justification-by-faith. But the latter are not slaves to gift language. The concept of gift illuminates God's gracious action; but divine action comes first and our theological reflection in light of the concept of gift comes second. What we can expect from the gift of the Holy Spirit placing the living Christ in our souls is power, excitement, transformation, and vigorous activity on behalf of loving our neighbor.

9

"Return to Your Baptism Daily": Baptism and Christian Life

Susan K. Wood

The fundamental principle of receptive ecumenism is that each tradition focuses on the question: "What can *we* learn, or *receive*, with integrity from *our* various others in order to facilitate our own growth together into deepened communion in Christ and the Spirit?"[1] Receptive ecumenism calls dialogue partners to receive gifts from each other. As Paul Murray expresses it, receptive ecumenism is based on the conviction that the life of faith "is always in essence a matter of becoming more fully, more richly, what we already are;

---

1. Paul D. Murray, "Preface," in *Receptive Ecumenism and the Call to Catholic Learning: Exploring a Way for Contemporary Ecumenism*, ed. Paul D. Murray (New York: Oxford University Press, 2008), ix-x.

what we have been called to be and are destined to be and in which we already share, albeit in part."[2] In what seems to be a paradox, this means that Catholics may deepen their Catholic identity, and Lutherans their Lutheran identity, by looking to their dialogue partner for elements preserved in the other tradition that they may also authentically claim as their own. This essay explores how Catholics can be more truly Catholic by appropriating more fully several aspects of Luther's baptismal theology.

Luther had little quarrel with baptism as practiced in the Roman Catholic Church. In *The Babylonian Captivity of the Church* (1520), he comments,

> Blessed be God and the Father of our Lord Jesus Christ, who according to the riches of his mercy [Eph. 1:3, 7] has preserved in his church this sacrament at least, untouched and untainted by the ordinances of men, and has made it free to all nations and classes of mankind, and has not permitted it to be oppressed by the filthy and godless monsters of greed and superstition.[3]

Catholics, however, were not so sanguine about Luther's theology of baptism. The seventh session of the Council of Trent in its "Decree Concerning the Sacraments" (March 3, 1547) issued fourteen canons on baptism in which it condemned positions attributed to the reformers that it considered to be heretical. Not all of these pertained to Luther's teaching, because both Luther and Trent were concerned to refute Anabaptist teaching, but Canons 6-10 were directed against the Lutheran teaching on baptism as a perpetual sacrament:

> Can 6. If anyone says that one who is baptized cannot, even if he wishes, lose grace, however much he sins, unless he refuses to believe: let him be anathema.

---

2. Paul D. Murray, "Receptive Ecumenism and Catholic Learning—Establishing the Agenda," *Receptive Ecumenism*, 6.

3. *LW* 36:57; *WA* 6:526-7.

Can 7. If anyone says that those baptized are obliged to faith alone, but not to the observance of the whole law of Christ: let him be anathema.

Can 8. If anyone says that those baptized are exempt from all the precepts of holy church, whether they are in writing or handed down, so that they are not bound to observe them, unless of their own free will they wish to submit themselves to them: let him be anathema.

Can. 9. If anyone says that people must be recalled to the memory of the baptism they received, thereby understanding that all vows made after baptism become of no effect by the force of the promise already made in their actual baptism, as if such vows detract from the faith they have professed and from the baptism itself: let him be anathema.

Can. 10. If anyone says that, solely by the remembrance of receiving baptism and of its faith, all sins committed after baptism are forgiven or become venial: let him be anathema.[4]

Today the limitations of these canons are recognized insofar as they are responses to texts extracted from primarily early texts of Luther before his later struggle with the Anabaptists and taken out of context. They do not do justice to Luther's sacramental theology when viewed within the totality of his theology, for his teaching on the relationship between faith, sacrament, and word is very nuanced.

One might also argue that Trent's teaching does not present a comprehensive Roman Catholic sacramental theology, but reduces it to a limited number of concerns such as the septenary number of the sacraments, their institution by Christ, and the principle of their causality *ex opere operato* on those who place no obstacle. Missing elements from the teaching include the ecclesial dimension of the sacraments, their fuller context in terms of Christ and his redemptive action, and their nature as a personal encounter in faith with Christ.[5]

---

4. Council of Trent, Session 7 (3 March 1547): Canons on the Sacrament of Baptism; in *Decrees of the Ecumenical Councils*, ed. Norman P. Tanner, SJ (Georgetown: Georgetown University Press, 1990), 2:685–686.

5. Godfrey Diekmann, "Some Observations on the Teaching of Trent Concerning Baptism,"

Trent also does not do justice to the Roman Catholic teaching on the necessity of faith for efficacious reception of the sacraments, on which the council fathers were agreed. As Godfrey Diekmann explains, "not faith *alone*" implied "faith plus something else."[6] Finally, Trent's emphasis on causality overshadowed the teaching on sacraments as signs.

Later study has determined that the Roman Catholic condemnations "underestimate the *ecclesial and soteriological importance* which the sacraments have in the Protestant churches as *means of salvation.*" Nor did the reformers "play off justification by faith alone (*sole fide*) against the celebration of the sacraments, as they were accused of doing,"[7] and which seems to be reflected in canon 7. Canon 6 does not accurately represent the Lutheran viewpoint, although it may apply to the Zwinglian position. It must also be noted that the phrase "contain grace" (*continere gratiam*), used in canon 6 of the canons on the sacraments in general, does not reflect the Protestant understanding of the relationship between a sacrament and the promise of grace. Arguably, it also is not the best expression of a contemporary Catholic understanding of grace. Perhaps Lutherans and Catholics could agree that sacraments communicate the grace that they signify if it is clear that the primary actor in the sacraments is Christ, something which both affirm. Finally, Lutherans do not find themselves targeted by canon 10 since 'they do not hold that persons who fall into grave sins after baptism and persevere in them without true and earnest repentance receive forgiveness of sins merely be recalling in a perfunctory and purely historical way that they were

in *Lutherans and Catholics in Dialogue II: One Baptism for the Remission of Sins*, ed. Paul C. Empie and William W. Baum (New York: U.S.A. National Committee of the Lutheran world Federation and the Bishops' Commission for Ecumenical Affairs, 1967), 61-70, at 65.

6. Diekmann, "Some Observations," 66.

7. Karl Lehmann and Wolfhart Pannenberg, eds., *The Condemnations of the Reformation Era: Do They Still Divide?* (Minneapolis: Fortress Press, 1990), 78.

once baptized, so that they have no need of genuine repentance and the ministry of the keys."[8]

Sacraments for Luther were not mere signs pointing to grace, but the necessary efficacious instruments of God who is present in them. Luther's *Large Catechism* (1529) states:

> Our know-it-alls, the new spirits, claim that faith alone saves and that works and external things add nothing to it. We answer: It is true, nothing that is in us does it but faith, as we shall hear later on. But these leaders of the blind are unwilling to see that faith must have something to believe—something to which it may cling and upon which it may stand. Thus faith clings to the water and believes it to be baptism, in which there is sheer salvation and life, not through the water, as we have sufficiently stated, but through its incorporation with God's Word and ordinance and the joining of his name to it. When I believe this, what else is it but believing in God as the one who has bestowed and implanted his Word in baptism and has offered us this external thing within which we can grasp this treasure?

> Now, these people are so foolish as to separate faith from the object to which faith is attached and secured, all on the grounds that the object is something external. Yes, it must be external so that it can be perceived and grasped by the senses and thus brought into the heart, just as the entire gospel is an external, oral proclamation. In short, whatever God does and effects in us he desires to accomplish through such an external ordinance. No matter where he speaks—indeed, no matter for what purpose or through what means he speaks—there faith must look and to it faith must hold on. We have here the words, "The one who believes and is baptized will be saved." To what do they refer if not to baptism, that is, the water placed in the setting of God's ordinance? Hence it follows that whoever rejects baptism rejects God's Word, faith, and Christ, who directs and binds us to baptism.[9]

Thus, for Luther, God's word is joined to the sign of baptism, the water, through which God enacts God's promise. Catholics, using the

---

8. Arthur Carl Piepkorn, "The Lutheran Understanding of Baptism: A Systematic Summary," *Lutherans and Catholics in Dialogue II*, 27–60, at 43.

9. Martin Luther, *Large Catechism*, Fourth Part: Concerning Baptism, §§28–31; *BC* 460.

language of metaphysics, would call baptism an instrumental cause of God's grace. The explanation may differ, but the reality is the same.

In 1966, the second U.S. bi-lateral official ecumenical conversation of the Lutheran-Catholic dialogue sponsored by the U.S.A. National Committee of the Lutheran World Federation and the bishops; Commission for Ecumenical Affairs issued a joint statement written by Bishop T. Austin Murphy and Paul Empie saying, "We were reasonably certain that the teachings of our respective traditions regarding baptism are in substantial agreement, and this opinion has been confirmed at this meeting."[10]

What Catholics Can Receive from the
Lutheran Doctrine of Baptism

In the spirit of receptive ecumenism, Catholics can profit from several themes in Luther's theology of baptism. This essay develops these three themes:

1. Catholics can better emphasize the role of baptism in governing and directing the whole of Christian life. Although received in its entirety with the invocation of Father, Son, and Spirit with immersion or effusion, all of Christian life is properly baptismal. Luther's injunction to put on baptism daily aptly applies to all of the baptized.

2. Catholics can bring out more strongly the promissory character of the sacraments and the need to appropriate them through faith.[11]

---

10. In *Lutherans and Catholics in Dialogue II*, 85. Also available in *Building Unity: Ecumenical Dialogues with Roman Catholic Participation in the United States*, ed. Joseph A. Burgess and Jeffrey Gross, F.S.C., Ecumenical Documents IV (New York: Paulist, 1989), 90.

11. This is a recommendation of the study group which produced *The Condemnations of the Reformation Era: Do They Still Divide?*, ed. Lehmann and Pannenberg; see p. 76.

3. Catholics can better recognize the eschatological orientation of baptism.

1. Return to Your Baptism Daily

In his *Large Catechism,* Luther emphasized the importance of baptism for daily life:

> Therefore let all Christians regard their Baptism as the daily garment that they are to wear all the time. Every day they should be found in faith and with its fruits, suppressing the old creature and growing up in the new. If we want to be Christians, we must practice the work that makes us Christians, and let those who fall away return to it. As Christ, the mercy seat, does not withdraw from us or forbid us to return to him even though we sin, so all his treasures and gifts remain. As we have once obtained forgiveness of sins in baptism, so forgiveness remains day by day as long as we live, that is, as long as we carry the old creature about our necks.[12]

Through baptism, the Christian is accepted into a relationship with Father, Son, and Spirit in a unique and fundamental way. A person assumes the name Christian, indicating that he or she has put on Christ when plunged into his death and resurrection and has assumed an identity that reorients the whole of life. It is irrevocable and unrepeatable regardless whether or not a person later renounces this allegiance. Baptism is a reality that cannot be destroyed once received even though the benefit of baptism, reception of God's grace, cannot be fully realized without a response in faith.

Even though baptism truly creates intimacy with God in a graced relationship, this relationship is capable of growth into likeness to God and deepening, what we call growth in sanctification.[13] In this

---

12. Luther, *Large Catechism,* IV:84-86; *BC,* 466-67.
13. The Council of Trent also speaks of a growth in justification. Session 6 (13 January 1547): Chapter 10, "On the Increase of Justification Received"; in Tanner, *Decrees of the Ecumenical Councils,* 675.

sense baptism is an inauguration of a Christian life that is open-ended even though the sacrament is itself complete. In baptism we are made holy and yet can grow in holiness. Baptism, which incorporates us into the once-for-all death of Christ, calls us to a daily dying to sin and rising to new life. Thus it is a continuing call to repentance, faith, and obedience to Christ. As Luther's *Large Catechism* puts it, living in repentance is a walking in baptism.[14]

Catholics would agree with this insofar as the sacrament of penance returns a person to the state of grace initially effected by baptism. Even though Trent in Canon 10 condemned the position "that by the sole remembrance and the faith of the baptism received, all sins committed after baptism are either remitted or made venial," this canon does not take into account the role of repentance in the return to baptismal justification. The Catholic and Lutheran positions are similar in the effect produced even though differences remain in how that effect is produced, Lutherans emphasizing the role of faith in the process of repentance and Catholics the objective role of the sacrament of penance within repentance, which of course also requires faith for fruitful reception. Where Lutherans would say that we always have access to baptism,[15] Catholics would say that we always have the possibility of returning to the condition initially established by baptism.

Luther opposed setting up penance as a replacement for baptism and in effect making penance into a kind of second baptism. For example, he thought that Jerome's allusion to penance as "the second plank on which we must swim ashore after the ship flounders" takes away the value of baptism by making it of no further use to us. He acknowledged that we slip and fall out of the ship, but said that those

---

14. *Large Catechism*, IV:75; BC 466.
15. *Large Catechism*, IV:77; BC 466.

who do fall out should immediately swim to the ship, that is, baptism, and hold fast to it.[16]

Using another conceptual system, the Catholic teaching on the sacramental character imparted by baptism certainly affirms the enduring permanence of baptism. The sacramental character means more than simply that baptism cannot be repeated. It confers a competence, a commission within the visibility of the church.[17] This is an authorization to participate in in the public worship of the church. A sacramental character is therefore a type of "ordination" which makes it possible for the worship acts of the baptized to be acts of the risen Christ since the baptized is incorporated into the body of the risen Christ in baptism. St. Thomas identified the sacramental character or competence a participation in the high priesthood of Christ, which varied depending on whether the character was conferred by baptism, confirmation, or the ordained priesthood.

Thomas's theology of sacramental character remains a theological view and is not official doctrine of the church. The dogmatic definitions of the Council of Florence and of Trent simply stated that the character is indelible such that the sacraments conferring a character can be received only once, but did not specify what a character actually is.[18] Catholic theological consensus, however, is that "a person who bears a character or mark bears a certain relation to the visible ecclesial community."[19] The Lutheran Confessions nowhere reject a character in baptism, but do not operate with this construct due to its late appearance in western theology, the lack

16. *Large Catechism* IV:81–81; *BC* 466.
17. Edward Schillebeeckx, *Christ, the Sacrament of the Encounter with God*, trans. P. Barrett (Kansas City: Sheed and Ward, 1963), 157.
18. Council of Florence, "Bull of Union with the Armenians" (1439); in Denzinger's *Enchiridion Symbolorum*, §1313; Council of Trent, "Decree on the Sacraments" (1547); Denzinger §1609.
19. Schillebeeckx, *Christ, the Sacrament of the Encounter with God*, 158.

of a biblical basis for it, the metaphorical nature of the term, and uneasiness about the Hellenistic doctrine of the soul inherent in it.[20]

For our purposes here, it is significant that this relationship to the church is not lost through sin. Thus even though baptismal grace can be lost through serious sin, baptism is not left behind, but endures. Since Lutherans would also say that loss of salvation remains a possibility for a Christian and that baptism is never left behind, for both communions there is something permanent in baptism and something that can be lost. Both communions would affirm that that which is permanent is on the side of God's activity in the sacrament, Lutherans describing this as promise and Catholics speaking of a definitive character of the sacrament. Both communions speak of the possibility of a subjective turning from baptism by the baptized. Finally, both speak of a return to baptismal grace, while Lutherans speak of this as a clinging to baptism through faith in God's promise and Catholics hold that this occurs not through faith in baptism, but through recourse to the sacrament of penance and contrition. Perhaps this account shows unity as well as difference in Lutheran and Catholic accounts of the permanence of baptism and the return to baptismal grace.

The task of remembering our baptism is a recollection of who we are in Christ and bringing to mind that our Christian life is a journey in union with Christ back to the Father within the process of a reconciliation of all in Christ. Baptism calls us to walk daily in the newness of Christian life in which we undertake a Christian ethic. Christian ethics connect the new creature we have become in Christ with the goal of humanity as revealed in Christ. Living out our baptismal identity leads us to sacrificial service. Thus the faith with which we receive baptism finds expression in love, which in turn impels us to mission. As Christ was sent on mission, so we are sent

20. Piepkorn, "The Lutheran Understanding of Baptism," 57.

to build up the city of God on earth. As he returns to his Father after completing his task, so too do we look forward to a union with the Father when we will see him face-to-face.

Luther's belief in the sufficiency of baptism received in faith is one reason why he rejected religious vows. He thought that all vows should be abolished and that everyone should be recalled to the vows of baptism: "For we have vowed enough in baptism, more than we can ever fulfill; if we give ourselves to the keeping of this one vow, we shall have all we can do."[21] Furthermore, he saw vows as multiplying laws and works and as extinguishing the liberty of baptism. In his view, in many ways religious life, interpreted as a new baptism, abrogated to itself the meaning and honor due to baptism.

An alternative view of this regards religious life as being based on baptism and a specific form of living out baptismal identity. For instance, the Sisters of Charity of Leavenworth, Kansas, state in their Constitution, "As Christians united personally by Baptism to Jesus Christ and to his body, the Church, the Sisters of Charity of Leavenworth . . . are women who view Baptism as the most significant event in our lives. . . ."[22] Similarly, recent work on lay and ordained ministry roots all ministries in baptism.[23] In part, this is the result of situating all ministry within the context of an ecclesial community. Baptism establishes a person as a member of the community and ministry, lay and ordained, proceeds from baptism as does all discipleship. Sacramental ordination is a further specification of a person's relationship within the community, out of which relationship derives the power to act in the name of the community

21. *LW* 36:75-76; *WA* 6:539.
22. *Constitution of the Sisters of Charity of Leavenworth* (1983), §3.
23. Susan K. Wood, ed., *Ordering the Baptismal Priesthood: Theologies of Lay and Ordained Ministry* (Collegeville: Liturgical Press, 2003). See especially the conclusion, pp. 256-265, and Richard Gaillardetz, "The Ecclesiological Foundations of Ministry within an Ordered Communion," 26-51.

and in the name of Christ. Baptism is a prerequisite for ordination as it is for marriage and membership in a religious community recognized by the church. Within this view, lay and ordained ministry and consecrated life are a "re-positioning" of a baptized member within the baptismal community according to the specific character of each.

Despite the relationship between ordained ministry and baptism, neither Lutherans nor Catholics entrust the public proclamation of the gospel and presiding over the Eucharist to anyone who is baptized apart from that person also being ordained. For Lutherans "a regular call" and ordination are normally required, although the Evangelical Lutheran Church in America permits lay presidency in cases of need. Nevertheless, this practice is not without controversy among Lutherans.

The imperative to live out baptism daily means that the whole of Christian life is paschal both in its structure and in its spirituality. Baptism is truly foundational in that baptism is the once-for-all opening insofar as it contains all of Christian life in a nutshell. It elicits a life-long response in faith and discipleship. It represents a journey of ever-deepening communion with God and fellowship with other Christians.

2. Appropriating the promissory character of baptism through faith

Luther said, "the *first* thing to be considered about baptism is the divine promise, which says, 'He who believes and is baptized will be saved' [Mark 16:16]."[24] The sacrament of baptism is an enacted form of word. This theology, of course, comes from Augustine, who called a sacrament "a visible word." The connection between

---

24. *LW* 36:58; *WA* 6:527. Note that Luther accepts as canonical the longer ending of Mark's Gospel.

"word" and "sacrament" so clearly emphasized by Augustine had, during the Middle Ages, passed out of view. In the words of Harnack, "the *verbum* disappeared entirely behind the sacrament's sign" with the result that the conception had become "still more magical, and consequently more objectionable."[25] For Luther, this loss seemed to undervalue the recipient's role in the sacramental encounter.

Luther's concept of a sacrament involved three elements: 1) A sacrament is a sign instituted by God and connected with a promise of grace; 2) The sacrament only becomes efficacious through the individuals faith in the promise;[26] and 3) The effect of the sacrament is forgiveness of sin and reconciliation with God. The recipient's role in the sacramental encounter, then, is to receive the word of promise embodied in the sacramental sign with the response of faith. Faith does not make the sacrament valid, but it does make it efficacious.

Catholics historically have had an under-developed theology of the Word. Even now after efforts to address this after the Second Vatican Council and the requirement to have scripture texts included in the revision of each of the sacramental rites, the notion of a sacrament as a visible word received in faith is not in the consciousness of most Catholics, even though sacramental theologians are attempting to remedy this.[27] The danger remains of regarding word and sacrament as two separate entities rather than as an interrelated whole.

25. Adolf von Harnack, *History of Dogma,* trans. N. Buchanan (New York: Russell and Russell, 1958), 6:200.
26. Luther's conviction of the need for a personal response of faith was problematic with respect to infant baptism. His answer to the problem varied. At times he viewed baptism as the prime example of the absolute gratuity of salvation. At another time he believed that the community of believers that needed to be present, allowing faith to be vicariously present. On yet other occasions, he suggested that infants were capable of faith. He vigorously defended infant baptism against the Anabaptists. This essay does not engage this aspect of Luther's thought.
27. See, for example, Louis-Marie Chauvet, *Symbol and Sacrament: Sacramental Reinterpretation of Christian Existence,* trans. M. M. Beaument and P. Madigan (Collegeville: Pueblo, Liturgical Press, 1995); Kevin W. Irwin, *Context and Text: Method in Liturgical Theology* (Collegeville: Pueblo, Liturgical Press, 1994); David N. Power, *Sacrament: the Language of God's Giving* (New York: Herder and Herder, Crossroad, 1999).

Karl Rahner is the theologian after Vatican II who incorporates a robust theology of the word in his account of sacramentality and comes closest to Luther's concept of sacrament. He identifies a sacrament as a "quite specific word-event within a theology of the word. Rahner even says, "the word constitutes the basic essence of the sacrament and that by comparison with the word the 'matter', the *elementum* has at basis the merely secondary function of providing an illustration of the significance of the word."[28] This word is an event of grace, a saving event made effective by the power of God.

Louis-Marie Chauvet, a Catholic liturgical theologian, in addressing what he calls the "false dichotomy between Word and Sacrament," speaks of the "word that deposits itself in the sacramental ritual as well as in the Bible" such that it is better to speak of "a liturgy of the Word under the mode of Scripture and of a liturgy of the Word under the mode of bread and wine." One avoids a magical or automatic effect of the sacrament by remembering that the communication of God in the sacraments is always "under the mode of communication by word." For Chauvet, the baptismal formula is "the precipitate of the Christians Scriptures" since the baptismal formula, "In the name of the Father, and of the Son and of the Holy Spirit" is like a "concentrate of all the Scriptures."[29] The baptismal formula functions as the symbol par excellence of Christian identity, is inscribed in the body, which is to say, in the fabric of life.[30] Thus word is understood on three levels: the Christ-Word, the Scriptures, and the sacramental formula itself pronounced "in the person of Christ."

Chauvet's theology of the connection between word and sacrament extends beyond Luther's theology of the word as promise

---

28. Karl Rahner, "What is a Sacrament?" *Theological Investigations*, vol. 14, trans. D. Bourke (London: Darton, Longman & Todd, 1976), 135-160 at 138.
29. Chauvet, *Symbol and Sacrament*, 221.
30. Ibid., 222.

and its reception in faith, but it bridges what is too often a dichotomy between word and sacrament and thus retrieves in a contemporary key Augustine's notion of a sacrament as a "visible word." Chauvet makes the connection with faith by recalling that contemporary exegesis of John 6 does not consider it to be a discourse about the Eucharist as such, but "a catechesis on faith in Jesus as the Word of God who has undergone death for the life of the world."[31] Faith is a chewing on the mystery of this scandal. Chauvet comments, "The thoughtful chewing of the Eucharist is precisely the *central symbolic experience* where we encounter the bitter scandal of the faith until it passes through our bodies and becomes assimilated into our everyday actions."[32] Where the predominant scholastic notion of faith tended to be intellectual assent to truths, and Luther's notion of faith was mainly fiduciary trust, Chauvet takes us to an embodied, enacted faith through participation in sacramental action. We literally enact that which we believe. This is made possible through sacramental sign and the identification between Christ's word and sacrament. Where Luther emphasized sacrament as enacted word, Chauvet emphasizes sacramental action as embodied faith. For both Chauvet and Luther, faith and sacrament, word and sacrament—perhaps better expressed as sacramental word received in faith through embodied sacramental participation—are entwined in sacramental action.

3. Recognizing the eschatological orientation of baptism

For Luther, the fulfillment of the death and resurrection experienced in baptism lies ahead of us. The task of conforming to the death and resurrection of Christ is a lifelong process that will only reach completion on the last day. He describes the eschatological orientation of baptism in his *Commentary on Romans* (1515-16):

31. Ibid., 225.
32. Ibid.

[I]t is not necessary for all men to be found immediately in this state of perfection, as soon as they have been baptized into a death of this kind. For they are baptized "into death," that is, toward death, which is to say, they have begun to live in such a way that they are pursuing this kind of death and reach out toward this their goal. For although they are baptized unto eternal life and the kingdom of heaven, yet they do not all at once possess this goal fully, but they have begun to act in such a way that they may attain to it—for Baptism was established to direct us toward death and through this death to life. . . .[33]

Luther has described the "already" and "not yet" of baptism in a 1519 sermon:

Therefore, so far as the sign of the sacrament and its significance are concerned, sin and the man are both already dead—he has risen again, and so the sacrament has taken place. But the work of the sacrament has not yet been fully done, which is to say that the death and resurrection at the last day are still before us.[34]

Baptism is essentially eschatologically oriented because the newness effected in baptism, although complete insofar as we are justified in baptism, remains incomplete or at risk insofar as the new creation is not fully realized in historical time. Thus aspects of the "already" and the "not yet" are intrinsic to baptism as they are to all sacraments, although Lutherans and Catholics express this through different conceptual systems. Lutherans express this through their affirmation of a person being simultaneously justified and a sinner, *simul iustus et peccator*. Catholics, while affirming that the forgiveness of sin received in baptism effects a state of grace, consider that due to human free will, victory over sin is never definitive until death.[35]

---

33. *LW* 25:312; *WA* 56:324.

34. *The Holy and Blessed Sacrament of Baptism* (1519); *LW* 35:32; *WA* 2:729-30.

35. The purpose of the present essay does not permit a discussion of a possible resolution of these two anthropologies here. See Pieter de Witte, *Doctrine, Dynamic and Difference: To the Heart of the Lutheran-Roman Catholic Differentiated Consensus on Justification* (New York: T&T Clark, 2012), and a forthcoming dissertation by Jakob Karl Rinderknecht, *Seeing Two Worlds: the*

This is to say that the new creation effected in the modality of sacramental sign, although real and efficacious in terms of grace, is lived out and comes to full embodiment in the everydayness of human interactions and in social realization only in a process involving duration and development within historical time. We die to sin and rise in the grace of God over a lifetime.

Baptism, as the sacramental realization of the end time proleptically breaking into the life of the baptized individual and the church, is inaugurated eschatology.[36] The connection between baptism and eschatology lies in the incarnation of Jesus Christ who brought eternity into historical time when he became human and thereby united divinity with humanity. In that moment eternity became enfleshed in history. Jesus Christ, the one who has come and entered our history, who comes in the present through word and sacrament, will come again. Incarnation and redemption rather than being the bookends of Jesus' life, represent an unbroken continuum through which creation becomes the new creation. Just as Jesus did not bypass the materiality of creation, so do Christians use the water and words of baptism to unite themselves to divinity and begin to live an eschatologically transformed life through sacramental mediation.

Through our participation in the death and resurrection of Christ in baptism, these past events are brought into the present historical moment. That sacramental event anticipates the final trans-historical event of our bodily resurrection in the fullness of the new creation. This sacramental view is consistent with the Pauline eschatological view of baptism in Romans 6, 2 Corinthians 5:1, and Galatians 6:15, which consider the present experience of Christians to be a

Eschatological Anthropology of the Joint Declaration on the Doctrine of Justification (Marquette University, 2015).

36. See Susan K. Wood, Chapter Two: "Baptism, Eschatology, and Salvation," in *One Baptism: Ecumenical Dimensions of the Doctrine of Baptism* (Collegeville: Liturgical Press, 2009), 1-19, at 1.

participation in eschatological reality. Pauline eschatology, while emphasizing what God has done in the death and resurrection of Jesus, develops the meaning of baptism in the daily life of the Christian, but then acknowledges that the full working out of the power of the resurrection remains to be fully accomplished. The dynamism of dying and rising with Christ sacramentally in baptism and in the daily choice to live that out in a life lived for others and for God identifies the hope of Christians and becomes the grammar of how they structure their lives.

Clearing Up Mutual Misunderstandings

In addition to naming gifts we receive from our ecumenical partners, receptive ecumenism requires that we clear up mutual misunderstandings of one another's theology of baptism. The first of these is whether a spiritual power resides in the baptismal water. The *Smalcald Articles* (1537) incorporates Augustine's definition of a sacrament as the Word added to the element. However, on the basis of this Luther says: "Therefore we do not agree with Thomas and the Dominicans who forget the Word (God's institution) and say that God has placed a spiritual power in the water which through the water, washes away sin."[37] He has made a similar point in *The Babylonian Captivity of the Church*, where he comments: "A great majority have supposed that there is some hidden spiritual power in the word and water, which works the grace of God in the soul of the recipient."[38] Here he is referring to a medieval dispute regarding how sacraments cause grace. Hugh of St. Victor held that the grace of the sacrament was contained in the sacramental sign and directly imparted through it. Others, such as Bonaventure and Duns Scotus,

---

37. *Smalcald Articles* III.5; BC 320.
38. *LW* 36:64; *WA* 6:531.

contended that the sign was merely a symbol, but that God imparted the grace of the sacrament when the sign was used. Luther appears to misunderstand Thomas, who specifically says that "grace is not in the sacrament as in a subject, nor yet as in a vessel inasmuch as a vessel is a certain kind of place, but rather inasmuch as a vessel or instrument is said to be the tool by means of which some work is performed. ..."[39]

A related misunderstanding is whether Catholics consider grace to be a substance. For instance, John Tonkin, in an otherwise fine article on Luther's understanding of baptism, says,

> This view of grace is perhaps the most basic difference between Luther's theology and the theology of the Church of Rome. In the Roman view, grace is, in effect, an impersonal substance which can be manipulated and brought into the present through the sacramental actions of the priesthood. For Luther, grace was no substance, but the personal presence of Christ and therefore Baptism was not the communication of a divine substance, but the creation of a personal relationship.[40]

Certainly, Luther had a lively appreciation for the interpersonal character of grace. Piet Fransen has suggested this may be due to his familiarity with the personalist language of the German mystical tradition.[41] Despite some popular misconceptions, for Catholics grace is also a personal category, referring to God's gracious commitment to human beings.[42] However, Catholics have distinguished between uncreated grace, which is the very presence of the Holy Spirit in the soul of the justified, and uncreated grace, itself not a substance, but an accidental modification of the soul empowering it to exceed the proportions of any created nature or disposing the soul for uncreated grace. Rahner has insisted that even "created grace" is an essentially

---

39. Thomas Aquinas, *Summa theologiae,* III, q. 62, a. 4, ad. 1.
40. John Tonkin, "Luther's Understanding of Baptism: A Systematic Approach," *Lutheran Theological Journal* 11:3 (December, 1977): 96-111, at 101.
41. Piet Fransen, *The New Life of Grace* (New York: Herder and Herder, 1972), 91.
42. Pannenberg and Lehmann, eds., *The Condemnations of the Reformation Era,* 76.

relational reality, having no absolute existence of its own and argues that even in Scholastic terms created grace must be seen as a secondary element in justification.[43] He further asserts that it is not sanctifying grace, a created entity, which effectively relates us to God in justification or sanctification, but uncreated grace. His work as well as more recent theology has retrieved a greater emphasis on uncreated grace borrowed from the insights of the Greek patristic tradition. Grace is always inherently relational and interpersonal, even though the Aristotelian categories of substance, nature, virtue, *habitus*, etc., have not always communicated this as clearly as one might wish. Finally, in the spirit of receptive ecumenism, since our righteousness is always the imprint upon us of divine righteousness, Avery Dulles has written, "the Reformation categories of *iustia aliena* and "imputed righteousness" convey an important truth that Catholics do not wish to ignore."[44]

A second misunderstanding of Catholic theology was the reformers' interpretation of sacramental efficacy *ex opere operato*. Studies have shown that one source of the misunderstanding may be because the Protestant side looks at the *reception* of the sacrament, while Catholics interpret the terms from the point of view of the *dispensation* of the sacrament.[45] Accordingly, Protestants viewed the teaching of *ex opere operato* as affirming an automatic salvific sacramental efficacy when the ritual was rightly performed. The teaching on *ex opere operato* was intended to stress that the divine offer of grace is independent of the worthiness of the one administering the sacrament and the one receiving it. Lutherans

---

43. Karl Rahner, "Some Implications of the Scholastic Concept of Uncreated Grace," *Theological Investigations*, trans. C. Ernst (Baltimore: Helicon, 1961), 1:328.

44. Avery Dulles, "Justification in Contemporary Catholic Theology," in *Lutherans and Catholics in Dialogue VII: Justification by Faith*, ed. H. George Anderson et al. (Minneapolis: Augsburg, 1985), 256-277, at 258.

45. Pannenberg and Lehmann, eds., *The Condemnations of the Reformation Era*, 77.

would agree that sacraments are independent of the worthiness of the one administering them, but would say that sacraments effect salvation only through faith. Nevertheless, they would also affirm the objective validity of baptism apart from faith. For example in a sermon on the Catechism, Luther states, "My faith does not make the baptism, but rather receives the baptism, no matter whether the person being baptized believes or not; for baptism is not dependent on my faith but upon God's Word."[46]

Catholics interpreted the Protestant denial of the teaching on *ex opere operato* as a denial of sacramental efficacy in general, particularly when combined with a teaching of efficacy through faith. Both sides, however, taught that Christ is the primary actor in the sacraments. Catholic doctrine requires believing reception in order for the sacrament is to be "for salvation."

Undoubtedly, Catholics have also misunderstood Lutheran theology. Too often fiduciary faith has appeared to Catholics to be a form of "believe and do what you will" or a dispensation from the precepts of the law. This attitude is reflected in Trent's canon 7, which condemned the position that the baptized are obliged to faith alone, but not to the observance of the whole law of Christ, and in canon 8, which condemned the position that "those baptized are exempt from the precepts of holy church." The emphasis on the commandments in both Luther's *Small Catechism* and *Large Catechism* is evidence of the importance and obligation of Godly behavior for Lutherans.

In recent times Catholics have themselves appropriated a more personalist notion of faith, as for example, in the Catechism's reference to Abraham and Mary as models of faith.[47] This also

---

46. *Ten Sermons on the Catechism* (1528); *LW* 51:186; *WA* 30I:114; cited by Tonkin, "Luther's Understanding of Baptism," 100. See also *Large Catechism* IV:28-31; *BC* 460.

47. *Catechism of the Catholic Church*, 2nd ed. (Vatican: Libreria Editrice Vatican, 1997), §§145-149.

corresponds to an understanding of Christ as the fullness of revelation.[48] Within this understanding of revelation, faith is adherence to a person. This balances the notion of faith as an act of intellect and will assenting to propositions expressing the "eternal decrees" of God's will.[49]

Thanks to developments in both our traditions, good historical studies that elucidate and put into perspective past differences, and the mutual recognition we affirm of each other's baptism and the communion we share based on that, as imperfect as it might be, Lutherans and Catholics are more open today to learning from each other. Catholics can be enriched by a retrieval of many of Luther's insights regarding baptism.

---

48. Vatican II, *Dei Verbum*, §2.
49. Vatican II, *Dei Verbum*, §6, referencing the First Vatican Council's Dogmatic Constitution on the Catholic Faith, *Dei Filius*, ch. 2 (Denzinger §3005). Even though this was arguably the dominant notion of faith and revelation prior to Vatican II, an astute reader of *Dei Filius* will notice that the decree says that revealed not only the eternal laws of is will to the human race, but also revealed himself. Furthermore, the text cites the author of the letter to the Hebrews saying, "In many and various ways God spoke of old to our fathers by the prophets; but in these last days he has spoken to us by a Son" (Heb. 1:1-2). Vatican II can be read as picking up and building on this strand of Vatican I and thus as being in continuity with Vatican I even while it corrects an imbalance caused by an overly intellectual notion of faith and an overly propositional notion of revelation.

10

"Every one must fight his own battle with death by himself, alone": What this Episcopalian Learned from Martin Luther

Randall C. Zachman

I was raised in the Protestant Episcopal Church in northern Ohio. My diocese was reflective of the Evangelical wing of the Church of England. Though we used the 1928 *Book of Common Prayer*, the liturgy was fairly low, and the normal Sunday worship service was Morning Prayer, with an emphasis on hymns and especially the sermon. We only celebrated communion once a month, on the first Sunday of the month, yet this made communion even more haunting and mysterious to me, since the language in the service was so different from Morning Prayer, and involved our coming forward to kneel at the altar rail to receive the signs of the body and blood of Christ.

My mother was deeply involved in the life of the Church, even serving on the Bishop's Standing Committee in Cleveland. Hence she very much wanted her children to be as involved in the life of the Church as she was. Her family could trace their Anglican roots all the way back to Henry VIII, and they came over to the colonies in the 1640s. My father, on the other hand, was initially raised Methodist, as the name John Wesley Zachman would reveal, but his parents converted to Christian Science in his youth, and this led him to become very skeptical of religion and religious people. He would usually go to worship with us, but we could tell that he had one foot out of the door the whole time. I have definitely inherited both aspects from my parents, and often find myself agreeing with Simone Weil's description of herself as a "threshold Christian."

Without my being aware of it at the time, I was part of the reason why my mother was so devoted to God and the Church. When I was eighteen months old, I contracted spinal meningitis, and at that time it was almost always fatal. My parents had me baptized in the intensive care unit, and when I recovered, my mother dedicated her life even more deeply to God, out of gratitude for my having been healed. I cannot say for sure, but this experience may also have left its mark on me, for I have been aware of the horizon of death from a very early age. Even though death was distant from my family when I was growing up, my thoughts would often turn to death, especially when I was lying alone in bed at night, feeling the solitude of darkness all around me. I would wonder why it was that I had to die, and wonder what death would mean for me. One night, I remember thinking, "Well, where were you before you were born?" I had no sooner asked that question than I received a very clear and powerful intuition that has stayed with me ever since. I was nowhere, for I was nothing, and on that night, and many solitary nights after that, I came to know what awaits me, what awaits all of us: not heaven, not hell, but an infinite black void, an abyss of silent annihilation.

My own personal interest and involvement in religion has always centered on this question. Given that our lives are heading toward the black void of annihilation, how should we live our lives? I first turned for answers to the 1928 *Book of Common Prayer*, especially the communion service, for it spoke of the Eucharist itself as being instituted as "a perpetual memory of that his most precious death and sacrifice, until his coming again." I was haunted by the bread which represented Christ's body given for us, and the wine which represented his blood shed for us, and the repetitious poetry of the liturgy captivated me. But I did not understand what the death of Christ meant, nor how his death might address my existential question about the meaning of my own death. I also heard a great deal about resurrection, eternal life, and the kingdom of God, but all of this sounded like a denial of death to me, for all I could see was a black silent void, and not eternal light and life.

When I was in high school, my best friend got me interested in Thomas Merton, and at the same time my brother-in-law got me interested in Mahayana Buddhist thought. I was especially drawn to the way Merton combined the Christian monastic tradition of contemplative prayer with the Buddhist practice of contemplation and meditation, and thought that this would be the path to follow to be able to integrate my awareness of death and the void with the way to live truly in this life. Our illusion is that we think that we and everything we know and love have souls that will allow them to live forever, when they are instead all destined to die, as we are. When we cling to ourselves and others, we suffer when death tears them away from us. We must free ourselves of the illusion of their and our immortality, in order to live enlightened lives without attachment to the things of this world destined for death and annihilation. This enlightenment will lead us to have selfless compassion for the suffering of all sentient creatures, and not just human beings, and will lead us to dedicate our lives to their enlightenment. Thus I went to Colgate University to study religion, and went from there to a graduate program in comparative religion, convinced that the true answer to the horizon of death lay in the Christian appropriation of the Mahayana Buddhist ideal of the Bodhisattva, who dedicates her life to the enlightenment of all sentient and suffering beings.

So what am I doing here, at a conference exploring the ecumenical impact of Martin Luther? While I was a graduate student of comparative religion, a Therevada Buddhist monk who was a friend of mine pointed out to me that I knew far more about his tradition than I did about my own. He came to the United States from Sri Lanka at considerable personal risk to learn more about Christianity, but when he asked me about my own tradition, I told him about his own, which he already knew. This convinced me that I needed to study my own tradition far more deliberately, and so I left the PhD program and went to Yale Divinity School to get a Master of Divinity degree, after which I planned to go back to do a PhD in comparative religion. In my second year at Yale, I took a reading course on the theology of Martin Luther, during which I read all of his lectures on Galatians of 1535. By the time this course was over, I knew I would devote the rest of my life to studying Christian theology, and that I would write my dissertation on Martin Luther.

Why? What did this Mahayana Buddhist Benedictine Protestant Episcopalian learn from reading Martin Luther? In sum, I learned how to think about death—my death, our death—directly in light of the gospel of Jesus Christ, in a way I had not even imagined before. Like me, Luther taught that there is only one thing worse than thinking about the approach of death every day, and that is not thinking about death at all: "indeed, it is like those who run to their grave backwards, for these live riotously and ignore death until they suddenly tumble into the grave."[1] But unlike my own early intuitions, the hour of death does not reveal a silent abyss of annihilation for Luther—indeed, he would have viewed such a future as a relief. Instead, my march toward death brings me inexorably to an hour when my whole life will be held directly accountable to God. At the time of my death, I will be alone before God, and God will ask me about the meaning of my life. I will be the only one who can speak on my behalf, and I must do so directly before God. "The summons of death comes to us all, and no one can die for another. Every one must fight his own battle with death by himself, alone. We can shout into another's ears, but everyone must himself be prepared for the time of death, for I will not be with you, nor you with me."[2]

To make matters worse, I will discover—if I have not already—that my conscience has been monitoring my entire life, every thought, no matter how hidden, and every act, no matter how long ago. At the hour of my death, all that lies within my conscience will become as transparently clear to me as it already is to God. I knew from the prayer for illumination in the communion service that to God all hearts are open, all desires are known, and from God no secrets are hid, but I had not imagined that at the hour of my death all that I am and all that I have thought and done will be illuminated before God and before myself. No one will be able to answer for me, and no one else will be able to acquit me, no matter how many people may have cared about me in this life. "For in your death struggle and in the Last Judgment, it will not help you at all that others praised you. Others will not bear your load, but you will stand before the judgment seat

1. *Commentary on 1 Corinthians 15* (1534); *LW* 28:132; *WA* 36:581 [1 Cor. 15:26-7].
2. *Eight Sermons at Wittenberg* (1522); *LW* 51:70; *WA* 10III:1.

of Christ (Rom. 14:10) and bear your load alone. There your partisans will not be able to help you at all, for when we die, the voices of those who praise us will be stilled. 'On that day, when God judges the secrets of men' (Rom. 2:16), the testimony of your conscience will stand either for you or against you."[3] I will have to answer directly to God for what my own conscience testifies to me about the mystery and meaning of my life, and it will render me either condemned or acquitted before God.

If the hour of my death comes upon me suddenly, without my being prepared, I am lost, for I will have no way of knowing how to handle the transparency of my conscience before God. My own sins may lie completely dormant in my conscience, and I may think that they therefore have all been forgotten, or that time has mitigated their impact. But at the hour of my death the power of sin will manifest itself to my conscience, and if I am not prepared for this, I will die of despair. "For as long as a person goes his way and neither feels nor heeds sin, he does not feel and fear death either. But when the hour strikes that man must fidget and die, sin soon appears on the scene and tells him: 'Alas! What did you do! How you angered God!' When that really strikes the heart, man cannot endure it, but must despair. And furthermore, if this condition lasts long, he must die in despair. For it is impossible for a man to endure a bad conscience when it really lays hold of him and he begins to feel God's wrath. Thus we see some people dying suddenly, or committing suicide because of such terror and despair."[4]

However, the situation can be just as perilous if I become aware of the hour of death before it arrives, for both my reason and my conscience will strongly tempt me to ask for more time to perform a work that can give me confidence before the judgment seat of God.

---

3. *Lectures on Galatians* (1535); *LW* 27:120; *WA* 40II:154 [Gal. 6:5].
4. *LW* 28:208; *WA* 36:688 [1 Cor. 15:56-7].

"Just give me more time, and I will make it up to you! I will not waste my life any longer, but will dedicate it entirely to you! I will give away all my possessions and become a monk, and spend the rest of my days in prayer and contemplation! Just give me time!" According to Luther, this is the only way my reason and conscience can prepare me for the hour of death. They hold before me the need to do something, anything, so that my conscience can testify for me and not against me when I stand naked and alone before God at the hour of my death. "But such is human weakness and misery that in the terrors of conscience and in the danger of death we look at nothing except our own works, our worthiness, and the Law. When the Law shows us our sin, our past life immediately comes to mind. Then the sinner, in his great anguish of mind, groans and says to himself: 'Oh, how damnably I have lived! If only I could live longer! Then I would amend my life.'"[5]

If there is to be any hope for me in the hour of my death, I must completely ignore the urging of my reason and conscience to try to make amends, and instead honestly admit that my conscience is entirely right when it testifies against me. I must therefore admit and feel that my death is not a fate toward which I was innocently hurled when I was born, but is rather what I deserve as a sinner before God. "For just as the Law reveals sin, so it strikes the wrath of God into a man and threatens him with death. Immediately his conscience draws the inference: 'You have not observed the Commandments; therefore God is offended and is angry with you.' This logic is irrefutable: 'I have sinned; therefore I shall die.'"[6] The wages of sin are death, and if in the hour of my death I am held accountable for my life, I must concur with my conscience that my death is justly deserved due to my sin. Moreover, in spite of the urging of reason and conscience to

5. LW 26:5; WA 40I:41 ["The Argument of Paul's Epistle to the Galatians"].
6. LW 26:150; WA 40I:260; [Gal. 2:17].

do something to spare myself from death, I know deep in my heart that there is nothing I can do, for as the prayer of confession reminds me, the remembrance of my sin is grievous unto me, and the burden of my sin is intolerable. Luther asks me to imagine trying to bring just one good work before the judgment seat of God, so that God might approve of it, and therefore of me. "Let us take St. Paul or Peter as they pray, preach, or do some other good work. If it is a good work without sin and entirely faultless, they could stand with appropriate humility before God and speak in this fashion: 'Lord God, behold this good work which I have done through the help of Thy grace. There is in it neither fault nor any sin, nor does it need Thy forgiving mercy.'" Far from leading us to be hopeful, Luther asks the reader, "doesn't this make you shudder and sweat?"[7] But if such a good work will not stand at the hour of my death, what about my real and serious sins? And what about me? What will I do with myself? So here I am, facing the hour of my death alone, knowing I am completely responsible for my life and my actions, knowing that I must render an account directly to God for the meaning of my life, and now certain that my conscience will silence me, as I will not be able to make any appeal which can bring God's approval of me. "He sees that he is such a great sinner that he cannot find any means to be delivered from his sin by his own strength, effort, or works."[8]

And here is the next thing that I learned from Luther. Precisely when I take full responsibility for the mess I have made of my life, for all that I have said and done (or left unsaid and undone), and when I allow my conscience to silence any excuse or explanation I might offer to God, so that I can only stand silently condemned before God, then God, out of incomprehensible love, sends his only Son Jesus Christ, and asks him to make himself responsible for my

7. *Against Latomus* (1521); *LW* 32:190; *WA* 8:79.
8. *LW* 26:131; *WA* 40I:231 [Gal. 2:16].

sin, for my death, for my condemnation. "When the merciful Father saw that we were being oppressed through the Law, that we were being held under a curse, and that we could not be liberated from it by anything, He sent His Son into the world, heaped all the sins of all men upon Him, and said to Him: 'Be Peter the denier; Paul the persecutor, blasphemer, and assaulter; David the adulterer; the sinner who ate the apple in Paradise; the thief on the cross. In short, be the person of all men, the one who committed the sins of all men. And see to it that you pay and make satisfaction for them.'"[9] The one human being who could truly stand acquitted before God as being innocent of any sin, is sent by God to make himself responsible for the sin for which I alone am responsible, so that he might take this unbearable burden away from me, and suffer in himself the death and condemnation that is rightfully mine. "Whatever sins I, you, and all of us have committed or may commit in the future, they are as much Christ's own as if He Himself had committed them."[10] Even though I know that my sins are mine alone, and Christ is without sin, I must also acknowledge that God wants me to let Christ take full responsibility for my sin, even though he is completely free of sin himself. "And this is our greatest comfort, to clothe and wrap Christ this way in my sins, your sins, and the sins of the entire world, and in this way to behold Him bearing all our sins."[11]

When I allow myself to do this, then suddenly the narrative of the passion and death of Christ springs to life before my eyes. So long as I look at this narrative in a disinterested way, or as though I, like Christ, am innocent, then the passion can have no meaning for me. But once I see that what is happening to Christ is taking place because he has made himself completely responsible for my sin,

9. *LW* 26:280; *WA* 401:437 [Gal. 3:13].
10. *LW* 26:278; *WA* 401:435 [Gal. 3:13].
11. *LW* 26:279; *WA* 401:437 [Gal. 3:13].

my death, my condemnation, then I see how it is my sin that leads to his condemnation and death. Moreover, even though Christ was personally innocent and righteous, he allowed himself to experience my condemnation in the depth of his conscience, so that he faced the abyss of a God-forsaken death alone. "For the Law exercised its full function over Christ; it frightened Him so horribly that He experienced greater anguish than any other man has ever experienced. This is amply demonstrated by His bloody sweat, the comfort of the angel, the solemn prayer in the garden (Luke 22:41-44), and finally by that cry of misery on the cross (Matt. 27:46): 'My God, My God, why hast Thou forsaken Me?'"[12] This means that Christ was not able to see anything other than the finality of death when he confronted the hour of his death alone in Gethsemane and on the cross. "That is what Christ also experienced. When He died and was buried, there was no perception or expectation of life. And it was so very hard for the disciples to believe that the Christ lying in the grave behind the sealed rock was the Lord over death and the grave. They themselves said (Luke 24:21): 'We had hoped that he was the one to redeem Israel.'"[13]

All of this took place so that Christ could take the power of my death away from me, in order to put my death to death in himself. "As He died and lay under the sod as you and I must die and be buried, thus He also rose again for our sakes and made an exchange with us; as He was brought into death through us, we shall be restored from death to life through Him. For by His death He has devoured our death, so that we will also arise and live as He arose and lives."[14] Because Christ has made himself responsible for my sin and my death, I no longer need confront my own death alone, for I am to see my

---

12. *LW* 26:372; *WA* 40I:567 [Gal. 4:4-5].
13. *LW* 28:72; *WA* 36:496 [1 Cor. 15:1-2].
14. *LW* 28:109; *WA* 36:546-7 [1 Cor. 15:20-1].

own death in Christ, put to death in his own death, so that when I die I might also hope to live in him. "Therefore if sin makes you anxious, and if death terrifies you, just think that this is an empty specter and an illusion of the devil—which is what it surely is. For in fact there is no sin any longer, no curse, no death, and no devil, because Christ has conquered and abolished all these. Accordingly, the victory of Christ is utterly certain; the defects lie not in the fact itself, which is completely true, but in our incredulity. It is difficult for reason to believe such inestimable blessings."[15]

The problem is, even though I may believe that my death has been destroyed in the death and resurrection of Christ, Luther tells me that I will now feel even more strongly that the opposite is true. Once my conscience is struck by the awareness of what the hour of my death will truly mean for me, it should make me much more aware of the power of sin and death than I was before. "But a Christian has already been thrust into death by the very fact that he became a Christian. Wherever he may be, he occupies himself with this hourly. He expects death at any moment so long as he sojourns here, because devil, world, and his own flesh give him no rest."[16] Moreover, even if I believe in Christ, I cannot see anything beyond death any more than someone who does not believe, nor am I at all immune from the fear of death, as though death did not affect me any more. As a Christian, Luther tells me, I have "learned and experienced that there is no help on earth against death, which is innate in us. In fact, [I as] a Christian must also bear and suffer death the same as others. And of course, it frightens and pains [me]."[17] My reason still tells me the same thing it did before I came to have faith in the victory of Christ, for to all appearances it seems that death is the ultimate victor, and that

15. *LW* 26:284-5; *WA* 40I:444 [Gal. 3:13].
16. *LW* 28:133; *WA* 36:581 [1 Cor. 15:26-7].
17. *LW* 28:119; *WA* 36:561 [1 Cor. 15:22].

I must face the empty, silent abyss of death in the end. "For reason does no more than merely to observe the facts as they appear to the eye, namely, that the world has stood so long, that one person dies after another, remains dead, decomposes, and crumbles to dust in the grave, from which no one has ever returned; in addition, that man dies and perishes so miserably, worse and more wretchedly than any beast or carcass; also, that he is burned to ashes or turns to dust, with a leg resting in England, an arm in Germany, the skull in France, and is thus dismembered into a thousand pieces, as the bones of the saints are usually shown."[18]

I must therefore believe the Word of God, when it proclaims to me that Christ is the victor over my death, and ignore what my eyes and reason tell me, including my intuition that the silent black void is all that awaits me. I appreciate the way Luther does not try to explain away my intuition of the reality and finality of death, but rather asks me to confront it directly, even as he asks me to set it aside in order to hold fast to the Word of God. "To be sure, I feel and see that I and all other men must rot in the ground; but the Word informs me differently, namely, that I shall rise in great glory and live eternally."[19] I am not to try to free myself from the fear of death, for that is impossible, but am rather to realize that not even Christ was immune from the fear of death, and not even he saw anything beyond the darkness of the grave in the hour of his death. "He, too, suffered such anguish and fear of hell, but through His resurrection He has overcome all. Therefore, even though I am a sinner and deserving of death and hell, this shall nonetheless be my consolation and my victory that my Lord Jesus lives and has risen so that He, in the end, might rescue me from sin, death, and hell."[20]

18. *LW* 28:69; *WA* 36:493 [1 Cor. 15:1-2].
19. *LW* 28:71; *WA* 36:495 [1 Cor. 15:1-2].
20. *LW* 28:105; *WA* 36:540 [1 Cor. 15:16-19].

Not only is my awareness of death as great as it was before I believed, but Luther tells me that my faith in Christ will expose me to forms of suffering and death not experienced by those who do not believe. The world does not welcome the message that each of us must answer directly to God in the hour of our death, and that we must all stand guilty at that time, with no hope of escaping condemnation on our own. The world likes to believe that its works and achievements are stronger than sin and death, and will outlive us all. When the world is told that all of this is for naught before God, it opposes this message, often with violent and even lethal persecution. The world also mocks the message that by dying for us Christ has freed us from the power of death, for the world thinks that when we die, we are dead, so that no one will be able to hold us to account, and no one will be able to free us from the dust of the grave. "In contrast to them, we who want to be Christians endure all kinds of troubles and misfortunes, so that people despise and vilify, revile and slander us. The world is so hostile to us; it begrudges us our very life on earth."[21]

However, Luther thinks that the suffering and death caused by the world's opposition to the faithful is trivial compared to the spiritual suffering and trial experienced by the faithful every day in their consciences. "But this fear and woe caused by God's wrath really pierces his heart: the fear of eternal death, of becoming partners of the devil in the abyss of hell. This haunts him day and night. Against this the Christian has to contend, well-nigh sweating blood."[22] Ironically, Luther tells me that my faith that Christ has conquered sin and death does not make me happier than the world that does not believe, but rather makes my life the most miserable on earth, with much greater suffering than I would experience were I not to believe.

21. *LW* 28:103; *WA* 36:537 [1 Cor. 15:16-19].
22. *LW* 28:103; *WA* 36:538 [1 Cor. 15:16-19].

"Therefore a Christian is an especially wretched person, suffering more of whatever may be termed misery than others. He heart is daily roasted on the fire. He must always be terrified, fearful, and trembling when the thought of death and God's severe judgment occur to him."[23] This suffering is intensified when God strikes my conscience with wrath, making me feel that God has abandoned me and consigned me to death with no mercy at all. "Beyond all this is the highest stage of faith, when God punishes the conscience not only with temporal sufferings but with death, hell, and sin, and at the same time refuses grace and mercy, as though he wanted to condemn and show his anger eternally."[24] Even though I have never experienced the fear of God's wrath and of hell in the ways Luther describes, I can appreciate his teaching that God seems to abandon me and heightens my awareness of death to see if I have learned to look away from what my reason and conscience tell me about my death, so that I may look only to Christ, in order to see my death in him, not only when I am tried in this life, but especially when I am brought to the crisis of the hour of my death. "Thus, if I am to gain comfort in the struggle of conscience or in the agony of death, I must take hold of nothing except Christ alone by faith, and I must say: 'I believe in Jesus Christ, the Son of God, who suffered, was crucified, and died for me. In His wounds and death I see my sin; and in His resurrection I see victory over sin, death, and the devil, and my righteousness and life. I neither hear nor see anything else but Him.'"[25]

Far from wanting to free me from the fear of death, Luther thinks that such fear is the training ground of faith, preparing me for the final battle of faith, which takes place at the hour of my death. Ironically, for all that Luther tells me that Christ does for me, he

---

23. *LW* 28:104; *WA* 36:538 [1 Cor. 15:16–19].
24. *Treatise on Good Works* (1520); *LW* 44:29; *WA* 6:208.
25. *LW* 26:357; *WA* 401:546 [Gal. 3:28].

insists that when I face my death, I will do so entirely alone. In particular, God will ask that I give God an account of what I believe, and why I believe it. At that time, the devil will also be present as the prosecuting attorney, and he will try with all his might to undermine my faith, so that he may claim me as his own. I will only be able to stand at that time if I can appeal to the Word of God alone, and not to any other teacher, even as Jesus appealed to the Word alone in his solitary battle with the devil in the wilderness of the Jordan. It will not be enough for me to tell God that I believe what the Church taught me, for what if the Church is in error? Even if the Church has taught this for thousands of years, and with the unanimous consent of councils and theologians, what if the Church is wrong? "When the time comes for you to die, neither I nor the pope will be at your side; and if you know no reason for your hope and say: 'I want to believe what the councils, the pope, and our fathers believed,' then the devil will answer: 'But what if they were in error?' Then he has won, and he drags you into hell. Therefore we must know what we believe, namely, what God's Word says, not what the pope or the saintly fathers believe or say. No, you must rely on the Word of God alone."[26]

I will not be able to stand if I simply say that I chose to believe what everyone else believed, for the danger is that they could all be in error. This possibility—that the Church could be in error, even if it taught a given position with unanimity for thousands of years—is what separates a follower of Luther from a member of a Catholic or Orthodox tradition, and it places an eternal responsibility on the conscience of each Christian. It is not enough to form my mind according to the mind of the Church, as expressed in its Magisterium, dogma, or liturgy. In the hour of my death, God will ask me what

26. *Sermons on the First Epistle of St. Peter* (1522); *LW* 30:105; *WA* 12:360 [1 Pt. 3:13-16].

I believe, and will also ask the grounds of my faith, why I believe what I do. Hence I must be given the ability to read Scripture for myself, so that I can develop the ground of my faith myself, and not be dependent on another teacher for what I believe. "Therefore you should say: 'What do I care about what this or that person believes or decrees? If the Word of God is not preached, I do not want to hear what is said.'"[27] This holds not only for the pope, the councils, and the fathers, but it also holds for Martin Luther himself. It will not suffice at the hour of my death for me to tell God, "I believe this because Luther told me it is true." For what if Luther is wrong? How do I know he is not wrong? Moreover, both at the time Luther taught, and even more since his death, there is a tremendous amount of controversy in the Church about the truth of the Gospel. I cannot wait until an ecumenical council gets convened that will settle all of these disputed questions, for at the hour of my death I will be asked to give God an account of my faith, and to do so I must come to know for myself what the Word of God truly says to me, and give my own account of this Word to God, over against the accusations of the devil. "For when you are lying at death's door and do not know what to believe, neither I nor anyone else can help you. Therefore you yourself must know. You must pay no attention to anyone, and you must cling firmly to the Word if you want to escape hell. And it is also necessary for those who are not able to read to take hold of and retain several—at least one or two—passages from Scripture and to stand firmly on this ground."[28]

Included in my account of my faith and hope to God will be an account of my own life. Just as I must have the reasons for my faith within myself, based on my own reading of the Word of God in Scripture, so I must also have the witness to my own integrity in

27. *LW* 30:106; *WA* 12:360 [1 Pt. 3:13–16].
28. *LW* 30:106; *WA* 12:360 [1 Pt. 3:13–16].

myself, and not in what other people say about me. Even though I should strive to maintain a good reputation among people, so that no one has just cause to be offended by what I do or who I am, I cannot appeal to my reputation when I stand alone before the tribunal of God at the hour of my death. Paul reminds me of this fact when he teaches me that each person must bear his own load (Gal. 6:5). "It is as though Paul were saying: 'It is the height of insanity to look for the ground of your boasting in others, and not in yourself. For in your death struggle and at the Last Judgment it will not help you at all that others praised you.'"[29] Even though the testimony of my conscience to my own integrity does not free me from sin, condemnation, and death, I still need to have this testimony within myself at the hour of my death, for it reveals that my faith and love were sincere, and not hypocritical. "We have need of this testimony of our conscience that we have carried out our ministry well and have also lived a good life."[30] Even though I need to be forgiven by others in spite of my best efforts, I still need to have the testimony of a good conscience, that I have lived a life of faith with integrity, in obedience to the commands of God. "The consciousness of a life well spent is the assurance that we are keeping the faith, for it is through works that we learn our faith is true. And one day my conscience will bear witness before God that I have not been an adulterer, that I have loved my brother, and that I have come to the assistance of the poor, even though there are many things in which we have offended even a brother."[31]

The account I give to God of my integrity must also include my own understanding of what God requires me to do, so that I can give my own account of why I lived the way I did. It will not be enough for me to answer that I only did what I saw all the other Christians

---

29. *LW* 27:120; *WA* 40II:154 [Gal. 6:5].
30. *LW* 27:121; *WA* 40II:155 [Gal. 6:5].
31. *Lectures on the First Epistle of St. John* (1528); *LW* 30:279; *WA* 20:716 [1 Jn. 3:19].

doing, for what if they were wrong? For instance, if I came to see myself as being free of my monastic vows because Luther exercised such freedom, and decided to marry a former nun because Luther did so before me, then I would not be able to stand at the hour of my death, when questioned about why I acted the way I did. Even if I saw entire monasteries empty out following the example of Luther, I must have the ground of such action in myself, or I will not be able to stand at the time of my death. "It is not enough to say: this man or that man did it, I followed the crowd, according to the preaching of the dean, Dr. Karlstadt, or Gabriel, or Michael. Not so; every one must stand on his own feet and be prepared to give battle to the devil. You must rest on a clear text of Scripture if you would stand the test. If you cannot do that, you will never withstand—the devil will pluck you like a parched leaf."[32] Even if the crowd is in fact acting rightly, in accord with the Word and command of God, if I have no appeal other than the fact that others were doing it, I will not be able to stand at the hour of my death. "But who can stand in the presence of Satan and before the judgment seat of God except the man who can stand firmly on solid ground made strong by the most certain warrant of the word of God . . . able to say without hesitation or trembling heart, 'You, who cannot lie, have said these things?'"[33]

However, the testimony of my conscience to my own integrity, and to my understanding of the commands of God, is not enough to save me at the hour of my death, for my sin is a deeper mystery than my integrity, and the devil has a way of making even my good works appear to be sins. In spite of the fact that I bear my own load by having the testimony of a good conscience within me, and not in the opinion of others, I need to appeal to Christ at the hour of my death, for he is the only one who will free me from sin and

32. *Eight Sermons at Wittenberg*; LW 51:79-80; *WA* 10III:21-22.
33. *Judgment of Martin Luther on Monastic Vows* (1521); LW 44:399-400;*WA* 8:668-9.

condemnation, and hence from death. "Here, therefore, I must have something else, something I can hold on to when it comes to the last gasp and my abashed and terrified conscience cries out: I may very well have done what I could, but who knows how often I have done too little, for I cannot see and mark all things, as Ps. 19 [:12] says, 'Who can discern his errors?' Therefore I can put no trust whatsoever in my own holiness or purity."[34] I must turn from myself and my own life, and direct my appeal to Christ, who alone can free me from sin, death, and condemnation. "So long as sin, death, and the curse remain in us, sin damns us, death kills us, and the curse curses us; but when these things are transferred to Christ, what is ours becomes His and what is His becomes ours. Let us learn, therefore, in every temptation to transfer sin, death, the curse, and all the evils that oppress us from ourselves to Christ, and, on the other hand, to transfer righteousness, life, and blessing from Him to us."[35]

Moreover, I must give an account to God as to why I am turning from myself to Christ, and how I personally know that Christ wills to be my redeemer to free me from sin, death, and condemnation. "Hence, if someone tackles you, as if you were a heretic, and asks: 'Why do you believe that you are saved through faith?' then reply: 'I have God's Word, and clear statements of Scripture. Thus St. Paul says in Romans 1:17, "He who through faith is righteous shall live." And above (1 Peter 2:6), when St. Peter, on the basis of the prophet Isaiah (28:16) speaks of Christ, the Living Stone, he says: "He who believes in Him will not be put to shame." I build on this, and I know that the Word does not deceive me.' "[36] Luther sought to give his readers and listeners such clear, indubitable testimonies to the work of Christ on their behalf, for he thought such short statements were the

---

34. *On the Sum of the Christian Life* (1532); *LW* 51:276; *WA* 36:365.
35. *LW* 26:292; *WA* 40I:454-5 [Gal. 3:13].
36. *LW* 30:105; *WA* 12:360 [1 Pt. 3:13-16].

most certain way to defend our faith at the hour of our death, even if we could not read Scripture for ourselves. "And it is necessary for those who are not able to read to take hold of and retain several—or at least one or two—clear passages from Scripture and to stand firmly on this ground."[37] Luther was especially fond of the testimony of John the Baptist to Christ, "Behold the Lamb of God who takes away the sin of the world," for it not only succinctly points to the redeeming work of Christ, but it is also known to all Christians through the Agnus Dei sung in the liturgy. Hence at the hour of death, even were I illiterate, I could take my stand on this text, for if the Lamb takes away the sin of the world, and I am in the world, then it necessarily follows that the Lamb takes my sin away.

But how do I reply if my opponent raises the texts that speak of Christ as requiring works of me in order to be saved from sin and death? What of the statement of Jesus in Luke 6:46, "Why do you call me Lord, Lord, and not do what I tell you?" What of his statement in Matthew that to enter eternal life we need to keep the commandments (19:17), and that only those who leave everything to follow him will inherit eternal life (19:29)? How can I turn from my works to Christ at the hour of my death, when Christ himself seems to be asking me for my works, as though my eternal life depends on them? Luther thought that if this happens to me, I should leave Scripture itself behind, and appeal directly to Christ. "Therefore one should simply reply to them as follows: 'Here is Christ, and over there are the statements of Scripture about works. But Christ is Lord over Scripture and over all works.' "[38] Thus, even though Luther thinks that it is in fact possible to harmonize Matthew and Paul, he thinks that in the hour of death we should leave such an effort behind, and simply appeal to Christ over and above Scripture. "I have the

---

37. *LW* 30:106; *WA* 12:360–61 [1 Pt. 3:13–16].
38. *LW* 26:295; *WA* 401:458 [Gal. 3:14].

Author and the Lord of Scripture, and I want to stand on His side rather than to believe you."[39] This means that in order to stand in the hour of my death, I must not only know the short, indubitable Scriptural testimonies to Christ, but I must also have these testimonies confirmed by my own personal experience of the saving work of Christ himself. "But he who will be taught and not err must watch for these two points: who can adduce testimony for his doctrine from Scripture and from reliable experience. We are able to prove our doctrine and proclamation. I, too—praise God—can proclaim from experience that no works are able to help or comfort me against sin and God's judgment but that Christ alone can still and console my heart and my conscience. For this I have the testimony of all of Scripture and the example of many pious people, who say the same and have experienced it."[40] In trials of conscience, I can come to experience the fact that only Christ can remove sin and death from me, and not any work that I do. At the hour of my death, when I am alone before God, I can point both to the Scriptural portrayals of the saving work of Christ, and to my own personal experience of that work, which has taken place in the depth of my own heart and conscience.

So what did this Mahayana Buddhist Benedictine Protestant Episcopalian learn from Martin Luther? I learned that the hour of my death reveals to me that I alone am completely responsible for my own life, and that I must answer directly to God regarding what I have said, what I have done, and what I have believed to be true, including my relationship to Christ. No one else can answer for me, and I will answer when I am all alone. I learned that even if I believe that Christ has conquered my death in his death, I can still honestly acknowledge that all I can perceive in my future is the dark, silent

39. *LW* 26:295; *WA* 401:458 [Gal. 3:14].
40. *LW* 28:81–2; *WA* 36:506 [1 Cor. 15:8–11].

abyss of death. I learned that I am responsible to God for the way I read Scripture, and can depend on no one else to teach me about myself and my relationship with God, including Martin Luther. I also learned the paradox that the more I am willing to take responsibility for my life, the more Christ wishes to take responsibility for my life; and the more Christ makes himself responsible for me, the more deeply accountable I am to God, not only at the hour of my death, but every hour before then. Finally, I learned that the mysterious poetry of the Eucharist in the 1928 *Book of Common Prayer* was meant to give me both the Scriptural testimony to the death of Christ, and the personal experience of the power of that death, so that I might turn to the death of Christ as my only hope in light of the inevitability of the arrival of my own hour of death. "All glory be to thee, Almighty God, our heavenly Father, for that thou, of thy tender mercy, didst give thine only Son Jesus Christ to suffer death upon the Cross for our redemption; who made there (by his one oblation of himself once offered) a full, perfect, and sufficient sacrifice, oblation, and satisfaction, for the sins of the whole world; and did institute, and in his holy Gospel command us to continue, a perpetual memory of that his precious death and sacrifice, until his coming again."

11

The Threat of Death, the Promise of Baptism, and the Vocational Form of Justification: A Response to Susan Wood and Randall Zachman

Ian A. McFarland

Taken together, Susan Wood's and Randall Zachman's chapters generate an interesting counterpoint on Luther: Wood speaks of the relationship between baptism and the Christian life; Zachman points to Luther's emphasis on the individual's continuous confrontation with death. The two chapters can be conceived contrapuntally because of the way these two themes are related in Luther, for whom the call for daily return to our baptism (Wood's theme) is inextricably bound up with fighting our battle with death (Zachman's focus).

As is the case with good counterpoint, the two lines of argument play off each other without coinciding, as Zachman's essay focuses on our objective hopelessness before death—without any mention of baptism—while Wood's attention is on the role of baptism as that which serves as the continual reference point for Christian existence—without focusing on the threat of death. Each writer interprets Luther both generously and appreciatively, but from a different angle, one highlighting the judgment of death that stands over each of us, and the other the baptismal grace that has covered it in Jesus Christ.

These two themes—that we face death alone, and that Christ is the only power on which we may rely to vanquish this threat—arguably constitute both the greatest strength of Lutheran thought and source of its greatest tension with other Christian confessional traditions. The strength is clear: a single-minded insistence that the only ground of human hope in death or in life in Jesus Christ alone: *solus Christus* as Luther's fundamental (nominative!) soteriological claim, with *sola gratia* and *sola fide* as hermeneutical corollaries clarifying how (ablative!) the salvation achieved by Christ comes to be effective for us. The tension has to do with the worry that this foundational claim effectively swallows up all other dimensions of human life before God and neighbor. Thus, while few today would (at least publicly!) accuse Luther of explicit antinomianism, the worry that antinomian tendencies are at least implicit in Lutheran thought is sparked by Lutheran suspicion of the so-called "third use" of the law, Lutheran nervousness about the doctrine of sanctification, and the difficulty Lutherans have had in developing a coherent social ethic. The interplay between this strength and weakness was given particularly illuminating form for me by my former teacher, George Lindbeck, in his course on ecclesiology. He argued (in agreement with both Wood and Zachman) that Luther always imagined the human being eschatologically: standing before the throne of God, where in the face of the majesty of the Trinity and the burden of sin, it is manifestly the case that a person's only possible recourse is Christ's righteousness. By contrast, in greater or lesser measure (and, obviously, with important differences among them), the other great Christian traditions—Catholic, Orthodox, Anglican, Baptist, Wesleyan, Reformed—all prescind from this radical eschatologization of the human condition to claim that human beings' relationship to God is inseparable from their activity in time and space, and thus from their relationships with one another. Lutherans worry that this stance invariably qualifies the *solus Christus*; their critics worry that the lack of any anthropological complement in the Lutheran understanding of *solus Christus* renders salvation empty: how can human beings "glorify God and enjoy him forever" if the only agency effective in salvation is God's?

While neither Wood nor Zachman makes this question the focus of their chapter (indeed, Wood encourages Catholics to give greater attention to the eschatological focus of baptism, generously bypassing the degree to which Lutherans might do well to focus on its this-worldly implications), their contrapuntal examination of the way Christ defines death and life provides impetus for me, as a Lutheran, to explore of how it is that the complete reliance on Christ that both authors rightly emphasize as key to Luther's theology establishes rather than undermining human life in time and space. The traditional Lutheran approach to this problem is grounded in the anthropology of Luther's *The Freedom of a Christian*. With typical dialectical flair, Luther in this treatise describes the Christian as at once free and a slave: free insofar as she has been unconditionally liberated by Christ from the power of sin, death, and the devil; slave insofar as she, no longer anxious about her status before God, will spontaneously devote herself to the service of the neighbor. Especially as supplemented by the language of the *Augsburg Confession* (1530) ("a person must do such good works as God has commanded. . . ."[1]), this language makes it clear that the life of faith has concrete worldly effects.[2] Nevertheless, in no way do those works, which link us to other people, contribute in any way to our status before God: they in no sense effect salvation.[3] Therefore, though this solution absolves Luther from the charge of indifference to the shape of Christian life ("antinomianism" in the strong sense, as rejected in the fourth article of the *Formula of Concord*), it does not address the charge that salvation is secured independently of any human activity—and thus fails to be a genuinely human experience.

How might one construct a more integrated—and yet still distinctively Lutheran—account of the relationship between our life before God and before other human beings? Here, I think, Wood's and Zachman's essays provide helpful resources. Let me begin by referring back to the contention that Luther's anthropology is one that imagines us always at the judgment seat. As Zachman notes, this perspective naturally attenuates any sense of vibrant connection with other human beings, because whatever our place in life—our status *coram hominibus*—each of us faces death, finally, alone. As Zachman puts it,

my march toward death brings me inexorably to an hour when my

---

1. Article VI [German text]; *BC* 40.
2. "Our faith in Christ does not free us from works but from false opinions concerning works." *The Freedom of a Christian* (1520); *LW* 31:372-3; *WA* 7:70. Cf. *Formula of Concord* (1577): "We also believe, teach, and confess that all people...are obliged to do good works. In this sense the words 'necessary,' 'should,' and 'must' are used correctly, in Christian fashion, also in regard to the reborn" (*Epitome*, IV.8-9; *BC* 498). See also Luther's *Smalcald Articles* (1537): "...we also say that if good works do not follow, faith is false and not true" (III.13.3; *BC* 325).
3. "If works are sought after as a means to righteousness...they are made necessary and freedom and faith are destroyed; and...[they are] no longer good but truly damnable works." *The Freedom of a Christian*, *LW* 31:363; *WA* 7:63. Cf. *Formula of Concord*: "we reject and condemn the following manner of speaking: when it is taught and written that good works are necessary for salvation" (*Epitome*, IV.16; *BC* 499).

whole life will be held directly accountable to God. At the time of my death, I will be alone before God, and God will ask me about the meaning of my life. I will be the only one who can speak on my behalf, and I must do so directly before God.[4]

Luther's discussion of Gal. 6:5 is relevant here: "It is as though Paul were saying: 'It is the height of insanity to look for the ground of your boasting in others, and not in yourself. For in your death struggle and at the Last Judgment it will not help you at all that others praised you.'"[5] Others are of no help; rather, as Paul writes, "all must carry their own loads" (Gal. 6:5). As Zachman notes, the point here is not that we are justified by the testimony of our own conscience (see 1 Cor. 4:4!), let alone by our actions, but rather to emphasize the utter uselessness of others' ideas, opinions, or reputation. One dare not rely on the views of another by, say, pleading that "I did what a great saint—even Luther himself—said I should do"—even if the saint said that I should call on Christ! One's faith must be one's own; one's trust in Christ and not in any created reality (up to and including Scripture) other than Christ.[6]

Wood draws attention to the way in which for Luther baptism objectively mediates this knowledge of God's grace in spite of our unworthiness. As the pledge of God's love for us in Christ through the Spirit, baptism is irrevocable: "a reality that cannot be destroyed once received even though the benefit of baptism cannot be fully realized without a response in faith."[7] As the physical bearer of God's word of promise, baptism transforms our situation before God, so that our task as we daily confront the reality of our death and the judgment it entails is simply to look to our baptism to understand

---

4. Zachman, 219.

5. *Lectures on Galatians*; *LW* 27:120; *WA* 40II:154; cited in Zachman, p. 231.

6. See the quotation from Luther's *Lectures on Galatians* (1535); *LW* 26:295; *WA* 40I:458; in Zachman, p. 234-35.

7. Wood, 199.

that we have been claimed as children of God in grace. Thus, if Luther's anthropology is one that places us always directly before God's judgment seat, baptism points us proleptically to the eschatological resolution of that judgment: that we are vindicated, for Christ's sake. It is central to Luther's understanding of the human situation that we are destined for death, and this by our own fault. In baptism we experience that death, but because in baptism we are put to death in and with Christ, we experience our fault as covered and redeemed by the grace of Christ.[8] So, as Zachman insists, we confront death daily, but, as Wood reminds us, our baptism reminds us that we emerge from that confrontation with the assurance of God's favor in Christ.

In summing up Luther's vision of human life as life-in-the-face-of-death, Zachman offers a provocative conclusion: "the paradox," as he puts it, "that the more I am willing to take responsibility for my life, the more Christ wishes to take responsibility for my life; and the more Christ makes himself responsible for me, the more deeply accountable I am to God, not only at the hour of my death, but every hour before then."[9] I think that this is exactly right, and it is a crucial insight, because it points the way to answering the charge that the Lutheran position evacuates our lives of any meaning by re-establishing human agency as significant in the face of death.

In order to understand how this is the case, it is important to get the meaning of this paradox right. Specifically, the texture of Luther's thought precludes reading Zachman as arguing that Christ is only willing to stand with me to the extent that I am willing to stand with him. That would be placing a condition on salvation, thereby establishing a species of works righteousness inconsistent

---

8. See Luther's *Commentary on Romans* (1515-16); *LW* 25:312; *WA* 56:324; cited by Wood on p. 208.

9. Zachman, 236.

with Luther's soteriology. The idea that Christ's actions are conditional upon my own, so that it is finally me, or what I do, that matters soteriologically, is irreconcilable with *solus Christus/sola fide*. Zachman's point is rather that the intrusion of God's unconditional grace on our eschatological situation reveals the true character of human responsibility rather than undermining it, in line with Paul's interpretation of his own life as I but "not I, but the grace of God that is with me" (1 Cor. 15:10; cf. Gal. 2:20). Paul is certainly not claiming that Christ's activity cancels his own, but rather that it allows it to be reclaimed as his own (cf. Rom. 7:24-25). All this is perfectly consistent with Luther, whose aim in insisting on faith alone is to affirm both that it is *Christ alone* who ensures our status and that this is good news *for us*—and thus something we can and must actively, willingly receive and enjoy as free and responsible human beings. As Luther himself recognizes, this does not preclude human activity, so long as human activity is understood as rooted in God. So, when he interprets Gal. 6:4 ("But let each one test his own work, and then his reason to boast will be in himself alone and not in his neighbor," RSV), he argues that the "phrase 'in himself alone' . . . must be interpreted in such a way that God is not excluded, namely, that everyone should know that his work . . . is a divine work, because it is the work of a divine calling and has the command of God."[10]

In this way, Luther recognizes that divine and human activity need not be conceived as a zero-sum relationship. The question that remains is whether this means of affirming the significance of human agency as a manifestation of divine agency can be extended beyond the individual to the others who are part of one's life. While it can be tricky to invoke Luther himself to this end, I think that such an argument can be constructed in defensibly Lutheran terms, and I

---

10. *Lectures on Galatians*; *LW* 27:120; *WA* 40II:153.

think Wood's essay carries important clues as to how this might be done. To be sure, we face death individually, and we are baptized individually. Our guilt is our own, and because God's address of pardon is equally in the singular, it can only be received as such and not as a general truth. As Wood points out, Luther's insistence on the final and irrevocable character of baptism was the basis for his rejection of religious vows, since he took them as implying that something beyond baptism was necessary, or at least helpful, to secure an individual's place before God. The worry is a fair one, but does the fact that baptism is *final* imply that its focus is irreducibly *individual* (or, perhaps better, does the fact that baptism is intensely *personal* communication render it *private*)? Wood points out that Catholics do not think so. For them baptism and post-baptismal vows are not in competition, because baptism "establishes a person as a member of the community. . . . In this sense baptism is an inauguration that is open-ended even though the sacrament itself is complete."[11]

There would seem to be significant biblical support for this view. After all, just a few verses before Paul tells the Galatians that each person must bear her own load, he writes, "Bear one another's burdens, and in this way you will fulfill the law of Christ" (Gal. 6:2). Of course (and as I already noted in connection with the anthropology of *The Freedom of a Christian*), Luther is not in any sense averse to helping others; but he insists that this aid, though made possible by the gracious gift of forgiveness, does nothing to affect the individual's place before God. This insistence is to be applauded insofar as it extinguishes any basis for works righteousness, but it seems to be false to the equally Pauline insistence that human

---

11. Wood, 203, 200. This point can be connected with her later endorsement of Chauvet as one who moves beyond Luther's theology as a word of promise to be accepted in faith to "an embodied, enacted faith through participation in sacramental action. We literally enact that which we believe" (p. 207).

beings are baptized not only into Christ's death, but also into Christ's body (1 Cor. 12:13), where they are members in relationship with other members, such that "If one member suffers, all suffer together; if one member is honored, all rejoice together" (1 Cor. 12:26). This at least suggests that in the same way that Christ allows us to reclaim our own agency for relationship with God, so Christ also enables us to engage our life with others to that same end.

But how concretely is it possible to do this without compromising the *solus Christus*—to affirm both that human beings are saved by Christ's promise independently of their work (or lack of work) in community, and also that their salvation is not independent of their relationships with others? I think the key here is (only somewhat paradoxically) to follow through on the implications of the character of justification as rooted in God's personal address to the sinner. To be justified is to have one's sin forgiven and so to be acquitted before God's judgment seat. What is sin? According to Scripture it is lawlessness (1 John 3:4), and since God is the author of the law, we might define sin as resistance to God's will. But because God's will is specifically that human beings should have life (John 10:10; cf. Rom. 11:32, discussed in this context in the *Formula of Concord* XI.10-11), it is probably more accurate to speak of sin as the refusal of God's grace. What is the life that God intends us to have in grace? In line with Luther's comments on Gal. 6:4 cited above, what God intends is that we answer God's call to life in the body of Christ; that is, that we live out our vocation. Our vocation is certainly our work, but it is also "a divine work, because it is the work of a divine calling and has the command of God." And, crucially, its shape will be different for each member (1 Cor. 12:17-19), so that what counts as sin—and thus forgiveness of sin—cannot be generalized, but is particular to each member, so that what counts as sin for me may not so count for another. And how do I know what my calling is—and thus what sorts of acts are sin that lead me from it? By discerning God's voice in the voices of those around me, that is, by living within the community and attending to what effects its upbuilding, from which my own cannot be separated.

It remains the case that we each bear our own loads. My dependence on others for discerning my calling does not make it any less my calling, as though I could acquit myself on Judgment Day by blaming someone else for my actions. But it is also different from viewing our interactions with others as simply works of service that are utterly unrelated to our justification. I am not saved by my works to or for others; I am saved only by faith in the good news that my sins are forgiven freely, for Christ's sake. But how do I know *my* sin? Here I must attend to others as I work out my calling. I look to others only as I know that God has called me to a place in Christ's body; but I can find that place only in and through constant interaction with the other members.[12] So one might interpret communally the first of Luther's *Ninety-Five Theses*: that the entire life of the believer is to be one of repentance.

In summary, while I face death alone, the fact that death is defeated *precisely in my being called to life with others* through baptism means that salvation does not evacuate my words and deeds in space and time of soteriological significance, even though it remains true that salvation is God's work even when my agency is involved. Paul's words in Phil. 2:12-13 are a good guide here: "Therefore, my beloved . . . work out your own salvation with fear and trembling, for it is *God* who is at work in you, enabling you both to will and to work for his good pleasure." Clearly our "working out" of our salvation is not a matter of earning, but rather of discerning—living into the freedom that has been won for us by Christ by living into the body

12. Cf. Wood, p. 202-04.

of Christ. The content of this life is inseparable from others, since it is through interaction with them (and theirs with us) under the one head that the reality of salvation is experienced. I am justified by Christ alone, but what it means to be justified is to live a member of Christ's body in a way that entails not the elimination of human agencies, but their complex interweaving in the power of the Spirit. In this way, vocation, conceived as life in community, is in no respect a *means* of justification, but it can be claimed as the concrete *form* justification (and, for that matter, sanctification) takes.

From this perspective, the "problem" of human agency associated with Luther's account of salvation as *solus Christus—sola gratia—sola fide* arises when divine and human agency are viewed as standing in competition with one another. There is such competition when we view things outside the context of the gospel, by (for example) seeing God as an agent on the same plane as ourselves, with whom we have to negotiate to achieve a particular end. To put it in traditional Lutheran terms, that is the relationship of law. But the good news of the gospel is that God is not this kind of agent. Because God is the source and end of our being, to confess the sufficiency of God's action in salvation is in no sense to undermine our own agency in community with others, but rather to set it in its proper frame as the action of a creature whose flourishing is at every moment dependent on the grace of its Creator.

12

Luther's Principle of *sola scriptura* in Recent Ecumenical Discussion

Johannes Zachhuber

Among the many theological ideas that Luther and the Reformation have bequeathed to their intellectual heirs, the Scripture principle, often expressed in the Latin formula *sola scriptura*, today seems one of the least plausible.[1] It is seen, at best, as a position that has become

---

1. As is well known, the formula *sola scriptura* is not found in Luther's works, but the central idea that Scripture's authority stands above the authority of the church is evidently central for the reformer's thought. Relevant texts include Luther's famous words at the Diet of Worms refusing to recant unless condemned by the testimony of Scripture or by obvious reasons ("testimoniis scripturarum aut ratione evidente": *LW* 32:112; *WA* 7:838) and the opening section in his *Assertio omnium articulorum M. Lutheri per bullam Leonis X. novissimam damnatorum* (1520); *WA* 7:96-100. I wish to acknowledge my indebtedness to Derek Nelson, Piotr Małysz and the other participants in the Ecumenical Luther conference at Wabash in the summer of 2014, and also to Philip McCosker, Philip Endean, Julia Meszaros, and Shaun Blanchard who helped me at various stages of the process that led to the present paper.

untenable with the advent of historical criticism, at worst, as a propaganda tool that could never deliver in the first place, given the reliance of all orthodox theology (including Luther's own) on post-biblical developments.

Yet in the midst of all the theological criticism, something important tends to get lost: there are indications that the Bible has never been more fundamental for ecumenical and global Christianity than it is today. This is not merely due to the fact that more people than ever before can read and therefore have access to the Bible in their own language. What is forgotten or overlooked when the Scripture principle is said to have crumbled under the fire of critical exegesis is that all the other elements of the Christian tradition have been affected by historicism too, and it is arguable that in general they have suffered worse than the New Testament.

I shall therefore, in my essay, sound a dissenting note. In the face of widespread skepticism towards the Scripture principle, I shall suggest that it is not an idea that should be laid to rest. On the contrary, there are good reasons why the notion that the Bible is Christianity's ultimate authority and the most fundamental source of Christian beliefs and practices resonates, today more than ever, with Christians and theologians across denominations.

My argument does not, admittedly, come without qualifications and caveats. First of all, against influential evangelical versions of the *sola scriptura*, it is crucial to recall that the Scripture principle for Luther and for the Lutheran (and Calvinist) tradition never excluded reference to patristic and even medieval authorities. Scripture is *norma normans* as opposed to the *norma normata* of later tradition, yet this is not meant to denigrate the contributions by theologians through the ages, but to indicate that their authority is secondary, derived from that of Scripture.[2]

Secondly, any affirmation of the Scripture principle today, I believe, has to come with the awareness that the Bible itself has a historical origin, which is connected (though not simply identical) with the early history of the Church. This was not really an issue in the sixteenth century,[3] but came to the fore with the subsequent rise of historical thought. In this sense, I am conscious of defending a modified historicized version of Luther's original principle which emphasizes the Bible's unique place within Christian history. I shall argue that this version of the *sola scriptura* has supporters, or at least quasi-supporters, way beyond traditional Protestantism. While doing so, I shall have to face the counter-argument, presented most uncompromisingly by Karl Barth, that it is anything but a legitimate development of the reformers' Scripture principle, but its ultimate betrayal.

1. Joseph Ratzinger on the "Geiselmann thesis" and the Relation of Scripture and Tradition

Let me begin my reassessment of the *sola scriptura* in what may seem a somewhat unlikely place. In his early paper, "The question of the concept of tradition. A provisional response,"[4] Joseph Ratzinger offers some highly instructive reflections on the problem of the relationship between the Catholic doctrine of Scripture and tradition and Luther's

---

2. For the early Lutheran attitude, see Martin Chemnitz, *Examination of the Council of Trent*, 4 vols., trans. Fred Kramer (St. Louis, MO: Concordia, 1971-86), 1:256-66; David Hollatz, *Examen theologicum acroamaticum*, prol. III, qu. 50, obs. V (Stargard: Jenisch, 1707 = Darmstadt: Wissenschaftliche Buchgesellschaft, 1971), 1:276-277. Notably, a *catalogus testimoniorum*, written by Jacob Andreae and Martin Chemnitz, was added to the *Formula of Concord* in 1580. It collects a large body of biblical and patristic passages illustrating the doctrine of the Incarnation, specifically the communication of the divine attributes to Christ's human nature (genus maiestaticum); see Robert Kolb and James A. Nestingen, eds., *Sources and Contexts of the Book of Concord* (Minneapolis: Fortress Press, 2001), 220-44.

3. Cf. however the Catholic argument "ecclesia est antiquior Scriptura," discussed, e.g., in Hollatz, *Examen theologicum acroamaticum*, 186.

4. Joseph Ratzinger, "The Question of the Concept of Tradition: A Provisional Response," *God's Word: Scripture—Tradition—Office*, ed. P. Hünermann and Th. Söding, trans. H. Taylor (San Francisco: Ignatius, 2008), 41-89.

position. The text originally appeared in 1965 in a book co-authored by the young Ratzinger and Karl Rahner, *Offenbarung und Überlieferung*. It shows the future pope at his theological best, combining sharp analytical skills with extraordinary learning and, in particular, a keen awareness of the theological significance of Reformation teaching. Ratzinger's objective is, unsurprisingly perhaps, to defend the Catholic view, but the way in which he does so suggests to me that he is much closer to Luther's position than he himself is aware or, at least, wishes to admit.

The Background: Geiselmann's Interpretation of the Tridentine Decree on Scripture and Tradition

In order to appreciate Ratzinger's theological contribution in his article, it is helpful briefly to consider its immediate context in the Catholic theological debate of the time. Ratzinger's argument was in many ways triggered by the groundbreaking, if controversial, research of Josef Rupert Geiselmann (1890-1970), who taught dogmatics and the history of theology at Tübingen until the late 1950s. Geiselmann's work was much discussed during the 1950s and 60s, but he is now, as far as I can see, all but forgotten.[5] His major work, *Die Heilige Schrift und die Tradition* (1962), covers much ground in patristic and medieval theology; most fundamentally, however, it is an attempt to re-interpret the way the Council of Trent considered

---

5. For a survey of Geiselmann's reception and, in particular, names of those theologians who accepted his views cf. Hans Küng, "Karl Barth's Lehre vom Wort Gottes als Anfrage and die katholische Theologie," in *Einsicht und Glaube*, 2nd ed., ed. Joseph Ratzinger and Heinrich Fries (Freiburg: Herder, 1963), 105, n. 25. For very different early Protestant assessments of his theory, see Heinrich Ott, *Glaube und Bekennen: Ein Beitrag zum ökumenischen Dialog* (Basel: F. Reinhardt, 1963), 59-60 (positive), and Hans Geisser, "Hermeneutische Probleme in der neueren römisch-katholischen Theologie," Joachim Lell (ed.), *Erneuerung aus der einen Kirche* (Göttingen: Vandenhoeck & Ruprecht, 1966), 200-229, here: 214-216.

the relation between Scripture and Tradition.[6] This relationship is summarized in the following words:

> this truth and rule [i.e., of the Gospel] are contained in the written book and unwritten traditions that have come down to us, having been received by the apostles from the mouth of Christ himself or form the apostles by the dictation of the Holy Spirit, and have been transmitted, as it were, from hand to hand.[7]

In these words, the Council Fathers expressed their view that the deposit of faith, handed down from the apostles, was contained both in the written documents that make up the Bible *and* in the oral tradition.[8] To the unbiased reader, it may seem fairly obvious what they meant to say. In opposition to the reformers' emphasis on the unique significance of Scripture, they affirmed that the Church relied for her doctrinal teaching not on one, but on two sources. Of those, one was public, the other, we might say, hermetic. The public part was contained in the Bible,[9] specifically the New Testament; but this could not be properly understood without taking into account the other part which the apostles had passed on to their successors. Both the written and the unwritten tradition, the Council Fathers add in memorable and frequently quoted words are "receive[d] and venerate[d] with the same sense of loyalty and reverence."[10] The necessary reliance on both parts, consequently, is the reason why the

---

6. Josef R. Geiselmann, *Die heilige Schrift und die Tradition* (Freiburg: Herder, 1962).

7. "Hanc veritatem et disciplinam [sc. Evangelii] contineri in libris scriptis et sine scripto traditionibus, quae ab ipsius Christi ore ab apostolis accepta aut ab ipsis apostolis Spiritu sancto dictante quasi per manus traditae ad nos usque pervenerunt." Council of Trent, "Decree on the Reception of the Sacred Books and Traditions" (1546); in Denzinger's *Enchiridion Symbolorum*, §1501.

8. John Thiel argues that this is a misreading and that the *libri scripti* of the Tridentine decree contain biblical and nonbiblical writings. Only by conflation with the later usage of "Scripture and Tradition" did the conventional interpretation emerge: *Senses of Tradition: Continuity and Development in Catholic Faith* (Oxford: Oxford University Press, 2000), 22.

9. Subsequently, the decree gives a full and authoritative list of the biblical books including what the Reformation churches consider "The Apocrypha"; Denzinger §1502.

10. Denzinger §1501. Cf. Hollatz, *Examen theologicum acroamaticum*, 278.

full truth of Christianity is only available within the Catholic Church, as it is only she who fully possesses both parts.

Geiselmann's intent was to reject this *prima facie* interpretation of the Tridentine decree. In his reading, the teaching of the Council was far more open than theologians normally recognized; in fact, it permitted a reading that came close to the recognition of the sufficiency of Scripture. His argument was subtle.[11] It relied heavily on the observation that an earlier draft, read at the Fourth Session of the Council, used what he thought was more unequivocal language. It said that the truth of Christianity was revealed partly in Scripture and partly in unwritten tradition (*partim . . . partim*). A small, but vocal minority opposed the *partim . . . partim* formula,[12] and the Council subsequently replaced it with the weaker *et . . . et*. By doing so, Geiselmann concluded, the Council wished to remain agnostic about the precise relationship between Scripture and tradition and left it to theologians to work out in detail what the relationship was.[13] Geiselmann's own view was, by Catholic standards, quite radical but still, he maintained, in line with Tridentine principles. Scripture, he declared, was materially sufficient even though it depended for its interpretation on the tradition of the Church.[14]

There is no doubt that Geiselmann's work was inspired by genuine ecumenical motivation. As his *Die Heilige Schrift und die Tradition* makes clear, he was attacked for advocating what amounted to a Catholic version of the *sola scriptura*.[15] And yet, it may not be entirely

---

11. Geiselmann, *Heilige Schrift*, 91-107; 274-282; and Josef Geiselmann, "Das Konzil von Trient über das Verhältnis der Heiligen Schrift und der nicht geschriebenen Tradition," in *Die mündliche Überlieferung*, ed. Michael Schmaus (München: Hueber, 1957), 123-206, esp. 163.

12. Augustino Bonuccio, general of the Servites, and Bishop Giacomo Nacchianti held that Scripture "cannot be deficient as a source of revelation. Its truth cannot be partial" (Thiel, *Senses of Tradition*, 20).

13. Geiselmann, *Heilige Schrift*, 93.

14. Geiselmann, *Heilige Schrift*, 282. For decisions about ritual and other practices, Geiselmann held, Scripture was insufficient.

unfair to find another motive in his scholarly argument as well. This is the sheer embarrassment in the face of a theory that, by the standard of today's historical awareness, has become quite simply untenable. It is, of course, the case that many doctrinal as well as practical decisions the Church made throughout her history cannot be fully justified on the grounds of the Bible alone, and it is also true that in arguments about these matters from patristic times onwards, the apostolic tradition is cited as a source of authority. Recognizing this, however, is one thing; the stipulation of an unwritten tradition going back to the apostles quite another. Quite apart from the lack of any evidence that Jesus was at all concerned with a written transmission of his revelation, which makes the juxtaposition of written and unwritten somewhat awkward in the first instance, it is not at all obvious which of the more controversial later decisions such a hypothesis would help explaining: debates about the Creed of Nicaea, for example, turned on the question of which biblical passages are relevant; how they are to be understood; and what, if any, non-biblical terminology can legitimately be employed in the clarification of doctrine.[16] They also occasionally involved an examination of the earlier theological tradition: did Bishop Dionysius of Alexandria, for example, condemn the use of *homoousios*; did the Council of Antioch in 268 do so?[17] This use of patristic authority was to become more

15. Heinrich Lennerz, "Scriptura sola?" *Gregorianum* 40 (1959), 38-53; 624-635.

16. Cf. the subtle discussion of the role scriptural interpretation played in fourth-century theology in Lewis Ayres, *Nicaea and its Legacy* (Oxford: Oxford University Press, 2004), 31-40. Interestingly, the example of the fourth-century trinitarian controversy and, in particular, the *homoousion* is invoked in Chemnitz, *Examination of the Council of Trent*, 1:254-5. Chemnitz points out that Athanasius and Cyril of Alexandria did not rebut the charge that the Nicene watchword was unscriptural by affirming the church's authority but with the assertion that it *corresponds* to how the Bible speaks about God. Cf. also Luther, *Assertio omnium articulorum* (1521), *WA* 7:98.7-12.

17. R. P. C. Hanson, *The Search for the Christian Doctrine of God* (London: T&T Clark, 1988), 70-76. Characteristically perhaps, Chemnitz adduces the example of Dionysius of Alexandria to illustrate that the teachers of the church could and did err: *Examination of the Council of Trent*, 1:262-3.

prevalent in subsequent debates, but apart from the problem of the historical veracity of these claims, it seems safe to say that nobody today would argue that it implies an origin of these "traditions" with Christ and the apostles.

Or take a celebrated example from ritual rather than doctrine, the baptism of infants. Anyone who thinks that this practice can be traced back to oral instruction by the apostles (and this was the assumption of both Catholics and Lutherans in the sixteenth century) has to explain why they not only chose to be silent about it in their written works, but quite on the contrary, gave many indications of following a very different practice. And while it is the case that examples of infant baptism go back to the church's early history, there is little to suggest that it was the universally accepted practice until much later.[18]

Geiselmann's effort to reinterpret the Tridentine decree on Scripture and Tradition is of interest to us because it highlights the context, usually ignored today, in which Luther's notion of the sufficiency of Scripture was originally formulated. Consequently, the discussion about the legitimacy of the Scripture principle is conducted along very different lines. For example, it is argued that *sola scriptura* abstracts from the historical, and ecclesial, context of Scripture itself. Even the emergence of a canon of Scripture, it is pointed out, cannot be explained except with reference to the Church. Scripture thus is, in a way, part of the tradition of the Church and cannot therefore simply stand above it. These are valid points, and I shall address them further below; however, constructing the problem along these lines arguably obscures the question that originally gave rise to Luther's emphasis on the sufficiency of Scripture: what are the sources and criteria of the Church's doctrine

---

18. Cf. the comprehensive and authoritative account in: Everett Ferguson, *Baptism in the Early Church: History, Theology, and Liturgy in the First Five Centuries* (Grand Rapids, MI: Eerdmans: 2009), esp. chapter 23.

and practice? As we have just seen, the standard interpretation of Tridentine doctrine until well into the twentieth century assumed two principal sources of revelation that can both be traced back to the apostles. Since one of them is by definition tied to the teaching magisterium of the Church, there is simply no way the latter can be called into question on the basis of biblical witness alone.

Yet the assumption that Scripture and oral tradition are equal sources of the church's teaching and practice is historically untenable. Geiselmann's response to this situation, which perhaps smacks a bit too much of wishful thinking, was to deny that they were ever really meant to be two separate sources. While admitting that the Council of Trent in its reaction to Reformation teaching came close to such a position and that its subsequent interpretation beginning with Melchior Cano actually emphasized the 'co-dignity' of the two,[19] Geiselmann argued that even in the sixteenth century the Catholic Church ultimately steered clear of this theory. From the nineteenth century, according to Geiselmann, an alternative view, which accepted the sufficiency of Scripture, began to emerge in the work of theologians like Johann Adam Möhler and John Henry Newman, and it is this view, the Tübingen theologian urges, that in his own time is increasingly gaining ground. Among those belonging to this growing group, Geiselmann mentions Joseph Ratzinger.[20]

Ratzinger's Own View: Scripture as a 'Relatively Independent Criterion' of the Church's Teaching

It is probably fair to say that Joseph Ratzinger, while never denying

---

19. Geiselmann, *Heilige Schrift*, 113-15.

20. Geiselmann, *Heilige Schrift*, 270-271. Geiselmann, incidentally, notes with approval his agreement with the revisionist Lutheran position of his time, which emphasized the reformer's view of Scripture as the *viva vox evangelii* rather than the dead letter of a historical text (p. 95, with reference to Hanns Rückert, *Schrift, Tradition, Kirche* [Lüneburg: Heliand, 1951], 22-23).

the scholarly quality and the ingenuity of Geiselmann's work, moved over the years from moderate to polemical critic of his Tübingen predecessor.[21] In "The question of the concept of tradition," he is still attempting a balanced assessment in a moderate tone.[22] His main criticism of Geiselmann's theory is, I would argue, a fair one. Ratzinger queries the usefulness of Geiselmann's claim that Scripture is "materially" sufficient for the Church's teaching. Is that really the case? Is it not, rather, almost a matter of honesty to admit that crucial elements of, say, trinitarian doctrine cannot "materially" be fully derived from the testimony of the Bible? Is not to pretend otherwise detracting from the way Christian doctrine has in fact developed over the centuries, taking into account experience the Church accumulated along the way?[23]

At the same time, Ratzinger observes, an answer to the questions raised by the Reformation requires the recognition that *sola scriptura* does not only, perhaps not even primarily, pertain to the "matter" of Church doctrine; it rather is, as much if not more, a "formal" principle: reference to Scripture provides a standard by which to gauge the appropriateness of existing traditions within the Church. Affirming the full "material" sufficiency of Scripture is therefore not merely inherently problematic, it is also lacking as a Catholic answer to the questions raised by the reformers. It affirms, one might say, both too much and too little: too much, in that it obscures the amount of actual doctrine and practice of the Church that cannot "materially" be derived from the Bible; too little, because it ignores the "formal" use of Scripture to critique existing practices within the Church and

21. In 1987, Ratzinger called the "Geiselmann thesis" an "insufficiently thought through and premature theory"; *Joseph Ratzinger in Communio*, vol. 1: *The Unity of the Church* (Grand Rapids, MI: Eerdmans, 2010), 91.
22. Ratzinger, "The Question," 47-51.
23. Ibid., 49-50: "Does it [i.e., the notion of the "sufficiency of Scripture"] not threaten to become a dangerous self-deception, with which we deceive ourselves, first of all, and then others (or perhaps do not in fact deceive them!)?"

thus the potentially most important aspect of the reformers' criticism of the pre-Reformation Church.[24]

Ratzinger therefore suggests a different approach based on the tensional unity of past and present in the Church's existence.[25] A successful negotiation of these two poles, he argues, has to recognize *both* the *ephapax* of the Christ event as testified in the Bible *and* its continuing presence within the Church of Jesus Christ. So, for him, the confrontation of the sixteenth century is caused by one-sided affirmations of these dual points of reference. Luther was right, the later pope says, to emphasize the uniqueness of the Christ event and protest attempts to merge it with the continuing existence of the Church. But his opponents were right to protest a tendency to isolate the two and affirm one at the total expense of the other.

It is interesting to see quite how far Ratzinger is willing to go in his appreciation of the Protestant position. Let me therefore quote a few lines from his text.

> It is essential that, just as there is an office of watchman for the Church and for her inspired witness, so also there be an office of watchman for exegesis, which investigates the literal sense and thus preserves the connection with the *sarx* of the Logos against every kind of Gnosis. In that sense there is then something like an independence of Scripture, as a self-sufficient and in many respects unambiguous criterion, vis-à-vis the teaching office of the Church. There is no doubt that Luther's insight was correct and that not enough space was accorded to it in the Catholic Church because of the claims of the teaching office, whose inner limitations were not always perceived clearly enough. ... Whatever can be known unambiguously from Scripture, through academic study or through simply reading it, has the function of a real criterion, against which even the pronouncements of the Magisterium must be tested.[26]

---

24. Ratzinger, "The Question," 50: "The question of the sufficiency of Scripture is only a secondary problem within the framework of a far more fundamental decision . . . that concerns the relationship between the authority of the Church and the authority of Holy Scripture."

25. Ratzinger, "The Question," 58–67.

By affirming reference to the historical voice of the Bible as a "relatively independent criterion" for the establishment of theological truth and by accepting that the teaching magisterium is required to take this voice into account when making theological decisions, Ratzinger comes in fact, it seems to me, as close to accepting the *sola scriptura* as Geiselmann did before him. Elsewhere, he cited both Bonaventure and Aquinas with affirmations of the primacy of Scripture using words, Ratzinger admits, that sound "offensive to us" (sic):

> "All saving truth is either in Scripture, or flows from it, or can be traced back to it." (Bonaventure)

> "We do not believe the successors of the prophets and apostles unless they announce to us what the latter left in writing." (Aquinas)[27]

This said, Ratzinger's major concern seems not so much with Scripture but with its interpretation by scholarly exegetes: "Can the word be set up as independent, without handing it over to the arbitrariness of the exegete, to be emptied in the disputes of historians, and thus to the complete loss of normative authority?"[28] For those who know Ratzinger's later work in the Congregation for the Doctrine of the Faith, an early pattern becomes apparent here: the Church loses its message if it makes itself entirely dependent on those with a purely historical interest in the Bible. It is hard to imagine that Luther would have disagreed with that view! In fact, even the later Lutheran divines, who are now often blamed for creating a barren, dogmatic version of the Scripture principle, are quite clear about the importance of ecclesial traditions of biblical interpretation.[29]

---

26. Ibid., 66.
27. Jared Wicks, "Six texts by Prof. Joseph Ratzinger as *peritus* before and during Vatican Council II," *Gregorianum* 89:2 (2008), 233-311 at 275-6. Cf. also Geiselmann, *Heilige Schrift*, 222-249.
28. Ratzinger, "The Question," 46.

More important for me, however, is another observation. Whatever his disagreements with Geiselmann, Ratzinger has no intention whatsoever of defending the Council of Trent along the more traditional lines of some of Geiselmann's earlier opponents. While Ratzinger' is concerned not to permit a detachment of the Church's proclamation from its historical source of revelation, he effectively agrees with Geiselmann (and Luther) that *qua* historical source the Bible is of unique value. In blunt terms he told the German-speaking bishops at the Second Vatican Council that the assumption of an oral, apostolic tradition had become historically untenable:

> History can name practically no affirmation that, on the one hand, is not in Scripture but, on the other hand, can be traced back even with some historical likelihood to the apostles. There are three classic examples given in textbooks, namely, the canon of Scripture, the existence of seven sacraments, and infant baptism. But these do not pass the test.[30]

Ratzinger's question is one we might call post-historicist: how far should purely historical knowledge be allowed to determine the life of the Church? One might paraphrase this problem in Nietzschean language as "the use and abuse of historical scholarship for the life of the Church." I would argue that Ratzinger's position—at least as much as Geiselmann's—is a fully justified concern flowing from the fundamental acceptance of the Scripture principle. Recalling at this point once again the historical confrontation in the sixteenth century, which, as I have shown, essentially concerned the existence of an unwritten apostolic tradition within the Church to complement the written record of the Bible, Ratzinger quite clearly stands on the

---

29. Chemnitz, *Examination of the Council of Trent*, 1:244-8; Hollatz, *Examen theologicum acroamaticum*, 276-77.
30. Wicks, "Six texts," 274.

side of the reformers, even though he does not, of course, accept the practical consequences the latter drew from this view.[31]

My provisional conclusion at this point is this: once we keep our eye on the original issue that divided Luther and his followers from his Catholic opponents in the sixteenth century, an ecumenical consensus of sorts has been reached for quite some time. And this consensus is in its fundamentals much closer to Luther's original view than it is to that of his adversaries. The Bible is the unique source of the Christian doctrine of faith, and its *sensus historicus* is a necessary criterion by which the Church's proclamation and practice has to be measured.

The reason for this development is largely the recognition that the Tridentine affirmation of an unwritten apostolic tradition as a source for the church's doctrine and practice has lost all historical credibility. If, then, it now often seems that it is really the *sola scriptura* that lacks plausibility, this may ironically be the result of its considerable ecumenical success as a theological principle, which has let slip into obscurity its historical rival. In a way, the Scripture principle may have become the victim of its own success, as it is no longer considered relative to an alternative, but entirely on its own merits.

2. The Scripture Principle in Historicist Transformation

I have been careful so far to say that Luther's view of the *sola scriptura* has become ecumenically accepted when viewed against the

---

31. In his lecture to the German-speaking Bishops at Vatican II, he presented his own modified understanding of Scripture and tradition as the only bulwark *against* the *sola scriptura*: "Characterizing Scripture and tradition as the sources of revelation means in effect that one identifies revelation with its material principles. This brings with it the acute danger of slipping into 'scripturalism', that is, holding *sola Scriptura* and identifying Scripture and revelation. One only has to affirm that tradition adds no supplementary content to Scripture and the outcome is that Scripture is the whole of revelation, that Scripture and revelation are identical in extent, and so you have *sola Scriptura* in a strict and exclusive sense" (Wicks, "Six texts," 271).

historical alternatives at the time, in particular against the Tridentine concept of tradition. This is not to deny, of course, that more recent appropriations of the Scripture principle have transformed its original form. This observation is crucial in the present place not least because it can be argued that the same factors that influenced modern transformations of the Scripture principle on the Protestant side were also influential for the position espoused by Geiselmann and Ratzinger and are therefore at least partly responsible for the ecumenical rapprochement I have sketched thus far.

The factor I have in mind is historicism. Around the turn of the nineteenth century, the emergence of a new type of historical thought led to one of the most fundamental transformations ever of Western intellectual life, including but not limited to religion and theology.[32] The shorthand of "historical criticism" is insufficient to describe what happened in those decades. Rather, all aspects of human life were increasingly seen as unfolding in the ever-developing and ever-changing frame of historicity. Historical understanding therefore became indispensable for *any* interaction with past events and ultimately for human self-understanding as such. While this development was not exclusively, perhaps not even primarily targeting religion, it was bound to have an impact on the theological interpretation of Christianity, especially given the historical character of this religion.[33]

Generally speaking, historicism entailed both a promise and a risk. The promise was that the new toolkit provided by modern

---

32. For an overview, see Johannes Zachhuber, *Theology as Science in Nineteenth Century Germany: From F.C. Baur to Ernst Troeltsch* (Oxford: Oxford University Press, 2013), 4-12.

33. For this assessment cf. J. F. W. Schelling, *Vorlesungen über die Methode des akademischen Studiums*; in *Sämmtliche Werke*, ed. K. F. A. Schelling, vol. I/5 (Stuttgart/Augsburg: Cotta, 1858), 291: "This is the great historical thrust of Christianity; this is the reason for which a Christian science of religion must be inseparable from, indeed wholly one with history. But this synthesis with history, without which theology itself could not be thought, in turn requires as its condition a higher Christian view of history."

historiography would permit unprecedented access to people and events of the past, far superior to traditional modes of their appropriation. The risk was that, by recognizing their historical place, distance could turn into detachment, and those figures of Europe's classical and Christian heritage, who had previously co-existed with their more recent readers as literary quasi-contemporaries, would now merely appear figures of the past. Initially, the promise seemed more evident and the potential gain well worth the risk. Increasingly, however, the dangers ensuing from the historical approach became the more prevalent notion.[34]

Perhaps the ambiguity of historicism with regard to our relationship to the Bible, and its development throughout the nineteenth century has never been as powerfully described as in the words of Albert Schweitzer:

> The study of the Life of Jesus has had a curious history. It set out in quest of the historical Jesus, believing that when it had found Him it could bring Him straight into our time as a Teacher and Saviour. It loosed the bands by which He had been riveted for centuries to the stony rocks of ecclesiastical doctrine, and rejoiced to see life and movement coming into the figure once more, and the historical Jesus advancing, as it seemed, to meet it. But He does not stay; He passes by our time and returns to His own. What surprised and dismayed the theology of the last forty years was that, despite all forced and arbitrary interpretations, it could not keep Him in our time, but had to let Him go. He returned to His own time, not owing to the application of any historical ingenuity, but by the same inevitable necessity by which the liberated pendulum returns to its original position.[35]

What did this development mean for the Scripture principle? In a seminal, early paper, Wolfhart Pannenberg identified two interrelated issues.[36] The original *sola scriptura*, he argued, relied on

34. Zachhuber, *Theology as Science*, 276-85.
35. Albert Schweitzer, *The Quest of the Historical Jesus*, trans. W. Montgomery (London: A&C Black, 1910), 399.

two implicit assumptions: first, the identity between the stories of the Bible and real history; secondly, the quasi-contemporaneity of the Bible to its readers. Both were shattered by the historical turn, and this led to the emergence of historical-critical exegesis and hermeneutics as twin disciplines aimed at recovering the Bible both as a historical document *and* in its contemporary relevance.

Pannenberg spoke in this context of a "crisis" of the Scripture principle. I would, however, add that the damage historicism did to some central tenets inherent in the original *sola scriptura*, affected Christianity's historical basis in general, not just the Bible. I have pointed out above how the notion of an unwritten apostolic tradition became a fatality of modern historical consciousness; the same can be said about that famous competitor of the Scripture principle, the idea of a *consensus quinquesaecularis*. The crisis of the latter principle can be studied particularly well in John Henry Newman, who as late as 1837 offered a spirited defense of Bishop George Bull's rebuttal, in 1680, of Dionysius Petavius' (1583-1652) argument "that the Rulers and Fathers of the Church [prior to Nicaea] were nearly all of the very same sentiments as Arius."[37] For the Newman of 1837, Petavius provided a prime example for the "Roman teaching as neglectful of antiquity";[38] in other words, for a tendency in post-Tridentine Catholicism to take refuge from historical uncertainty in a legalistic affirmation of the authority of the teaching magisterium. Only a few years later, however, Newman's own further research had led him to recognize as fictitious the traditional Anglican affirmation of a "consensus of doctors" in the early centuries of the church.[39]

---

36. Wolfhart Pannenberg, "The Crisis of the Scripture Principle," *Basic Questions in Theology*, trans. G. H. Kehm (Minneapolis: Fortress, 1970), 1-14.

37. John Henry Newman, *The Via Media of the Anglican Church: Illustrated in Lectures, Letters, and Tracts*, 2 vols. (London: Greens and Co., 1901), vol. 1: *Lectures on the Prophetical Office of the Church*, 61.

38. Newman, *The Via Media*, 47.

His *Development of Doctrine* necessitated his conversion *because* for him the only response to the uncertainty of historical conclusions lay in the embrace of ultimate institutional authority. In that sense, his famous words that "to be deep in history is to cease to be a Protestant"[40] are not free from ambivalence: while the Catholic principle of tradition was intended to hold together its apostolic origin and its presence in the teaching magisterium, Newman's case shows how delicate the balance between these two elements was, especially under the conditions of historicism. More often than not, the Catholic Church faced the unenviable choice of either rejecting historical criticism not only of the Bible but of the history of doctrine as well, or permitting the impression that the authority of the magisterium was one of arbitrary legality.

By contrast, Scripture could be given, and was given, a historicist lifeline by means of the observation that it stood at the very beginning of Christianity as a historical entity and, for that reason, could be seen as its ultimate source. This was Friedrich Schleiermacher's view, according to which "the Christian writings, which are derived from the period of Primitive Christianity are . . . objects of Exegetical Theology . . . insofar as they are held capable of contributing to the original and therefore, for all periods, normal representation of Christianity."[41]

This hypothesis obviously has its own considerable historical and consequently theological problems given that dating the writings of the New Testament is difficult and that the historical reconstruction of their relationship to the actual origins of the Christian religion

---

39. John Henry Newman, *An Essay on the Development of Doctrine* (London: Greens and Co, 1909), 14–20.

40. Newman, *An Essay on the Development of Doctrine*, 8. The sentence is absent from the first edition.

41. Friedrich Schleiermacher, *Brief Outline of the Study of Theology*, trans. W. Farrer (Edinburgh: T&T Clark, 1850), 132 [§ 103].

depends crucially on more or less plausible exegetical and philological assumptions. Yet it is interesting that against all the more radical hypotheses that have inevitably been put forward—among them, for example, Baur's famous view according to which only the major Pauline epistles clearly belong to the Apostolic age whereas many of the remaining writings have been written much later, some of them only far into the second century[42]—the insight that the core writings of the New Testament, the Pauline corpus and the gospels, belong to the first fifty years after the death of Jesus and are thus, more or less, the earliest extant pieces of Christian literature, has practically won the day. Difficulties remain, but they cannot be engaged here in any detail.[43] I do take this very general observation, however, as justification to concentrate on a different problem with this new perspective on the Bible.

For, even if it is granted that the New Testament can be identified as the historical origin of Christianity, cannot this insight be taken as confirmation for the position that the Bible is *nothing but* the earliest part of the Church's tradition? In other words, could it not be precisely the upshot of a historicist transformation of theology that the Bible loses its uniqueness and becomes merely one part within Christianity's historical and literary heritage? And, if so, does it not have to be admitted that any special authority Scripture may possess must be derived from the authority of the Church and that, consequently, Scripture could never possess authority over the Church, as the reformers had claimed?

Schleiermacher himself accepted that reference to Scripture (like all theology) made sense only from within the Church. The authority granted to Scripture, he argued, always presupposes faith in Jesus.

---

42. Cf. Zachhuber, *Theology as Science*, 92-95.

43. A further major problem concerns the Old Testament. It is no coincidence that many of the "historicist" biblicists focus heavily on the New Testament.

"The authority of Holy Scripture cannot be the foundation of faith in Christ; rather must the latter be presupposed before a peculiar authority can be granted to Holy Scripture."[44] But some of his readers felt he should have gone further than that. I am thinking in particular of Johann Adam Möhler, who, in *Die Einheit in der Kirche*, used a Schleiermacherian framework to develop a novel, yet distinctively Catholic, account of the relationship between the Bible and tradition.[45] In a manner that anticipated Newman's later theory in *The Development of Doctrine*, Möhler applied the romantic category of organic unity to the historical character of the Church which, for him, is the continuation of the Incarnation. In this perspective, any distinction between Scripture and tradition is ultimately blurred; the body of Christ in its concrete, hierarchical constitution is the overarching principle and the one seat of ultimate authority.

Mentioning Möhler at this point makes sense for yet another reason. It is arguable that the more recent Catholic positions discussed earlier in this chapter owe much to his appropriation of a historicist perspective within the Catholic tradition. And yet we have seen that, for both Geiselmann and Ratzinger, the upshot of this perspective is not a complete blurring of the distinction between Scripture and tradition but the complete opposite. I think the explanation for this is quite simple. Möhler's synthetic view of Christian unity (much like Newman's) does not necessarily offer criteria for decisions about ecclesiastical doctrine and practice. In fact, as the example of

---

44. Friedrich Schleiermacher, *The Christian Faith*, trans. H. R. Mackintosh and J. S. Stewart (Edinburgh: T&T Clark, 1999), 591 [§128].

45. Johann A. Möhler, *Die Einheit in der Kirche: Oder das Prinzip des Katholizismus*, ed. J. R. Geiselmann (Darmstadt: Wissenschaftliche Buchgesellschaft, 1957). For Schleiermacher's influence on its conception cf. Michael J. Himes, " 'A Great Theologian of our Time': Möhler on Schleiermacher," *Heythrop Journal* 37:1 (January 1996): 24-46. On p. 25 Himes quoted Möhler's famous protestation that the reason for any similarities between their works is Schleiermacher "catholicizing." An excellent historical contextualisation of Möhler's early work is Geiselmann's "Introduction" to his edition of Möhler's work.

Newman illustrates, the ambiguity of any given historical analysis can be used to defer decisions in principle to the legal authority of the teaching magisterium. If any authority was to be granted to a historical aspect of Christianity (as opposed to its contemporary, "living" existence), it made sense to focus on the texts that directly reflect the historical reality of the Incarnation.

3. Scripture or Tradition? Karl Barth's Defense of the Scripture Principle in *CD* I/2

The strongest advocate of the interpretation that Möhler understood Schleiermacher better than the latter had understood himself was Karl Barth. In a highly polemical (and entirely un-ecumenical), but at the same time extremely engaging section in *Church Dogmatics* I/2, Barth argued that the Neo-Protestant historicization of the Scripture principle was tantamount to its betrayal and that Möhler and others were perfectly right in perceiving Schleiermacher's theory as a pale reflection of the traditional Catholic view.[46] Barth's position is so emphatic because for him the major purpose of the *sola scriptura* was to retain the Bible as a criterion of truth over and above the Church and her proclamation.

Interestingly, in the previous volume of his *magnum opus*, Barth himself had developed his famous theory of the three-fold form of the Word of God, of which Scripture was only the second and, as such, inferior to the Word Incarnate himself.[47] To this day, as is well known, Evangelicals have accused Barth on this basis of a betrayal of the Scripture principle. Yet in *CD* I/2 there is little to mitigate the sense that Scripture's authority must be absolute and total. Barth is

---

46. Karl Barth, *Church Dogmatics*, vol. I/2 (1938), trans. G. T. Thomson and H. Knight (Edinburgh: T&T Clark, 1956), 559-64.
47. Barth, *Church Dogmatics*, vol. I/1 (1932), trans. G. W. Bromiley (Edinburgh: T&T Clark, 1975), 88-124.

not, of course, ignorant of the critical work done by historians over several centuries, but ultimately, he insists, the Church is faced with a simple decision: does she think she possesses in some form or another her own source of authority, or does she accept Scripture in this position? If the former, then, Barth argues, Scripture will inevitably be relegated to an inferior position and eventually lose its significance altogether. For that reason, any attempt to tamper with the simple truth that the Bible is the Word of God and, as such, the ultimate source of all authority in the Church must be resisted.

Barth's argument in §20 of *CD* I/2 is significant in two ways: on the one hand, I agree with his historical claim about the factual *rapprochement* of Catholic and Protestant views of Scripture and tradition in the nineteenth and twentieth centuries following the historicist turn. Given that Barth did not know (or certainly did not use) Newman and that authors such as Henri de Lubac had not even come to prominence at all, it shows some considerable perceptiveness on his part to see this historical alignment so clearly. I would, therefore, take Barth as a prominent witness in support of my initial thesis that on the basis of its historicist reconstruction the Scripture principle has gained something like ecumenical recognition.

On the other hand, of course, Barth is also, in effect, offering the most antagonistic counter-argument to my own claims in this chapter. I therefore have to defend my view against his criticism, but I can also hope that, by defending it against Barth's view, I am addressing some of the strongest theological objections to my own theory. In fact, I do not think that this defense is too difficult. Contrary to what Barth says, the willingness to accept the word of Scripture as a criterion of the Church's proclamation does not depend on the premise, which after all is difficult to defend in a post-historicist world, that we can abstract the Bible from Christian history. On the contrary, historical contextualization has often helped discern more clearly what Scripture is saying on a particular issue. Nor does Barth say, positively, how his model would always guide the Church in times of difficult challenges. "The Bible," as everyone knows, does not simply communicate absolute truths. It speaks with many voices, and different people find different insights in it. While it is true that any "human" attempt to discern the most relevant aspect of the biblical message for a time or a situation, inevitably blurs the boundary between the Word of God and its human interpretation, there is no way this risk can be avoided.

It is always important to remember that Barth published this volume in 1937; he cannot be blamed for the fact that the uniquely painful experience of the church struggle was before his eyes when he wrote it. Yet from the historical distance we can also perceive that the situation he was faced with was fairly exceptional: the threat of a group within the Church (the "German Christians") who sought to introduce a new revelation into the Christian faith. While we can sympathize with Barth's tendency to see all trajectories in more recent church history coalesce in this attack against the foundations of the faith, it is by now reasonably clear that this was a kind of tunnel vision that made him blind to many important nuances that we can find reflected in much of his earlier and later work.

I conclude therefore at this point that, while Barth was right to see a surprising gradual alignment of Protestant and Catholic views on Scripture since the early nineteenth century, his radical rejection of this emerging consensus throws the baby out with the bathwater. He is right, of course, that the new, historical view of Scripture has its dangers: we can perceive it on the Protestant side in the complete dissolution of the Bible into its historical sources with the resultant loss of its theological and spiritual dimension. The corresponding danger on the Catholic side is the one-sided emphasis on the "absolutist" power of the Petrine Office, as exemplified at Vatican I. Yet these dangers do not devalue the positive gain which, I believe, has led to an increasing awareness of the Bible as the most foundational and the most authoritative text the Christian churches possess.

Conclusion

I have so far consciously avoided defining what precisely *sola scriptura* amounts to. The late Catholic theologian, Edward T. Oakes, has suggested the formula "text precedes community."[48] While this may not be a perfect definition, it is a heuristically helpful starting point. With its assistance, we can immediately perceive that the historic Reformation churches have never solely relied on the Scripture principle. Children and indeed many adults were catechized; pastors were figures of authority, and a teaching magisterium continued to exist even though it was delegated in non-episcopal churches to the theological faculties at public universities. Moreover, for centuries all or most religious debates involving direct reference to the Bible were contextualized within Christendom, broadly speaking. This only began to change in the nineteenth century and did not become prevalent until much later.

At the same time, text has always preceded community to some extent within Christianity and not just in Protestantism. Why else would there have been the codification not just of a canon of the Scriptures but of major doctrines and practices? What is the purpose of creeds and conciliar decisions if not that these texts can, and are expected to, be used to correct communal beliefs and practices?

The Reformation, then, has hardly brought about a complete

---

48. Edward T. Oakes, "The Paradox of the Literal: The voice of canon criticism in Reformation and Counterreformation polemics," in *Reform and Counterreform: Dialectics of the Word in Western Christianity since Luther*, ed. J. C. Hawley (Berlin: de Gruyter, 1994), 15-29, at 15.

reversal in the history of Christianity; rather, it has readjusted the balance between text and community. And time has not stopped in the sixteenth century. It is arguable that one of the reasons why the Scripture principle has developed such a powerful dynamic over the centuries may well be that it has chimed with social tendencies that made authoritative references to communal traditions increasingly precarious.

This certainly seems to be the case today, and I would like to close by suggesting that current debates about the role of Scripture can be understood against the backdrop of declining patterns of primary communal belonging. In consequence, there is an overall tendency towards the erosion of the kind of authority that derives from such primary or natural communities; indeed, where individuals today affirm the need and the value of communal authority—and many of course emphatically do so—this is often the result of conscious decisions (for example, conversions), compensating for the felt loss of the intuitive security that used to come with one's sense of communal belonging.

This tendency to compensate, or should we say overcompensate, for the eclipse of communal authority is at work, I would suggest, in today's attacks against the reliance on Scripture, most brutally articulated perhaps by Stanley Hauerwas, who famously demanded that the Bible should be taken away from the American people.[49] But we should not be deceived, nor should we be distracted, by the noise created by this kind of intervention. Continuing changes to the religious fabric of most parts of Christianity mean that reliance on the "unwritten" traditions that guided much of religious life until very recently is on the way out. Consequently, text will inevitably (and in many cases now literally) "precede" community, and there are good

---

49. Stanley Hauerwas, *Unleashing the Scripture: Freeing the Bible from Captivity to America* (Nashville: Abingdon, 1993).

reasons to assume that in the long run no other text commands the same symbolic power as the Bible.

Hauerwas is not, however, writing against the grain of current developments only. He is also, I believe, mistaken in seeing appeals to Scripture as simply the outgrowth of religious individualism. In their own way, they also create community and could, in fact, be seen as supremely ecumenical. Not in the sense that reference to, and reliance on, Scripture inevitably leads to unity and agreement among Christians, but in the recognition that the acceptance and the use of the Bible is in many ways the one element that unites Christians of East and West, North and South, of antiquity and modernity. Gerhard Ebeling once sought to define church history as the history of the exegesis of the Bible.[50] This can easily appear not just hyperbolical but a typically Protestant narrowing of what Christianity has historically amounted to. However, if Ebeling's definition is not understood as excluding the wealth of the many forms of doctrine and worship that have developed over the centuries, but as drawing attention to the fact that the vanishing point behind the vast majority of them is to be found in Scripture, then his view is far less extravagant and far more plausible than one might intuitively think. We are continually more aware of the huge discrepancies between the Christianities that have emerged at different points in time and those that have existed, and continue to exist, in different parts of the globe. Perhaps it is time we accept that they cannot all be embraced in a single institution, nor even in the most elastic concept of Christian orthodoxy, whereas their willingness to accept the Bible as the foundation of their faith is the one bond that holds this variety together.

---

50. Gerhard Ebeling, "Church History Is the History of the Exposition of Scripture," *The Word of God and Tradition*, trans. S. H. Hooker (London: Collins, 1968), 3-33.

13

Learning from Luther: Reformed Appropriations and Differentiations

Anna Case-Winters

Introduction

For John Calvin, Martin Luther was "the pathfinder." Calvin's affirmation of Luther could not be stronger. At one point Calvin goes so far as to say of Luther, "we consider him a distinguished apostle of Christ whose labor and ministry have done most in these times to bring back the purity of the gospel."[1] Surely there could be no higher praise. Calvin's acceptance of the *Augsburg Confession* signals his solidarity with Luther and his theology.[2] He would never have

---

1. John Calvin, *The Bondage and Liberation of the Will: A Defence of the Orthodox Doctrine of Human Choice against Pighius* (1543), ed. A. N. S. Lane (Grand Rapids: MI: Baker, 1996), 28.

identified himself over against Luther—as "Reformed" in contrast to "Lutheran" in the sense of later polemics and divisions. Both he and Luther were together "Evangelical"—champions of the gospel seeking reforms that would serve that end.

What we see in Calvin's relation to Luther is deep appreciation and extensive appropriation. Many Luther scholars have read Calvin through a Zwinglian lens that obscures his proximity to Luther and his differences from Zwingli. Considering Calvin in his own right reveals that he has in fact, at many points—including, notably, sacramental theology—a closer affinity to Luther's views than to Zwingli's. At the same time, there are a few differentiations from Luther that are distinctive to Calvin. Brian Gerrish has said that Calvin's was the "stance of a critical disciple," and as often happens with strong-willed disciples, he would leap vigorously to his master's defense, and yet claim for himself the right to criticize him freely.[3]

Of the many topics through which such could be fruitfully explored along these lines, I will zero in on the central matter of *sola scriptura*, which has been termed the "formal principle" of the Reformation. Calvin's appropriation and differentiation on this principle is at the heart of many of the differences in Lutheran and Reformed theology that carry forward even into our day. A final step will take an experiential turn as I offer some relevant observations from my term of service co-chairing the Joint Commission on Lutheran-Reformed Relations for the World Communion of Reformed Churches (WCRC) and the Lutheran World Federation (LWF) and some reflections on the way to Jubilee 2017.

---

2. B. A. Gerrish, *The Old Protestantism and the New: Essays in Reformation Heritage* (Edinburgh: T&T Clark, 1982), 29.

3. Gerrish, *The Old Protestantism and the New*, 29.

I. *Sola Scriptura/Tota Scriptura*

Luther came gradually to a clear and forceful articulation of *sola scriptura*. In July of 1519, he affirmed "scripture alone" in matters of faith.[4] In the *Babylonian Captivity of the Church* (1520), he went on to say that, "Whatever is asserted without scriptural proofs or an accredited revelation may be held as an opinion, but it need not be believed."[5] Then, at the Diet of Worms (April 1521), when he refused to recant, he took the matter further, "Unless I am convicted by Scripture and plain reason—I do not accept the authority of popes and councils, for they have contradicted each other—my conscience is captive to the Word of God."[6] What is decisive here is his bold elevation of Scripture above popes and councils.

For Luther "the content of Scripture is Christ . . . all Scripture turns about him as its true center." His affirmation of the Old Testament reveals its character as the "swaddling clothes and the manger in which Christ lies."[7] This christological turning point meant for Luther that there is, in fact, a canon within a canon. As he says, "John's Gospel and St. Paul's epistles, especially that to the Romans, and St. Peter's first epistle are the true kernel and marrow of all the books." He dismisses the book of James as "strawy"—fit for a fire starter.[8] He says that it would be better if Esther was not in the canon and insists that Revelation is not an "apostolic" book.

At this point, Calvin's position on Scripture differentiates. For Calvin, it may be said that *sola scriptura* entails "*tota scriptura*." "All" of Scripture and sometimes the very words themselves are seen by him

---

4. Ibid., 54.
5. *LW* 36:29; *WA* 6:508.
6. *LW* 32:112; *WA* 7:838; cf. Ronald Bainton, *Here I Stand: A Life of Martin Luther* (Penguin: New York, 1995), 185.
7. "Preface to the Old Testament" (1523); *LW* 35:236; *WA* DB 8:12.
8. "Preface to the New Testament" (1522); *LW* 35:361-2; *WA* DB 6:10. Cf. Gerrish, *The Old Protestantism and the New*, 55.

as divinely inspired. Every part of Scripture carries the full weight of authority and validity for all times and places. Calvin, in fact writes commentaries on every book of the Bible excepting only two: Revelation and Song of Solomon. It was not that they were "strawy," but, as he reported, he simply did not know what to do with them!

Calvin concurs with Luther that Christ is the centerpoint of Scripture. Both he and Luther share a vision of the one covenant of grace through all times and places; a covenant mediated by Christ. However, for Calvin, the Old Testament is more than the "swaddling clothes and the manger in which Christ lies." For Luther, the right way to read the Old Testament is to do so christologically. For Calvin these texts have their own integrity as a story of God's way with God's people in their own right, antecedent to the coming of Christ. These hermeneutical differences have their effect in the theologies of Luther and Calvin.

Calvin's *tota scriptura* has a unifying and leveling effect. Both Old Testament and New Testament carry the full weight of authority. There is no contrasting of the Old Testament (as law) with New Testament (as gospel). Because of this unity, Old Testament and New Testament writings can be read synoptically. Like Luther, Calvin read Christ into the Old Testament without hesitation. He went to draw a parallel between the sacraments of baptism and the Lord's Supper and the practices of circumcision and Passover. Calvin identified the people of Israel as, in some sense, "the church." It is this presumption of the unity and equal authority of the texts of Scripture that makes it possible to follow the principle of "letting Scripture interpret Scripture."

II. The "Third Use" of the Law

Taking a *tota scriptura* approach has a number of important ramifications for Calvin's theology and for that of the Reformed churches that inherit his legacy. Perhaps the most significant differentiation from Luther that Calvin's "*tota scriptura*" approach yields is Calvin's embrace of the Old Testament and "the law." Luther's work stays focused on the New Testament and in a manner consistent with Pauline writings and with the book of Galatians in particular, he draws a contrast between law and gospel which Calvin does not accept.

In any summation of our shared Reformation heritage[9] there will be delineation of three uses of the law:[10] 1) a "civil use" where the law serves to restrain wrongdoing, 2) a "pedagogical" use as a tutor to lead us to Christ by convicting us of sin and our inability to meet the demands of the law, and 3) a "normative" use, as a rule of life for believers. In his *Commentary on Galatians,* Luther acknowledges the first two uses:

> there is a double use of the Law. One is the civic use. God has ordained civic laws, indeed all laws, to restrain transgressions. Therefore every law was given to hinder sins. Does this mean that when the Law restrains sins, it justifies? Not at all. When I refrain from killing or from committing adultery or from stealing, or when I abstain from other sins, I do not do this voluntarily or from the love of virtue but because I am afraid of the sword and of the executioner. ... [T]he first understanding and use of the Law is to restrain the wicked. ... The other use of the Law is the theological or spiritual one, which serves to increase transgressions. This is the primary purpose of the Law of Moses ... to reveal to man his sin, blindness, misery, wickedness, ignorance, hate and contempt of God, death, hell, judgment, and the well-deserved wrath of God.[11]

This second use is the principal purpose of the law for Luther and

---

9. Ken Sawyer, "The Third Use of the Law" (unpublished lecture given at McCormick Theological Seminary in October 2012).

10. Ibid.

11. *Commentary on Galatians* (1535), *LW* 26:308; *WA* 401:479-81 [Gal. 3.19].

its most valuable contribution. Until self-righteousness is slain people are not ready to receive the good news of God's grace.

There is a running debate about whether Luther also recognized the third use of the law. I will leave it to the Luther scholars to settle that issue. It is certainly there in Melanchthon and in the Lutheran *Formula of Concord* (1577). Luther "was ever suspicious of the misuse of the law, and wary of the reintroduction of any teaching that would encourage works righteousness."[12] This concern may have "curbed his enthusiasm" for the third use of the law, even if he recognized its validity.

For Calvin, on the other hand, the third use of the law is its primary use. The law is a guide for living life in covenant relation with God. It is Torah, instruction, a good and gracious gift of God to the people of God. Calvin reads quite positively the text in the Gospel of Matthew, where Jesus says, "Do not think that I have come to abolish the law or the prophets; I have come not to abolish but to fulfill" (5:17, NRSV). The law is in no way abrogated. In Matthew's Gospel, Jesus is presented as the authoritative interpreter of the law who understands its true intent and can show us how to live in its light, loving God and neighbor. Jesus' interactions concerning the law in Matthew consistently avoid legalism, on the one hand, and antinomianism, on the other—both of which were problematic already in Reformation times.

To sum up, Reformed folk, following Calvin's lead, have always embraced a "Psalm 19" approach in their reading of the nature of the law: "The law of the LORD is perfect, reviving the soul; the decrees of the LORD are sure, making wise the simple; the precepts of the LORD are right, rejoicing the heart; the commandment of the LORD is clear, enlightening the eyes" (vv. 7-8). There is a difference

---

12. Sawyer, "The Third Use of the Law" (unpublished lecture).

of emphasis between Luther and Calvin on which use of the law is the primary one. Luther is concerned to establish that justification by grace through faith has set us *free from the demands and accusations of the law* and its system of rewards and punishments. The role of the law is fulfilled in judging and convicting and driving the Christian to Christ. In this sense, the law is at an end for the Christian, having served its purpose. The freedom of a Christian means living in the Spirit. This does not mean that there is no ethical imperative for the Christian. Life in the Spirit does entails "having the mind of Christ" and thus fulfilling the command to love God and neighbor.

Calvin's emphasis is different. He would maintain that the law has a continuing rule for the Christian. He does acknowledge the second use of the law, as we come to terms with how far short we fall, we know ourselves to be utterly reliant on divine grace. Our justification by grace through faith sets us *free to follow the law as we live our lives of gratitude to God.* This leads very naturally to Calvin's greater emphasis on sanctification.

III. Sanctification and the Good Works of the Justified

One difference leads to another. Calvin's *tota scriptura* orientation, which embraces the Old Testament and the law in turn, yields a differentiation with respect to the place of sanctification and good works in the life of the justified. On the way to that difference, it must be acknowledged that Luther himself certainly had a place for works. He countered the charge that justification by grace through faith would lead to laxity with the insistence that faith produces fruit. Calvin certainly agreed with him on this. There is a place for good works in the Christian life, but they are "the fruit and not the root" of our justification. That view continues to be a shared understanding between our communions. The balance is well expressed in the *Joint*

Declaration on the Doctrine of Justification (1999) which is clear, on the one hand, that "faith is active in love and thus the Christian cannot and should not remain without works," and equally clear, on the other hand, that "whatever in the justified precedes or follows the free gift of faith is neither the basis of justification nor merits it."[13] This, it seems to me, expresses well the view that Luther held and with which Calvin concurred.

The differentiation comes with respect to emphasis and the relationship between justification and sanctification. Luther's focus was single-mindedly on justification. Luther pressed the *simul iustus et peccator* (our being, at one and the same time, justified and a sinner). He had a clear conviction of the lifelong struggle for believers with the power of sin in our lives that is not removed by justification. Although he affirmed that good works were to be expected, he was reluctant to reintroduce much attention to works lest they undermine "the freedom of a Christian" and reintroduce the servitude and oppression that "works righteousness" entailed.

For Calvin, by contrast, justification and sanctification are seen together as a "twofold grace" that entails both reconciliation and regeneration. These are not sequential, and they are not separable. Not only is Christ's righteousness imputed to us, it is in a sense, *imparted* to us in our union with Christ. It is not a matter of "moving on to perfection" but a matter of growing in grace in our union with Christ. As Calvin puts it, "Christ is not outside us but dwells within us . . . [W]ith a wonderful communion, day by day, he grows more and more into one body with us, until he becomes completely one with us."[14] This way of understanding is carried forward in Reformed

13. *Joint Declaration on the Doctrine of Justification*, §25.
14. John Calvin, *Institutes of the Christian Religion*, ed. J. T. McNeil, 2 vols., The Library of Christian Classics (Philadelphia: Westminster, 1960), 1:570-1 [III.2.24].

confessions; the *Westminster Catechism*, for example, expresses this view in Question 77:

> Wherein do justification and sanctification differ? Although sanctification be inseparably joined with justification, yet they differ, in that God in justification imputeth the righteousness of Christ; in sanctification his Spirit infuseth grace and enableth to the exercise thereof; in the former sin is pardoned; in the other it is subdued.[15]

Gabriel Fackre has pointed out that there is a clear difference of understanding between Luther and Calvin concerning how the saving work of Christ is applied to us. Is it imputation or impartation, forensic justification or changed life? Fackre suggests that from this difference follow many related divergences between Luther and Calvin regarding such things as the place of works, the relation of law and gospel, and the prospects for personal and social transformation.[16] Though I trace the originating divergence to the differences between Luther and Calvin concerning the *sola scriptura*, I do think Fackre makes a keen observation here concerning how these differentiations are intertwined with one another. What happens when, as he puts it, "the Lutheran *simul* meets the Reformed *sanctificatio*?"[17]

For the Reformed, the place and purpose of good works is clarified in the *Second Helvetic Confession*. Good works have nothing to do with "earning eternal life"; they are rather "for the glory of God, to adorn our calling, to show gratitude to God, and for the profit of the neighbor."[18] Further on, the confession speaks in fairly strong language about the importance of good works. "We therefore condemn all who despise good works and babble that they are useless and that we do not need to pay attention to them."[19] It seems that

---

15. Presbyterian Church, (USA), *Book of Confessions* (Louisville: Office of the General Assembly, Presbyterian Church [USA]), 7.187.
16. Fackre, "The Joint Declaration and the Reformed Tradition" (unpublished paper, 2001), 22.
17. Ibid., 4.
18. *Book of Confessions*, 5.117.

the Reformed want to, at one and the same time, reject merit and affirm the importance of good works. A strong social ethic and a world-engaged orientation have grown out of Reformed sensibilities. A "Christ transforming culture" vision predominates, and Reformed folk tend to see involvement in social-political matters as part of the calling of a Christian. Life lived in covenant relation, life lived *coram Deo*, issues in work that expresses gratitude for the grace received. Another ingredient in this is the conviction of the sovereignty of God over all of life—not just the narrowly religious aspects.

While the Reformed accept the forensic character of justification as an event of God's grace, they readily connect this to sanctification as a process of growing in God's grace. *Both* justification and sanctification are God's work and not ours. As Question 35 of the *Westminster Shorter Catechism* puts it, "Sanctification is the work of God's free grace, whereby we are renewed . . . and are enabled more and more to die unto sin and to live unto righteousness."[20] Thus we are not only counted righteous but also are being made righteous, as justification and sanctification are grasped together.

IV. The Place of the Confessions in Relation to Scripture

Another difference we see between the magisterial reformers concerns the relation between Scripture and the creeds and confessions of the church. For both, it can be said, the affirmation of *sola scriptura* places the confessions, as *norma normata*, under the authority of Scripture as the *norma normans*. There is a differentiation between us, however, in level of authority granted to creeds and confessions. To some extent this difference may be a function of differing contexts and times, but I do not believe the difference is

19. Ibid., 5.118.
20. Ibid., 7.035.

reducible to that. The most recent shared statement of Lutheran and Reformed world bodies articulates the difference as still maintained these many centuries later:

> #143 Member churches of the LWF understand those confessional writings that form an integral part of their tradition as binding doctrinal references of constitutional relevance. #144 Member churches of the WCRC understand those confessional writings that form an integral part of their tradition as guidelines and standards for truthful interpretation . . . of Holy Scripture.[21]

Luther and the Lutherans who came after him accept creeds and confessions as *regula fidei.* For Calvin and the Reformed, "Scripture is the only clear and sufficient *rule of faith.*"[22] Tradition, as such,

> cannot be elevated to the status of an authority that gives a binding interpretation of Scripture. ... Instead of tradition being the authority that decides the correctness of scriptural interpretation, Scripture, which interprets itself, is the authority that decides the correctness of tradition.[23]

The *French Confession* (1559), following this principle, is clear that the Apostles', the Nicene, and the Athanasian Creeds are to be accepted "*because* they are in accordance with the word of God."[24] They are subordinate standards.

Consistent with this orientation toward Scripture as the only "rule of faith" is Calvin's refusal, in his debate with Caroli, to "subscribe"

---

21. *Communion: On Being the Church.* Report of the Lutheran Reformed Joint Commission between the Lutheran World Federation (LWF) and the World Communion of Reformed Churches (WCRC), 2006-20012.

22. Jan Rohls, *Reformed Confessions: Theology from Zurich to Barmen* (Louisville, KY: Westminster/ John Knox, 1998), 43.

23. Rohls, *Reformed Confessions*, 43.

24. Article V. Further, according to the *Belgic Confession* (1561), "Neither may we compare any writings of men, though ever so holy, with those of divine Scriptures; nor ought we to compare custom, or the great multitude, or antiquity, or succession of times and persons, or councils, degrees or statutes with the truth of God" (Article VII).

to the ancient creeds of the church. Caroli had accused him of not holding to an orthodox doctrine of the trinity because he was not using the terms "trinity" and "persons" in his writings. In the course of the debate, Calvin expressed dismay that the terms used in the formulation of the doctrine of the trinity went beyond what is there in Scripture. He criticized the idle "speculation" that characterized discussion of the inner workings of the divine life. As for subscribing to creeds, he felt this was an undue elevation. He urged that nothing should be raised to such a height; nothing should "take the place of Christ."

One of the out-workings of this orientation to creeds and confessions is that they are much relativized in Reformed tradition. Like statements of church councils, they are fallible. They may be faithful interpretations of Scripture, or they may be flawed. As the *Westminster Confession of Faith* (1646) insists, "All synods or councils since the apostles' times, whether general or particular, may err, and may have erred; therefore they are not to be made the rule of faith or practice but are to be used as a help in both."[25] Some Reformed confessions even have built in disclaimers. One such instance is the Preface to the *Scots Confession* (1560):

> If any man will note in this our confession any article or sentence repugnant to God's holy word, that it would please him of his gentleness and for Christian charity's sake, to admonish us of the same in writing. And we promise to him satisfaction of any errors found.

In the Reformed orientation to creeds and confessions, they are not only relativized, they are multiplied. There are numerous confessions among the Reformed today! This was truly baffling to the Lutheran representatives serving on the International Commission for Lutheran-Reformed Confessions. For Lutherans, the *Augsburg*

---

25. *Book of Confessions*, 6.175.

Confession (1530) has a singular authority fairly universally accepted. There is no parallel among the Reformed. Our confessions are many and they are understood to be time and context bound. Some typify our pattern as, "Here we stand, until further notice"—and that is not far off the mark. As we say, "Reformed confessions are attempts, repeatedly renewed, to meet differing situations and to explicate insights into God's revelation, attested to in Scripture, Jesus Christ, God's Word made flesh.[26] That the attempts are "repeatedly renewed" is why the Reformed hold to what can be called an "open" rather than a "closed" confessional tradition. Every "formally adopted confession takes its place in a confessional line up preceded by statements from the past and expectant of more to come as times and circumstances change"[27] In the PCUSA for example, we have a *book* of confessions. My colleague who teaches church history is fond of reminding us it is a "book without a back cover." He has been known to do this by dramatically ripping the back cover off a copy during class.

V. Delineating a Difference Differently

Interestingly, even as Luther and Calvin affirm *sola scriptura*, both of them are concerned to distinguish between Scripture and that to which it gives witness. They delineate the difference differently, however. For Luther, that something to which Scripture gives witness is "the Gospel;" for Calvin it is "the Word of God."

Luther's distinction finds the heart and center of Scripture in its teaching about Christ. His canon within a canon (discussed earlier) is consistent with this understanding. The message of Christ is "the gospel" and it is embedded in the larger work which is Scripture. It

---

26. According to the *Confession of 1967*, "In each time and place there are particular problems and crises through which God calls the church to act. The church, guided by the Spirit, humbled by its own complicity, and instructed by all attainable knowledge, seeks to discern the will of God and learn how to obey in these concrete situations" (*Book of Confessions*, 9.43).

27. Rohls, *Reformed Confessions*, xi.

is, borrowing Luther's wording, "the kernel in the nut, the grain in the wheat, and the marrow in the bones."[28]

Calvin draws his distinction between Scripture and that to which it gives witness differently. "The Word of God" (God's self-revelation) is what is key and it is something larger than Scripture. Scripture is an instance as "the word of God (written);" it is the "witness without parallel." God's self-revelation is present, not only in Scripture but also in the whole creation. The *French Confession* speaks of a two-fold revelation of God: "First, God reveals himself through his works, in creation and through its preservation and guidance. Second, and more clearly, God reveals himself through his Word, first revealed through the spoken Word, and later committed to writing in the books we call Holy Scripture" (Article II).

Scripture may provide the "spectacles" that sharpen our vision to see God's self-revelation in the wider world. By the activity of God's Spirit, revelation can happen in our encounter with Scripture and proclamation. But revelation does not simply lie there naked on the page. It is always a gift; never a given. At the center, of course, is God's self-revelation in Jesus Christ as the living Word of God. Some centuries after Calvin, Karl Barth spoke of three forms of the Word of God: proclaimed, written and living. Scripture and proclamation have their authority in a secondary and derivative sense, as witnesses—by the Holy Spirit—to Jesus Christ, the living Word of God. This feels a bit closer to Luther's way of speaking. Nevertheless, the "Word of God" expressed in Scripture and proclamation and preeminently in Jesus of Nazareth is not exhausted there.

Among the Reformed, there is a sense that God's self-revelation does not begin and end with Jesus of Nazareth. It is interesting to note that Reformed confessions do not even limit the "gospel" to

---

28. Gerrish, *The Old Protestantism and the New*, 1.

the message of Jesus Christ or even the New Testament as such. The *Heidelberg Catechism* (Question 19) speaks of the gospel, "which God first revealed in Paradise, afterwards proclaimed by the holy Patriarchs and Prophets, and foreshadowed by the sacrifices and other ceremonies of the law, and finally fulfilled by his well-beloved Son."[29] This is not exactly a decentering of God's work in Christ, but it assumes a larger frame.

Not unrelated to this is the infamous *extra calvinisticum*. The naming is meant as a criticism—that "Calvinist extra"! The Reformed in fact hold that while the Eternal Word incarnate in Christ is *fully* God (*totus*), it is not *all of* God (*totum*). God does not cease to be present and active in all things even when God becomes incarnate in Christ.

It should be noted, because of past misunderstandings, that there is nothing in Reformed theology to imply that the God we have come to know in Jesus Christ is somehow different in character from the God who continues to fill all things even as Jesus of Nazareth walks the earth. Some have misconstrued the *extra calvinisticum* as allowing for this. A connection is made with a notion of the *Deus absconditus* who is "unknown" and may or may not be like the good and loving God of the Incarnation (*Deus revelatus*). This has served as a kind of explanation for Calvin's acceptance of double-predestination. In fact, it is not the *extra calvinisticum* but rather Calvin's *tota scriptura* that accounts, in large part, for his acceptance of double predestination. There are texts in Scripture from which this is a logical inference. Augustine saw this, and Luther did as well. Calvin could not simply lay aside these difficult texts, but felt compelled to grapple with them. Furthermore, what he was affirming elsewhere about grace in relation to the bondage of the will compelled him. Luther himself

---

29. *Book of Confessions*, 4.019.

considered this conclusion, but finally rejected it. Most Reformed theologians would side with Luther here.[30]

There was much debate between Reformed and Lutheran thinkers on the matter of the *extra calvinisticum*. Different understandings of the mode of Christ's presence in the Eucharist are not unconnected to this difference in the understanding of the Incarnation, as will be argued in what follows. On the way, it should be noted in our defense, that the view expressed in the *extra calvinisticum* was in fact the view held by most prominent Catholic theologians (Athanasius, Augustine, Aquinas, and others). It could as easily have been called the *extra catholicum*.

VI. *Capax, non capax* and Sacramental Theology

A closely related question concerns whether and in what sense the finite may be said to contain the infinite. Differences in understanding the Incarnation, as described above, have their parallel in differences concerning sacramental theology. Gabriel Fackre observed that in his twelve years of the US Lutheran-Reformed dialogue leading up to the full communion agreement, the conversation partners regularly ran into a fundamental difference of orientation. He described it as "the Lutheran *finitum capax infiniti* . . . meeting the Reformed *finitum non capax infiniti*." Understanding this difference helps us to better understand why Luther could speak of a local physical presence of Christ in the sacrament while Calvin viewed this presence as spiritual in nature.

---

30. In fact, predestination—contrary to the popular view—is not a central doctrine for Calvin. It does not even arise until Book IV in the *Institutes* and there it is discussed in terms of the assurance that confidence in God's predestining grace gives to believers. Only in the 17th century protestant scholasticism of the *Westminster Confession of Faith* does it become a matter of "eternal decrees" and get placed up front and receive doctrinal status. Other confessions (and most all Reformed theologians) hold with single predestination and "cherish a good hope for all" as the *Second Helvetic Confession* commends.

While there are real differences here, they are perhaps not as great as the popular view—which tends to obscure Calvin's true perspective by superimposing a Zwinglian reading. Calvin, in fact, differed from Zwingli at least as much as he differed from Luther on the mode of Christ's presence in the Lord's Supper. Calvin is in complete agreement with Luther in rejecting the medieval doctrine of transubstantiation. He saw this as a confusion of the sign with the thing signified. Calvin would even take Luther's part against Zwingli on significant points. For example, he criticized Zwingli's symbolic approach as making of the sacraments "bare nude signs" which are nothing in themselves and accomplish nothing in us. Zwingli did not understand sacraments as "means of grace" at all but saw them primarily as an exercise of faith. They were "signs" in the sense of "badges" or "emblems" by which Christians identify themselves as Christian and pledge themselves anew to Christ, and no more than that. For Calvin, Zwingli too sharply separates sign and thing signified. Gerrish underscores that Calvin's position is "the exact opposite of Zwingli's." Where Zwingli sees symbolic language as allowing one to "use realistic language without meaning it realistically," for Calvin a sign function precisely because "it bestows what it signifies."[31] When seeking to articulate the relation between the "sign" and "the thing signified" in the sacraments, Calvin uses the christological formulation of "distinction without division."[32] The Roman catholic view fails to distinguish and the Zwinglian view falls into division. Calvin stands—with Luther—between these extremes. He holds, with Luther, that the sacraments are "efficacious signs."

For Calvin, just as for Luther, the sacraments are about what God does in using these "instruments" to mediate divine grace to believers. Calvin does concur with Zwingli's argument that God can work in

---

31. Gerrish, *The Old Protestantism and the New*, 123.
32. Ibid., 4.

us apart from any instruments, and that the sacraments cannot not bind the freedom of God—no *ex opere operato*. (Would Luther really disagree here?) Calvin then goes on to insist, that although God is not "bound," the sacraments are the "ordinary means" of the working of God's grace in the lives of believers. "Because sacraments are divinely appointed signs, and God does not lie, therefore the Spirit uses them to confer what they symbolize."[33] Why not seek grace in places it can dependably be found—in Word and sacrament? A distinctive Calvin adds to the discussion is his close joining of Word and sacrament. The sacraments are the Word made visible in an act of bodily cleansing (baptism) and an act of bodily nourishment (the Lord's Supper)."[34]

One point where Calvin agrees with Zwingli (against Luther) is that a local, physical presence of Christ is not what we experience in the Lord's Supper. As he argues, a physical body does not work like that. For him, the reality of the Incarnation is undercut unless Christ's body is like our bodies. So he will speak of a "spiritual presence" rather than a local, physical presence. Interestingly, for Luther as for Calvin, it is a concern for the reality of Incarnation that shapes his view of real. Genuine embodiment in the sacrament is crucial. Both Luther and Calvin intend "real presence" in what they set forth. In the Lutheran-Reformed dialogues of recent years, that shared understanding has eclipsed our differences on the mode of Christ's presence. We have declared that the historical differences in understanding are not "church dividing" differences.

How is Christ present? Calvin maintains that this is a mystery. "I rather experience than understand it," he says.[35] Calvin insists that something really happens to us—contra Zwingli—at the Lord's Supper. As he expresses it, we are "joined to Christ becoming one

---

33. Ibid., 123. See especially the *Geneva Catechism*, Qq. 312, 328, and 353.
34. Ibid., 4.
35. Calvin, *Institutes*, 2:1403 [IV.17.32].

with him, bone of his bone, flesh of his flesh." It is not so much that he comes down from the right hand of God to be with us, but rather we are raised to be with him. Our hearts are lifted up to the Lord: *sursum corda*!

One point where Calvin stands between Zwingli and Luther is in his understanding of the importance of faith for the efficacy of the sacrament. For Zwingli the exercise of our faith is really all that is happening in the sacrament. For Luther faith is not necessary for the sacrament to be the sacrament. Even the person who is without faith receives the sacrament—though unworthily and unto damnation. For Calvin the unbeliever does not truly receive the sacrament. It is not that faith "makes" the sacrament what it is, but rather that faith prepares people to receive what is offered in the sacrament. Without faith being present, it is as if water were being poured over a stone. The water is what it is, but the stone is not sufficiently porous to receive it. In summary, for Luther the sacrament is what it is with or without faith. For Zwingli, the sacrament is all about faith; it is an exercise of faith. For Calvin, those who believe, receive.

In a way Calvin's views stand between Luther and Zwingli, though, I would maintain, with a leaning toward Luther. Calvin believed that if only he had been at Marburg when Luther and Zwingli argued over the Lord's Supper, he could have mediated the differences and avoided the divisions that followed; so he argues in his *Short Treatise on the Lord's Supper*. Alas, Calvin came on the scene too late.

In the dialogues on the way to full communion the difference between Luther and Calvin and between Lutheran and Reformed folk who came after them have been reframed as an occasion for mutual teachability (or "mutual admonition"). Thus we find ourselves in a very different place today.

Conclusion: Jubilee 2017 and the Unfinished Business
of the Reformation

There are many considered and creative plans for celebrating and commemorating on the way to Jubilee 2017. The celebratory decade began with the Calvin Jubilee in 2009. That was a memorable year for Reformed Christians the world over as we joined in a truly remarkable celebration. New resources were generated: educational DVDs, a new Calvin biography, a compilation of his sermons and writings now available online. New CDs of music of the Reformation were created, and a hymn writing competition yielded a Calvin Jubilee hymn. On a lighter note: there are now Calvin chocolates—think Swiss chocolate—available with tiny images of Calvin stamped on them. The ad for them says, "*Reform* your taste buds." A favorite of many is a dry white wine that, playing on the Latin phrase *in vino veritas*, has been commissioned with the label "*In Calvino Veritas.*"

The years since have each had a special Reformation theme and exhibition. All this leads up to the Reformation Jubilee year which will begin on October 31, 2016 with a journey of sorts. Its starting point will be in front of the Cathedral in Berlin. Ninety-five Volkswagen buses will be lined up to begin to make their way to the Reformation cities throughout Germany and Europe, collecting from each one a "thesis" which together will add up to the "Ninety-Five Theses for Today's Church." Reformation cities will each have their own distinctive displays: Zurich, Marburg, Worms, Geneva and all the rest—each one will be different, reflecting the history and meaning of the Reformation in particular locations. Wittenberg will be turned into a World Exhibition of the Reformation in time for 2017. Churches from all around the world will be sending exhibits for a Ninety-five-day exhibition. It all culminates in a grand service of worship on October 31st 2017, at Wittenberg. Thousands of people are expected to be in attendance for the grand celebration.

This is a time of opportunity for Protestant churches and also a time of challenge. Our primary challenge, I think, as we look back to the Reformation at this Jubilee will be to reclaim the insights, give an honest appraisal of the oversights, and get on with the *unfinished business of the Reformation*. Our interpretation must make clear that we are not celebrating the division of the church. This is a time to shine a light on our good faith efforts toward more visible unity both among the churches of the Reformation and with the Roman Catholic Church. Our interpretation cast a compelling vision of how we together may make visible the unity which—by the grace of God—is already ours in Jesus Christ.

Reclaiming visible unity is, in my opinion, a large part of our interpretive project—and constitutes major "unfinished business of the Reformation." This is a *kairos* moment for the church. It portends reconciliation of what has become divided. This could be a time not only of celebration and commemoration but also of much needed reorientation—a *metanoia* if you will—a "turning around" and a turning toward those from whom we have long been estranged. Not only by that early original divide but also in the divisions that have arisen since then among the churches of the Reformation. Some say that the Reformation set a precedent for dividing in the face of difference. Now we have "developed a habit" of splintering—even our splinters have splinters. We have too often been content to live apart, complacent with separation.

I hope that churches of the Reformation will take this auspicious occasion to take some further steps toward reconciliation with the Roman Catholic Church. Though we hold that the Reformation was necessary, the divisions that followed were tragic. There is a brokenness that stands in need of healing. I am not saying, "Let's all return to the mother church." I am not assuming a unity of uniformity. There are alternative visions. What about the "reconciled diversity" of which we speak in ecumenical endeavors? What about something like what Cardinal Walter Kasper called "a communion of communions"?

Luther (and Calvin with him) thought the division in the church was scandalous. Neither aspired to founding a "new church." Martin Luther, even after his excommunication in 1521, constantly strove for dialogue. He was completely convinced that Rome would come to see the necessity of reform. He cherished a hope that that the Pope would convene a general council. In my more hopeful moments I think the day "the ecumenical Luther" hoped for might be drawing near.

John Calvin shared Luther's profound regret over the division of the church. He expressed his deep concern in a letter to the Archbishop of Canterbury, Thomas Cranmer. He declared that the division of the church "is to be ranked among the chief evils of our time. . . . Thus it is that the members of the Church being severed, the body lies bleeding. So much does this concern me, that, if I could be of any service, I would not grudge to cross even ten seas."[36] Calvin's depiction of Christ's "dismembered" body is a powerful and compelling image. His discussions of the Lord's Supper insist that we cannot separate communion with Christ from communion with one another.

I take hope when I think of some of the wonderful advances made in recent years. The signing of the *Joint Declaration on the Doctrine of Justification* was a momentous accomplishment of agreement upon one of the church dividing issues of the Reformation. It also offered a new model for reconciliation in its "differentiated consensus"

---

36. John Calvin, "Letter to Cranmer" (1552), *Selected Works of John Calvin: Tracts and Letters*, ed. Henry Beveridge and Jules Bonnet (Grand Rapids, MI: Baker, 1983), 5:355.

format—affirming what we can affirm together and then allowing remaining differences to be articulated rather than obscured. It testifies that differences need not divide. Progress toward reconciliation is possible.

Closer to home, I hope that churches of the Reformation will seize this moment to turn toward one another. Lutheran and Reformed communions have a shared history in the Reformation, a shared understanding of the church, and shared convictions of the centrality of Word and sacrament. We even have shared agreements such as Leuenberg that have been in place for decades. And yet churches have not claimed the fullness of shared life available to them. In the USA we have the *Formula of Agreement*, declaring "full communion" between us; yet our realizations of this communion are partial and fragmentary. One person proposed in good humor that our situation is the reverse of the practice of many young adults today who live together even though they are not sure about getting married. We are entirely willing to be married, but we are not so sure about living together.

Have we reached our ecumenical limits? By no means! I take hope in the moments of reconciliation/restoration we have seen in recent years. Some of these I myself have witnessed from the vantage point of serving as co-chair of the Joint Commission for Lutheran-Reformed relations:

- There is a growing commitment to union churches. An example would be the "United Churches" in Germany which combine Lutheran and Reformed traditions. I understand that the plan now is that new church developments will be undertaken together, and the churches will be founded as union churches.

- In Argentina, there is seminary in Buenos Aires (ISEDET-*Instituto Superior Evangelico de Estudios Teologicos*) that all Protestants attend together. They receive the same foundation in theological education with a few specialized courses in their particular traditions. They are set on a path of partnership in ministry.

- In France, the Lutheran and Reformed churches recently came together to form the "United Protestant Church of France."

- In Namibia, most all of the work done in the area of HIV-AIDS is done together. Church leaders there say, "Why have two separate mission efforts here? Why not pool resources, avoid reduplication of efforts, form a coalition for advocacy efforts?" Very wise. Common witness, common work.

- I had the privilege of attending, as a Reformed representative, the 2010 meeting in Stuttgart. I was there for the service of reconciliation where the LWF confessed the persecution of the Mennonites and engaged in an extraordinary act of repentance and a plea for reconciliation. It was beautiful, so moving, so much what was needed.

This is a hopeful time. This is a time for *ecclesial imagination*. What does it mean to be church? How may we live together as church in ways that better manifest our unity? This is time to embrace unity as both gift and calling. In ecumenical work we often say that our unity is a gift of God. If indeed it is a gift, then it seems to be the kind of gifts that is marked "some assembly required." Margot Kässmann, special envoy for Jubilee 2017, calls our attention a wall painting that depicts of twelve key figures of the sixteenth century who played a role in renewal of the church and of our view of the world. They are—*assembled*—reconciled at the foot of the cross.[37] It is a powerful image. May it be so for us!

37. The church of Alt-Staaken just outside Berlin houses a wall painting designed by Gabriele Mucchi and executed by one of his students. The persons depicted are (from left to right): Nicholas Copernicus, Ulrich Zwingli, John Calvin, Ignatius Loyola, Thomas More, Katharina von Bora, Martin Luther, Thomas Müntzer, Johannes Bugenhagen, Philip Melanchthon, Lucas Cranach, and Erasmus of Rotterdam.

14

Scripture as Matrix, Christ as Content: A Response to Johannes Zachhuber and Anna Case-Winters

Paul R. Hinlicky

I

I am delighted with this opportunity to attend to the "formal principle of the Reformation" by responding to the contributions of Johannes Zachhuber and Anna Case-Winters. Our shared hope is that the quest for a resource in the "ecumenical Luther" may help us to grow beyond "reconciled diversity" and even "differentiated consensus" in regard to the diverging ways in which Reformed and Lutheran theological traditions have parsed and applied the Scripture principle of Reformation theology. I would like also acknowledge a personal reason that I am delighted to make this response from my Lutheran perspective. While I have spent most of my theological career in dialogue with Orthodox, Catholic and Evangelical theologians, and more recently with Jews and Muslims, it was the encounter with Reformed Christian theology, and in particular with the theologies of Karl Barth and Jürgen Moltmann during graduate students days at Union Theological Seminary in New York, which awoke me from the dogmatic slumber of confessionalized Lutheranism. So the present contribution is an opportunity to be returned to that autobiographically decisive stimulus.

Over the years, I have in jest offered a trade to Calvinist friends: "I would be willing to give up Melanchthon, if you would be willing to give up Zwingli." Of course, that is a joke. The rationalism and crusaderism of Zwingli, and the intellectualism and conservativism of Melanchthon, are deeply woven into the fabrics of our respective traditions. By the same token, our traditions are each internally unstable if not conflicted in just these ways. Lutheranism, historically, is Luther mediated by Melanchthon. Reformed theology, historically, is Calvin always looking back over his shoulder in the direction of Zurich. The "ecumenical Luther," accordingly, might very well be the one of whom Calvin was the best disciple, if Calvin in turn might be exorcized of that ghost from Zurich who haunted him. I am especially appreciative, then, of Case-Winters' sharp differentiations in this regard. If this is at all right, the prospect of an "ecumenical Luther" could mean nothing less than shredding the fabrics of our respective traditions woven by such mutual but convoluted delimitations over these five hundred years. But "God kills in order to make alive." The ecumenically hopeful prospect would be to reweave retrievable strands from our traditions into the tapestry of a new future, just as Case-Winters so hopefully concludes.

As she expressly notes, this new future could not and should not, however, be some pan-Protestant alliance against Rome, as often was thought in the past, already by Philip of Hesse when he assembled the Marburg Colloquy (1529), or by Frederick the Great when he forcibly consolidated Lutheran and Reformed in the interest of the enlightened modern nation-state in the Prussian kingdom of the 19th century. On the contrary, today such a reweaving—I call it in my forthcoming systematic theology a christological "realignment"[1]—would have to incorporate fresh drafts of patristic theology from Eastern Orthodoxy, not to mention unflinching recognition today of post-Christendom in the West and surging Global Christianity in the South and East. From my jest about trading off Melanchthon and Zwingli, then, I derive a few modest principles for this project of a contemporary reweaving that would draw from the "ecumenical Luther" as a resource.

First, Lutherans should never blame others for believing, and thus being misled by, what Lutherans say about Luther. Second, non-Lutherans should not only read what Lutherans say about Luther but read Luther for themselves. Third, we all should read Luther neither as hero nor as villain but as a father in faith and teacher of the gospel who, alongside others, vigorously instantiated in his own life the principle *simul iustus et peccator*. And fourth, pray God, we should not imagine that on this level any of us will do any better than Luther than to become forgiven sinners, and, further pray God, even better than Luther that we may thus be transformed into forgiving people. That has not a little to do with ecumenical reconciliation. So much by way of preface.

---

1. Paul R. Hinlicky, *Beloved Community: Critical Dogmatics after Christendom* (Grand Rapids, MI: Eerdmans, 2015), 439–45, 711–20.

II

Since, if I read him rightly, I am in particularly deep agreement with Zachhuber, I will respond to his essay first, making two suggestions, one in terminology and then, later, another regarding methodology. The terminological suggestion turns on whether we take the Latin, *sola scriptura*, as a nominative or as an ablative, i.e. whether it means "only the Bible," as in the nominative, *solus Christus*, "Christ alone," or whether it means, "by the Bible only, only by way of, or means of, the Bible," in tandem with the ablatives, *sola fide*, by faith alone, *sola gratia*, by grace alone. I take it that Zachhuber's entire argument amounts to a case for the ablative reading, that is to say, that Christian theology as a doctrinal discipline and missiological methodology is unified across a plentitude of historical contexts by the interpretive work of *using* the Bible as "Christianity's ultimate authority and the most fundamental source of Christian beliefs and practices." In that case, the derivative authority of creeds and confessions emerges from acute episodes of disputed Scripture reading as nothing but, but also nothing less than, ecumenical, or ecumenically proposed clarifications about how to read the Bible as the Spirit intends. Classical examples of such clarifications would be the *homoousios* of the Nicene Creed concerning the Son's relation to the Father and the exclusive particle, *sole fide*, concerning the sinner's justification, as proposed by the Reformation. If, in the latter case of the Reformation's exclusive particle, the Scripture is the ablative, and Christ is the nominative, then it is further clarified concerning the sinner's justification: it is all about Christ, while faith, grace and Scripture variously modify the access, epistemic and otherwise, to Him in whom the sinner's righteousness is given as the gift of God.

But why should the Scriptures alone provide this epistemic access? What is it about the Scriptures that qualify them alone to do this work? To answer this question, terminologically, it would be more fitting to think of *prima scriptura* in the nominative—that is to say, as Zachhuber does, that *the Bible, as Luther's manger in which Christ is given and found, is the unique and irreplaceable* source *of Christian doctrine and theology.* As I put it in my systematic theology, the Bible opened and read and debated in the *ecclesia* is the *matrix* of Christian theological practice and thought;[2] with the word, matrix, I am playing on Luther's statement that the *ecclesia* "is the mother that begets and bears every Christian through the Word of God, which the Holy Spirit reveals and proclaims. . . ."[3] From this it is evident, as the postliberals have shown us, that *ecclesia* and *scriptura* are correlative concepts. The know-nothing, Bible Alone misreading of *sola scriptura* is hard to avoid, however, if *sola scriptura* is taken in the nominative—as if the Book were the saving self-donation of God that is Christ rather than the earthen vessel that bears this treasure, even when we also hold, as we should, that the chosen earthen vessels are sanctified ("inspired") and thus made the means by which the Holy Spirit works ("inspires") holiness.

My proposed terminology of *prima Scriptura* makes it clear that engagement with the world in the gospel's mission to the nations, as the font streams forth from the Biblical source into the world, therewith inevitably and rightly bathes non-Biblical words or concepts it discovers to clarify Christian doctrine in fresh ways and so enable the mission to go forward. Christian doctrine, in turn, is primarily *regula fidei*, rules for reading the Bible rightly to discern its gospel claim to truth. In that case, *homoousios* or *sola fide* are not human additions to the Word of God, but, on the contrary, the very practice and fruit of Scriptural reasoning in the Spirit that work

---

2. Hinlicky, *Beloved Community*, 171-91, *et passim.*
3. Martin Luther, *Large Catechism*, The Creed, §42; BC 436.

to articulate the gospel's claim to truth, namely, in Luther's simple and majestic words, that "Jesus Christ, true God begotten of the Father in eternity, and also a true human, born of the Virgin Mary, is my [saving] Lord."[4] To be sure, theology has to give an account of the Bible that warrants concretely and materially the privileging of this specific (canonical collection of) text(s), out of all possible texts in the world, as its epistemic primary. That warranting will concern my final methodological remarks to Zachhuber regarding the "widespread skepticism towards the Scripture principle" today that, of course, he acknowledges from the outset.

But let me next articulate what I have gleaned from Zachhuber's presentation. His chief claim is that "there are good reasons why the notion that the Bible is Christianity's ultimate authority and the most fundamental source of Christian beliefs and practices resonates more than ever with Christians and theologians across the denominations" today.[5] He argues for this claim by means of a discussion of Geiselmann's thesis that the "Scripture is 'materially' sufficient but has to be read and understood within the Church."[6] He sees that this, precisely, is what *sola scriptura* meant in "the context, usually ignored today, in which Luther's notion of the sufficiency of Scripture was originally formulated." The "point," raised by Ratzinger against Geiselmann, that Scripture as canon is "part of the tradition of the Church and cannot therefore simply stand above it," is, Zachhuber notes, "valid," yet it reflects contemporary concerns that obscure the ecclesial context of Luther's demand for "the sources and criteria of *the Church's* doctrine."[7] So the Bible is the Church's book and the Church is to be identified as the community that draws and judges from the Bible. The circle is not vacuous but analytical; church and

---

4. Martin Luther, *Small Catechism*, The Creed, §4; *BC* 355.
5. Zachhuber, 250.
6. Ibid., 254.
7. Ibid., 256. Emphasis added.

Scripture are correlative concepts as both are part of the gospel, taken as the Word of God spoken in the resurrection of the Crucified. Luther, accordingly, would quite agree with Ratzinger that "the Church loses its message if it makes itself dependent on those with a purely historical interest in the Bible"[8]—what Luther lambasted as a mere *fides historica* that even the devils have. On the other hand, the Tridentine contention for the authority of unwritten traditions, by means of which Ratzinger sought to safeguard the Bible as sacred Scripture from reduction to a purely historical interest, has "lost all historical credibility" today by the work of those same historical critics.

Yet that disillusioning result does not, according to Zachhuber, abandon the Bible to the critical intention of finding the books of the Bible in the past and leaving them there, as Ratzinger feared. Rather, an emerging ecumenical consensus on the authority of the Bible "is in its fundamentals much closer to Luther's view . . . [that] the Bible is the unique source of the Christian doctrine of faith, and its *sensus historicus* is a necessary criterion by which the Church's proclamation and practice has to be measured."[9] That can only mean that the Bible is warranted as normative (*auctoritas normativa*) on account of its material content (*auctoritas causativa*, that is, the nominative, Christ alone, *homoousios* with His Father, given as the sinner's righteousness to create the community of faith). It is not, then, the Bible by virtue of alleged formal qualities, like miraculous inspiration, or by virtue of an exalted status conferred upon it from an authority external to itself, as in ultramontane versions of magisterium. As Zachhuber indicates, the unhappy contemporary alternatives in the past two centuries have been the liberal "Protestant dissolution of the Bible into its historical sources," on one side, and "the one-sided emphasis on the 'absolutist'

---

8. Ibid., 260.
9. Ibid., 262.

power of the Petrine Office," on the other.[10] But we should also add here what goes unsaid, as I just hinted: the equal loss of "all historical credibility," not only of Catholic unwritten tradition but on the Protestant side, of the old Orthodox doctrine of the Bible's miraculously guaranteed inspiration.

That being noted, by way of trenchant analyses of nineteenth-century discussions, Catholic and Protestant, leading up to an *Auseinandersetzung* with Barth, Zachhuber rightly maintains that "[while] it is true that any 'human' attempt to discern the most relevant aspect of the biblical message for a time or situation [i.e., "contextualization"] inevitably blurs the boundary between the Word of God and its human interpretation, there is no way this risk can be avoided."[11] Indeed, undertaking precisely this risk is itself Biblically warranted, as Bonhoeffer famously pointed out: Jesus' historic question, "Who do you say that I am?" entails our contemporary asking and answering, confessing and following: "Who is Jesus Christ for us today?" Indeed, this risk of venturing to speak the Word of God from the Bible for us today is precisely what is intended by Luther's ablative, *sola scriptura;* then it sense as a norm is that our risky speaking today issues first from our disciplined listening and remains ever accountable to this primary source, the Bible. From this Zachhuber's conclusion follows: "text precedes community," as source precedes stream, as "the pure and clear fountain of Israel" (so the Lutheran *Formula of Concord* put it[12]) flows into contemporary theological acts of understanding and public confession. In turn, that community out of all communities in the world is critically identified as the holy community of Christ which is the one that is engaged theologically with the interpretation of

10. Ibid., 271–72.
11. Ibid., 271.
12. *Formula of Concord,* [Preface to the] Solid Declaration, §3; *BC* 527.

canonical Scripture for mission in its specific context. This amounts to Zachhuber's "recognition that the acceptance and use of the Bible is in many ways the one element that unites Christians. . . . "[13] Such *significant* clarity is not the least of what may be gained today from our "ecumenical Luther."

Yet the question remains: Why the Bible, i.e., this canonical collection? The formal, Scripture principle of the Reformation is not so much in question today because criticism has discredited the historical truthfulness of the Bible and thus the Orthodox doctrine of inspiration by verbal dictation. On the contrary, historical criticism has done much to open up that source and show how the Bible itself is already a process of continual re-reading of the promises of God (what Case-Winters will call the "one covenant of grace") by the persisting community of faith through the trials and testings of its earthly sojourn. Rather, the real challenge to *prima scriptura* comes from a different direction altogether. Even if in ("traditional") church circles Luther's version of the Scripture principle more and more prevails today as the book that sources and therefore norms the conversation that constitutes the Church in distinction from all other conversations and societies on the earth, Luther's *sola scriptura* is nevertheless profoundly challenged on *these same grounds* by contemporary history of religions perspectives. Here it is observed that already the very formation of a canon (assembling diverse texts into a new whole that de facto harmonizes them for boundary setting purposes) is the very essence of an ahistorical, retrospective, dogmatic imposition of alien meaning on the past that by its nature excludes other literature as alien or deviant.

In historical fact, the Scripture that Luther inherited and made use of so creatively owes its very existence to the struggle of second

---

13. Zachhuber, 274.

century church fathers, stretching from Ignatius of Antioch to Irenaeus of Lyons, to sustain the unity of the Testaments against Gnostic dualism and christological docetism. So the formal observation is correct: Scripture *qua* canon exists as a *dogma*, as a particularly Christian *rule* of ecclesial or orthodox faith, namely, ruling *out* the theological dualism and christological docetism of Gnosticism. Today, I submit, just this kind of warrant for the Bible must be again made, if Luther's *sola scriptura* is to have even a fighting chance in our rapidly Gnosticizing churches.[14]

Thus a methodological suggestion may be ventured. As Zachhuber recognizes, what makes theology Christian is its employment of the Bible as source and norm, yet this employment does not yield timeless truths but risky, concrete, historical, contextually specific ones that in some way venture *hic et nunc* to identify the Word of God with some words of a human creature. That happens *regularly* in every Christian prayer, every liturgy, every sermon, every testimony, every confession of faith, every good work done in Jesus' name and for His sake. If we join this insight to my contention that the material privileging of the canonical text is always and first of all a renewed dogmatic decision against the perennial Christian temptations of Gnostic dualism and christological docetism for the sake of the redemption of creation by Jesus Christ in His bodily death and resurrection, we can see that the inherited alternative, Scripture or tradition, is a classic binary forcing false choices on us, what Peter Ochs, the Jewish philosopher and advocate of Scriptural Reasoning calls a dyadic, either/or logic.[15] Drawing upon pragmatism, Ochs

---

14. Philip J., Lee, *Against the Protestant Gnostics* (New York: Oxford University Press, 1987). For the extended case, see Paul R. Hinlicky, *Divine Complexity: The Rise of Creedal Christianity* (Minneapolis, MN: Fortress Press, 2009).

15. Peter Ochs, *Another Reformation: Postliberal Christianity and the Jews* (Grand Rapids, MI: Baker Academic, 2011). See my review essay in *The Journal of Scriptural Reasoning* 13:2 (December 2014, published online by the University of Virginia).

recommends a triadic logic where the interpretation of Scripture is always to a concrete situation/audience for a "reparative" purpose. In this triadic way, we honor *both* the authority of Scripture as source and norm for speaking/acting in the name of the God who comes to bless (Ex. 20:24b)[16] *and* contextual pleas for redemption. In the process, we do not arise to timeless truth but deliver timely truths in the stream of a definite and recognizable "tradition of the gospel" (1 Cor. 15:3). We do not rest on repeating past confession but continuing in the confessing tradition we inherit in order to go forward: neither *quia* nor *quatenus*, but *ut confiteamur*.[17]

I would only add to this line of reasoning from Ochs the further stipulation that the unity of the church in employing the Bible this way is not only to be discerned spatially across the contemporary globe, as Zachhuber argues. It is also to be discerned temporally through the centuries in the sense that some few but henceforth irrevocable dogmatic decisions have been made about the right reading of Scripture; as argued in my systematic theology, these are the *canon* of Old and New Testaments, the *homoousios* of the Nicene Creed and the *sola fide* of the Reformation. The sense of this claim is that after the disruptions of Arianism, of Nestorianism and of Pelagianism, we cannot continue to tell the Biblical gospel truly without meaning in our own contemporary contexts that in the man Christ we meet the same being as the One whom He called Father, so that in meeting Christ crucified, we who are helpless truly find the help in the sending of their Spirit that is infinitely generous. This is exactly what the mature Luther taught when he argued that the *solus Christus* can be undone in three ways: by Arians who deny Christ's divinity, by Nestorians who separate this divinity from its

---

16. See R. Kendall Soulen, *The Divine Name(s) and the Holy Trinity*, vol. 1: *Distinguishing the Voices* (Louisville KY: Westminster John Knox, 2011).
17. Paul R. Hinlicky, "Confessional Subscription Today," *Lutheran Forum* (Spring 2012), 47-53.

own humanity, and by Pelagians who make the work of this one Person, the eternal Son incarnate, pointless.[18]

III

Anna Case-Winters argues the thesis that "Calvin's appropriation and differentiation on [the formal principle of the Reformation, *sola scriptura*] is at the heart of many of the differences in Lutheran and Reformed theology that carry forward even into our day."[19] I see an analogy here with the christological difference she later introduces and discusses: as the total Scripture is to the gospel of Jesus Christ, so the divine Son of God is to Jesus of Nazareth. And if that analogy is right, her thesis is incisive, at least as a theological account of historically divergent tendencies in spite of so much held in common. I do not always fully consent to the way in which Case-Winters articulates these differences. This may be little more than my own stubborn desire "to articulate the difference differently!" But this thesis as it stands is surely correct, and, as we shall see, points us in the end exactly in the right direction if we are seeking an ecumenical Luther that is neither Lutheranism's Luther or Calvinism's Luther but an ecumenical resource for a renewed Christianity.

Case-Winters writes that "all of Scripture and sometimes the very words themselves are seen by [Calvin] as divinely inspired," while for Luther, as is well-known, the Scriptures themselves demand differentiation between straw and wheat, husk and kernel, manger and Christ-child, what speaks to us and what does not, not to mention between God's Word as law that demands and as God's promise that gives what God demands.[20] Yet Case-Winters is right

---

18. *On the Three Symbols or Creeds of the Christian Faith* (1538) *LW* 34:201-29; *WA* 50:262-83; see the discussion in Hinlicky, *Beloved Community*, 542-4.
19. Case-Winters, 276.
20. Ibid., 277-78.

also to note that Luther holds with Calvin "one covenant of grace that spans" the Testaments, and that Calvin, just like Luther, "reads Christ into the Old Testament."[21] The question then remains whether a (shared) Christocentric view of the whole of Scripture requires, as it seems, certain kinds of differentiation in the theological weight assigned to texts, just as a view of the equally divine inspiration of every text does little more than beg this question of what weight should be assigned and why. But of course Case-Winters does not beg such questions; she probes them issue by issue.

For Calvin, the "third use of the law," Case-Winters writes, is Torah, and as God's gracious "instruction for life lived in covenant relation to God," it is the "primary use" of the law, while for Luther, by contrast, the Spirit's use of the law to accuse, convict and slay self-righteousness and so to reveal the lost creature's true impotence and need *coram Deo* is the law's principal purpose. A fallacy of equivocation, however, seems to haunt this differentiation. Torah is not a *use* of the law. Torah, *instruction*, is *what* the law *is*, knowledge of good and evil, right and wrong given by God. Usage, by contrast, concerns application of this knowledge, not its being; the Reformation doctrine of the *uses* of the law asks not what the Law is (it takes this for granted), but rather how divine instruction is to be *used and applied*. In this light, the *spiritual* or theological use is law in the usage *of the Holy Spirit* rather than the law's use in the hands of jurists or philosophers. For Luther, this usage denotes God's *juridical* activity, God at work as Judge to convict the world concerning sin, and righteousness and judgment. Correspondingly, then, if, being justified by faith we have peace with God, that can only be because God's judgment on our works by the measure of His own law has already now fallen in Christ's death; this is the execution of a divine

---

21. Ibid., 278.

death-sentence that now incorporates the sinner by baptism into Christ's death and just so delivers to new life in Christ. So this usage of law by the Spirit to accuse is finished, its mission is accomplished. God's juridical activity is complete in the sinner's justification by faith in Christ. The law in this sense is at its end so that, as Heiko Oberman famously put it, justification by faith alone in Christ alone is not the uncertain goal but the assured foundation of Christian life,[22] of the just who will *live* by their faith.

It is thus, in my view, better to see in Luther a second *use* of the Gospel,[23] namely to give the Spirit for the new obedience, rather than a so-called third *use* of the Law, which according to this understanding of the *uses* of the law would put believers back under the old political system of rewards and punishments, as demands can only do, thus back under the accusing judgment of God, *lex semper accusat*, back into a state of unpeace with God. Following the Apostle, Luther holds that those who are led by the Spirit are not under any law, but are rather given the mind of Christ by the Spirit to live as freed people, sons and daughters and no longer as slaves. But, of course, for Luther law in the ethical sense of love not only remains but is, he audaciously maintains, *fulfilled*. Not least because Christ has fulfilled the double love commandment, loving His Father above all by loving sinners as Himself; just this same mind of love is given by the Spirit to believers as was in Christ Jesus. Thus Luther, who made his living as a professor of Old Testament and published an outstanding commentary on Deuteronomy, teaches that this same Spirit of Christ is the One who spoke by the prophets so that, ethically, also for Luther, "the Law is holy, just and good" instruction

---

22. Heiko A. Oberman, *The Dawn of the Reformation: Essays in Late Medieval and Early Reformation Thought* (Edinburgh, UK: T&T Clark, 1986), 124.
23. William H. Lazareth, *Christians in Society: Luther, the Bible and Social Ethics* (Minneapolis: Fortress Press, 2001).

for living in proper relationship with God and all creatures. But it *does* this holiness, the law's demand for holiness is only *fulfilled*, in Spirit-given, gospel-formed *faith*.

Thus it is problematic in the same way to parse a Lutheran-Calvinist difference in sanctification and good works, since it is Luther's view, derived from Paul, that whatever is not done in faith is sinful. That is to say, it is Spirit-given faith that sanctifies the deed and makes it theologically good, that is, good *coram Deo*—even if the doer is one who remains otherwise a sinful member (though not citizen) of the fallen world. To make the same point another way: as justifying faith is the work and gift of the Holy Spirit, faith is already, for the historical Luther, "sanctification." The rigid scheme, "justification first, then sanctification," does not stand up to scrutiny.[24] To be sure, Lutheran Orthodoxy, in its allergic reaction to Osiander, imposed the scheme, "justification first by imputation, sanctification second by impartation." Yet Calvin is in this respect a good, orthodox Lutheran! He certainly maintains the strictly forensic account of justification as such, while the mystical union with Christ, to which Case-Winters happily points, is nothing other than Calvin's version of Luther's joyful exchange—though now it is made to follow after imputative justification rather than to ground it, as arguably it does in the historical Luther. What a labyrinth! In any event, there is no Lutheran-Reformed difference on Case-Winter's concluding point in this connection that "*[b]oth* justification and sanctification are God's work and not ours"—a conclusion that ought to send us all back the drawing boards.[25] We ought to learn to think instead of the passive and active aspects of the Holy Spirit's one work of

---

24. For this—controversial—claim, see Paul R. Hinlicky, "Staying Lutheran in the Changing Church(es)," Afterword in Mickey L. Mattox and Gregg Roeber, "Changing Churches" (Grand Rapids, MI: Eerdmans, 2011), 281-314.
25. Case-Winters, 284.

justification/sanctification—suffering God in the mortification of the sinful self, rising in Christ to newness of life.

Similarly, I suggest, the insightful discussion of the authority of church confessions points to differences that may be best attributed to the vicissitudes of historical circumstance, accidents, so to say, of each tradition's development. Calvinism remained embattled until the Peace of Westphalia (1648), while Lutheranism, via the *Augsburg Confession*, was legally tolerated from the time of the Peace of Augsburg (1555). This historical difference deeply stamped each tradition's take on the authority of confessions. I believe that while the case can be made that, for Luther, Scripture and ecumenical creeds together form a "hermeneutical whole," as I argued in analyzing Luther's late disputation on the divinity and humanity of Christ,[26] I don't believe we really get to the heart of the matter theologically until we come to the christological distinctions Case-Winters provides in the section, "Delineating a Difference Differently," although, as we shall see, they point to a *common* Western deficit in robust Trinitarian personalism.

Case-Winters acutely observes that, for Luther, the content to which Scripture attests is the specific word of the gospel concerning Jesus as the Christ, while for Calvin it is the generic, as it were, Word of God. Certainly this difference can be exaggerated. For Luther the gospel is *the* Word of God, precisely as the *divine* promise of renewal comes to surpass God's own judgment on sin, as resurrection surpasses crucifixion; for Calvin, the Word of God is *incarnate* as the gospel of Jesus Christ, the mirror of the Father's heart in whom believers are to seek and find their election. Yet, as she notes, this difference in emphasis, which can be exaggerated, is related to "the

---

26. Paul R. Hinlicky, "Luther's Anti-Docetism in the *Disputatio de divinitate et humanitate Christi* (1540)," Oswald Bayer and Benjamin Gleede (eds.), *Creator est creatura: Luthers Christologie als Lehre von der Idiomenkommunikation* (Berlin: de Gruyter, 2007), 139-85.

infamous *extra calvinisticum*," which she parses to mean from her Reformed perspective that "while the Eternal Word incarnate in Christ is fully God (*totus*), it is not all of God (*totum*)."[27] That is surely the right interpretation of the *intention* of Calvin's Christology, aimed against Johannes Brenz's exaggerated ubiquitism of Christ's body, itself an over-reaction to Zwingli's Eucharistic memorialism. Let us acknowledge, accordingly, that Lutherans like Brenz were inept, to say the least, in articulating their christological/incarnational affirmation of the *finitum capax infiniti est*.[28]

But the problem here arises because of Trinitarian *modalism*: one thinks of the "divinity" of Christ as a natural quality that can attend, so to say, on a sliding scale of intensity rather than as that eternal being of God in the way of being a Son. Perhaps within the historical horizon of the traditional Western tendency towards *modalism* going back to Augustine,[29] the christological issue raised here could not be solved. The Word of God external to the self as a result could either be located in the specificity of Jesus' cruciform humanity that hides the deity or in the transcendence of the divine nature fully but not totally incarnate in Christ. Given this choice, everything depended from the Lutheran perspective on whether we draw the necessary distinction between God in heaven and God incarnate christologically, that is within the Person of Christ, producing a Nestorianism, or Trinitarianly, between the eternal Son wholly incarnate and the God of Israel, whom He address Abba, Father in the power of the Holy Spirit—though admittedly few Lutherans attained full clarity on this, while Brenz utterly confused the issue by generalizing what is christologically specific on a road that ends up

27. Case-Winters, 289.
28. For the detailed argument here, see Hinlicky, *Beloved Community*, 544-65.
29. Colin Gunton, "Augustine, The Trinity and the Theological Crisis of the West," *Scottish Journal of Theology* 43:1 (February 1990), 33-58; see the discussion in Hinlicky, *Beloved Community*, 335-41, 434-39.

with the patripassianism of Hegelian theology. In any case, classically, Calvinism distinguished between the divine nature which transcends embodiment in principle and the body that is the man Jesus, while Lutheranism distinguished between the person of the eternal Son who is (now, having once for all become) the body that was born of Mary and suffered under Pontius Pilate and the persons of His Father and their Spirit that together, as a living "totality" constitute divine nature as the *perichoresis* of the Beloved Community, the eternal Trinity.

The salience of the issues raised here may be appreciated in light of what has gone under-accounted in Case-Winters' delineation of the Lutheran-Reformed difference. The doctrinal topic that was surely the most divisive historically, as may be seen already in Formula of Concord XI, was Calvinism's embrace, already in Theodore Beza,[30] of an absolute and secret decree of reprobation in order to safeguard the sovereignty of God, also in the damnation of the wicked. This is not unrelated to the problem of the *extra calvinisticum*. If God is secretly, and indeed taken as a totality, infinitely beyond the finite Jesus Christ, friend of sinners, then clear and rigorous theological thinking has no choice, in view of the evident withholding of repentance and faith to some, than to draw the inference that God reprobates according to His own sovereign will. This gives us a non-christological *deus exlex*, not the *esse deum dare* of classical Trinitarianism. Theologically, such diverging visions of God's sovereignty *had* to divide.

Historically speaking, then, we today cannot take for granted Karl Barth's great achievement in delivering the Reformed tradition from

---

30. See especially Reid's Introduction in John Calvin, *The Eternal Predestination of God*, trans. and ed. J. K. S. Reid (Louisville: Westminster John Knox, 1997), and Jill Raitt, *The Colloquy of Montbeliard: Religion and Politics in the Sixteenth Century* (New York & Oxford: Oxford University Press, 1993).

the straightjacket of this line of thought, which in reality goes back more to Zwingli's *De providentia Dei* than to Calvin's sober and really marginal reflections on the "horrible thought," as Case-Winters rightly describes it. In fact, we should acknowledge in Barth's revision of Reformed theology a healthy borrowing from the Orthodox Lutheran teaching on the unlimited universality of the atonement against corresponding Reformed views of an atonement "limited" to the elect. Likewise, of course, we have to acknowledge historically that Luther toyed with double predestination in *De servo arbitrio* (the work against which Zwingli wrote *De providentia Dei!*), though, as Robert Kolb has shown, the debate, including Zwingli's reaction, caused Luther to qualify, if not recant those heretical[31] speculations.[32] As I argued in my *Paths Not Taken*, Barth's teaching on election is the fulfillment of the old Lutheran Orthodox contention for universal atonement, the intention of which Orthodoxy itself had neither the clarity nor the courage to follow out. If that is right, we need today further mediation of these classical Lutheran-Reformed differences that actually moves the argument forward, as Barth did in his day. That will draw upon an ecumenical Luther, that is, a Luther liberated from Lutheranism (and a Calvin liberated from Zwinglianism), teachers who belongs to the whole Church as teachers of the Holy Scriptures.

---

31. To reference a God who is in reality other than and over His own Word is Arianism; to argue that apart from Christ, God appears as hidden in His sovereign intention for us, is not a comment on the divine ontology but on the human perspectives of unfaith in contrast to faith.

32. Robert Kolb makes a strong case for Luther's reconsideration of his reckless language in the treatise on bound choice. See *Bound Choice, Election, and Wittenberg Theological Method: From Martin Luther to the Formula of Concord*, (Grand Rapids, MI: Eerdmans, 2005), 17, 40, 65, 131, 146, 161-4, 178, 222, 227, 262. On Barth's "Lutheran" revision of the doctrine of election, see Paul R. Hinlicky, *Paths Not Taken: Fates of Theology from Luther through Leibniz* (Grand Rapids, MI: Eerdmans, 2009), 112-9, and *Luther and the Beloved Community: A Path for Christian Theology after Christendom* (Grand Rapids, MI: Eerdmans, 2012), 149-69.

Contributors

Matthew Myer Boulton (Disciples of Christ) is President and Professor of Theology at Christian Theological Seminary in Indianapolis, Indiana. He is the author of *Life in God: John Calvin, Practical Formation, and the Future of Protestant Theology* (Eerdmans, 2011) and *God Against Religion: Rethinking Christian Theology through Worship* (Eerdmans 2008). He is husband to filmmaker Liz (saltproject.org), and father to Jonah and Maggie.

Brian Brewer (Baptist) is Associate Professor of Christian Theology at the George W. Truett Theological Seminary, Baylor University, where he teaches historical theology of the Reformation and post-Reformation periods. He holds degrees from Baylor University, Truett Theological Seminary, Princeton Theological Seminary, and Drew University, and has focused his research on magisterial reformers, the Anabaptists, and the early Free Church movement.

Anna Case-Winters (Presbyterian) is Professor of Theology at McCormick Seminary. She has served the Presbyterian Church in various ecumenical endeavors, most recently as Co-Chair of the International Commission for Lutheran-Reformed Relations with the World Communion of Reformed Churches. Her published works include: *God's Power: Traditional Understandings and Contemporary Challenges, Reconstructing a Christian Theology of Nature: Down to Earth,* and *A Theological Commentary on the Book of Matthew.*

Paul R. Hinlicky (Lutheran) is Tise Professor at Roanoke College, a Docent of the Protestant Theological Faculty in Bratislava, and Professor of Systematic Theology at the Institute of Lutheran Theology. He is author of a systematic theology, *Beloved Community: Critical Dogmatics after Christendom* (2015) among many other books and articles.

Matt Jenson (Evangelical Covenant Church) is Associate Professor of Theology in the Torrey Honors Institute at Biola University. He is the author of *The Gravity of Sin: Augustine, Luther, and Barth on 'homo incurvatus in se',* and, with David Wilhite, *The Church: A Guide for the Perplexed.* He is a licensed minister.

Piotr J. Małysz (Lutheran) teaches history and doctrine at Beeson Divinity School in Birmingham, Alabama. He is the author of *Trinity, Freedom and Love: An Engagement with the Theology of Eberhard Jüngel* (T&T Clark, 2012), and articles on Pseudo-Dionysius, Luther, Hegel, Barth, and more broadly the Lutheran tradition, including a chapter in the forthcoming *Oxford Handbook to the Reception of Christian Theology.* He was ordained in the Lutheran Church—Missouri Synod.

Ian McFarland (Lutheran), a lay theologian of the Evangelical Lutheran Church in America, is Regius Professor of Divinity in the Faculty of Divinity at the University of Cambridge. Prior to his appointment, McFarland was Bishop Mack B. and Rose Y. Stokes

Professor of Theology and Associate Dean of Faculty and Academic Affairs at Emory University's Candler School of Theology.

Derek R. Nelson (Lutheran) is Associate Professor of Religion and Director of the Wabash Pastoral Leadership Program at Wabash College. An ordained pastor in the Evangelical Lutheran Church in America, Nelson is the author or editor of nine books, including *Resilient Reformer: The Life and Thought of Martin Luther* (Fortress, 2015), *Theologians in Their Own Words* (Fortress, 2013) and *Sin: A Guide for the Perplexed* (T&T Clark, 2011).

Ted Peters (Lutheran) is a pastor, as well as Research Professor Emeritus of Systematic Theology and Ethics at Pacific Lutheran Theological Seminary and the Graduate Theological Union in Berkeley, California. He is former editor-in-chief of *Dialog, A Journal of Theology*; and currently he co-edits the journal, *Theology and Science.* Among his newest books is a book on meditation, *Short Prayers,* and an espionage novel about "the black op in the white collar," *For God and Country.* His *magnum opus* is *GOD—The World's Future* (Fortress, 3rd ed., 2016). Visit his website: tedstimelytake.com.

David Tracy (Roman Catholic) is the Greeley Distinguished Service Professor Emeritus of Theology and the Philosophy of Religions at the University of Chicago Divinity School and the Committee on Social Thought. His publications include *Blessed Rage for Order* (1979), *The Analogical Imagination* (1981), *Plurality and Ambiguity* (1987), and *On Naming the Present: Reflections on God, Hermeneutics, and Church* (1994).

Jared Wicks, SJ (Roman Catholic) grew up in Columbus, Ohio, and entered the Jesuit order in 1949. His doctoral studies were at the University of Münster, with a dissertation on Luther. He taught at Jesuit School of Theology in Chicago and at the Gregorian University in Rome. In late 2011 he was called back to Columbus to be scholar-in-residence at the Pontifical College Josephinum, where his research and writing concentrates on Vatican Council II and on topics contributing to U. S. Lutheran–Catholic ecumenical dialogue.

Susan Wood, S.C.L. (Roman Catholic) is a professor of theology at Marquette University. She serves on the U.S. Lutheran-Roman Catholic Dialogue, the North American Roman Catholic-Orthodox Theological Consultation, and the International Lutheran-Catholic Commission on Unity. Her most recent ecumenical books are *One Baptism: Ecumenical Dimensions of the Doctrine of Baptism* (Liturgical Press, 2009) and, co-edited with Alberto Garcia, *Critical Issues in Ecclesiology* (Eerdmans, 2011).

Johannes Zachhuber (Evangelische Kirche in Deutschland, "uniert") is Professor of Historical and Systematic Theology at the University of Oxford. He specializes in the Eastern Patristic tradition of theology, its philosophical background, and its development up to John of Damascus, and in modern theology from the Reformation to the present, with special interests related to nineteenth-century German theology. His books include *Human Nature in Gregory of Nyssa* (Brill, 1999) and *Theology as Science in Nineteenth-Century Germany* (Oxford University Press, 2013).

Randall C. Zachman (Episcopalian) is Professor of Reformation Studies at the University of Notre Dame. He is the author of *Reconsidering John Calvin* (Cambridge University Press, 2012), *Image and Word in the Theology of John Calvin* (University of Notre Dame Press, 2007), *John Calvin as Teacher, Pastor, and*

Theologian (Baker Academic, 2006), and *The Assurance of Faith* (Westminster John Knox Press, 2005).

Index of Names

Index of Subjects